Multicultural Issues in Literacy
Research and Practice

Multicultural Issues in Literacy Research and Practice

Edited by

Arlette Ingram Willis
Georgia Earnest García
Rosalinda B. Barrera
Violet J. Harris
University of Illinois at Urbana–Champaign

LEA LAWRENCE ERLBAUM ASSOCIATES, PUBLISHERS
2003 Mahwah, New Jersey   London

Lawrence Erlbaum Associates, Inc., Publishers
10 Industrial Avenue
Mahwah, NJ 07430

Cover design by Kathryn Houghtaling Lacey

Library of Congress Cataloging-in-Publication Data

Multicultural issues in literacy research and practice /
    edited by Arlette Ingram Willis . . . [et al.].
        p.   cm.
Includes bibliographical references and index.
ISBN 0-8058-3240-8 (cloth : alk. paper) — ISBN 0-8058-3241-6 (pbk. : alk. paper)
    1. Literacy–Social aspects–United States.   2. Multicultural education–United States.
I. Willis, Arlette Ingram.

LC151 .M85   2002
370.117—dc21   2001054845
                                                                      CIP

Books published by Lawrence Erlbaum Associates are printed on acid-free paper,
and their bindings are chosen for strength and durability.

Printed in the United States of America
10 9 8 7 6 5 4 3 2 1

Contents

Preface

This book grew out of our desire to inform and broaden understanding concerning the intersection and complexity of multicultural issues in literacy research and practice. We have gathered together a distinctive set of writings that focus on issues of difference in the field of literacy. The diverse group of authors raises issues that often are overlooked and undervalued in literacy education. Our book is aimed at a wide audience that includes literacy researchers, teacher educators, preservice and inservice teachers, and policymakers.

Each fall throughout our nation a new crop of eager undergraduates enters the field of education seeking to become the nation's schoolteachers. Many of these students hail from very homogeneous suburban lifestyles and are representative of the typical education undergraduates, European American, middle-class, English-speaking, able-bodied, and female. In addition, each fall a new class of graduate students enters professional schools seeking to expand their knowledge of educational issues and practices. We have found that both groups, generally, bring little understanding of multicultural issues in literacy research and practice. Moreover, they often resist when presented with information that would assist them in connecting multicultural issues and literacy research and practice. Yet, we also know that both groups are likely to face increasing numbers of students of color in their classrooms.

Although literacy research in the United States has existed for more than a century, we are alarmed to discover that in the 21st century there are many students and classroom teachers who have not read research on multicultural issues in literacy. Much like the Colorforms used by children at play, in which thin pieces of lightly colored plastic are peeled on and off a background storyboard, notions of difference often are mentioned to "cover" the topic, but not to address root issues in theory, research, and practice. There appears to be a pattern in literacy research that marginalizes cultural and linguistic needs of children of color.

We note that the tendency of researchers in the field not to embrace and deconstruct these issues continues. For example, current national research reviews and initiatives continue to downplay the importance of addressing cultural and linguistic difference. It is our position that discussions on research and practices that specifically address the literacy needs of children from culturally and linguistically diverse backgrounds are missing.

In this volume, we attempt to reverse the pattern of marginalizing these issues. We explore multicultural issues in research and practice informed by researchers of diverse backgrounds who address the literacy and linguistic needs of children of color. We have organized the chapters so that the first three explore the complex relation among culture, language, literacy, and identity. The next four chapters describe and evaluate the development and implementation of curricula, assessments, and materials for students from diverse linguistic, cultural, and racial backgrounds. The last five chapters focus on preservice and in-service teachers as well as teacher education issues related to the implementation of multicultural literacies. Thus, the chapters in this volume offer a fresh perspective that (a) explores the complex relation among culture, language, literacy, and identity; (b) describes and evaluates the development and implementation of curricula, assessments, and materials for students from diverse linguistic, cultural, and racial backgrounds; and (c) focuses on preservice and in-service teachers and teacher education issues related to the implementation of multicultural literacies.

INTRODUCTION
Giving Voice to Multicultural Literacy Research and Practice

Georgia Earnest García
University of Illinois at Urbana–Champaign

Our society increasingly is becoming more diverse. According to the U.S. Census Bureau, by the year 2020 more than 37% of the U.S. population will be Latina/o, African American, Asian/Pacific Islander, and Native American. Yet, the literacy field has been relatively slow to embrace this diversity. Multicultural perspectives still have not made a significant impact on the research canon, national research reports, national and state educational decision making, or classroom instruction (Au, 2000; García, Willis, & Harris, 1998; Gee, 1999; Willis & Harris, 2000). This volume confronts this situation by giving voice to the work of researchers and teacher educators, and the participants in their studies, who strive to enact multicultural literacy research and practice.

Various definitions of multicultural literacy have been proposed (Barrera, 1992; García & Willis, 2001; Harris & Willis, 2002). Most advocates of multicultural literacy reject neoclassical views (Tollefson, 1991) of literacy that emphasize the mental processes and mechanics involved in an individual's reading and writing acquisition, instruction, and performance in favor of literacy views that are socially, culturally, and ideologically constructed (Lankshear & McLaren, 1993). In this view, literacy is not a universal or neutral construct devoid of cultural and political influences. Rather, the cultural, political, historical, and economic realities that shape students' literacy acquisition, instruction, assessment, and performance are investigated, acknowledged, and incorporated into theory

1

and practice (Freire & Macedo, 1987; Giroux, 1993). Due to the variation inherent in such realities, the term multicultural literacies often is
used to reflect the different cultural meanings and multiple forms of literacy that exist (Courts, 1997; Gee, 1999; The New London Group, 1996).

Similar to what has happened in the field of multicultural education
(Banks, 1997; Sleeter & Grant, 1987), there is considerable variation in
how the field of multicultural literacies has been interpreted and implemented. Some educators assume they have implemented multicultural
literacies when they introduce texts written about diverse cultural groups
into their classroom instruction (for critiques, see Barrera, 1992; Harris,
1993). Others view literacy acquisition, instruction, and performance
from a sociocultural perspective. Informed by Lev Vygotsky (Moll, 1990;
Wertsch, 1985), this theory asserts that children initially develop their
understanding of literacy through their observations and participation
with others in social settings. Children then internalize their understanding, mentally creating cognitive structures on which they can later draw
for future application. The cultural and social settings through which
children acquire and develop their literacy affect their literacy understandings, practices, and attitudes (John-Steiner, Panofsky, & Smith,
1994; Tharp & Gallimore, 1988). Researchers and educators in the field
of multicultural literacies who subscribe to a sociocultural theory of literacy embrace culturally responsive literacy pedagogies that build on and
extend children's cultural and social experiences with literacy (Au, 1998;
Moll & González, 1994; Trueba, Jacobs, & Kirton, 1990).

Another perspective, sometimes held in conjunction with a sociocultural perspective, is that of critical literacy. Critical literacy has its roots
in critical theory (García & Willis, 2001), and requires a historical appraisal of hegemonic literacy policies and practices. Paulo Freire's (1970)
work in Brazil, with his emphasis on getting oppressed people to "read the
world" as they learned to "read the word," has been a cornerstone of this
perspective. Henry Giroux (1993) explained that critical literacy involves
raising participants' consciousness by making them aware of others' experiences (current and past), causing them to reflect on their own experiences,
and motivating them to take action to confront and dismantle inequity in
literacy definitions, purposes, practices, and policies.

García and Willis (2001) argued that if the full import of multicultural
literacies is to be understood and influential, then the following are necessary: a complex understanding of culture and its relation to literacy, a
strong commitment to social justice, a transformative mission, and implementation of the emancipatory paradigm. Rosalinda Barrera (1992)

pointed out that literacy is a set of practices that develops to meet the needs of a particular culture or cultural group. As a result, literacy embodies cultural meanings according to the cultural contexts that help to shape its manifestations. This variation occurs both within a single culture and between cultures. Therefore, the educational community needs to understand how dynamic cultural forces both within and between cultures shape the forms, purposes, and meanings of literacy; literacy access, instruction, and assessment; literacy goals, motivation, and identities; and the use of literacy to construct and further knowledge (García & Willis, 2001).

A commitment to social justice and an enactment of the transformative mission not only should be informed by what is known about culture and literacy, but also should occur in tandem. According to García and Willis (2001), a commitment to social justice requires critical self-examination and reflection on the economic, historical, social, and political forces that have resulted in students' differential literacy acquisition and performance. Educators, researchers, and policymakers need to investigate and confront the historical and political forces that have shaped the literacy experiences of diverse groups (Harris & Willis, 2002; Willis & Harris, 1997). In the words of Patrick Courts (1997), they should "recover that knowledge which we choose not to know" (p. 135). Informed by critical literacy (Freire & Macedo, 1987; Giroux, 1993), the transformative mission involves changing how literacy has been interpreted, taught, researched, and used so that it helps to create a more just society.

In terms of instruction, a commitment to social justice and a transformative mission means offering students problem-solving opportunities that raise their consciousness, empower them, and enable them to use literacy to confront inequities and the tensions that diversity creates in their daily lives (Weil, 1998). To do this, educators should reflect on both the content and process aspects of literacy instruction. Hilda Hernandez (1989) explained that content refers to the curriculum or the literacy materials, instructional activities, and literacy tasks that generally are visible to an observer, whereas, process refers to how the curriculum is enacted or aspects of instruction that often are hidden. The latter includes how teachers interact with students, their attitudes and expectations, and the messages that teachers send about what is valued and who may participate. In addition, educators need to remember that the instructional context is situated within and affected by larger cultural contexts, such as the school, community, and society (Schulman, 1986). These contexts also need to be interrogated and taken into account in the development of transformative curricula.

Finally, researchers and policy makers need to implement an emancipatory paradigm. Donna Mertens (1998) explained that an emancipatory paradigm involves

> directly address[ing] the politics in research by confronting social oppression at whatever level it occurs, . . . go[ing] beyond the issue of the powerful sharing power with the powerless and relinquish[ing] control of the research to the marginalized group. (p. 15)

An emancipatory paradigm includes the perspectives of the researched, not only through the choice of topics and participants, but also through the acknowledgment and heralding of the work and voices of those researchers from the very groups being studied.

In this volume, we have allowed the voices of researchers and participants from diverse groups who portray varied dimensions of multicultural literacies to be heard. A common theme throughout the chapters is "an emphasis on the manner in which elements of difference—race or ethnicity, gender, class, language, sexual preference—create dynamic tensions that influence literacy access, acquisition, instruction, performance, or assessment" (García, Willis, & Harris, 1998, p. 183). We have organized the chapters so that the first three explore the complex relation among culture, language, literacy, and identity. The next four chapters describe and evaluate the development and implementation of curricula, assessments, and materials for students from diverse linguistic, cultural, and racial backgrounds. The last five chapters focus on pre-service and in-service teachers and teacher education issues related to the implementation of multicultural literacies.

The first set of chapters explores how the literacy development and performance of individual children are affected by their cultural and linguistic identities and the social contexts in which these identities are embedded. In the first chapter, Eurydice Bouchereau Bauer uses a case study to examine a young bilingual (German–English) preschooler's responses to different genres of literature. She focuses on the child's responses to literature read in each language, her use of code-switching in her responses, and the role that different genres play in the child's responses. Bauer's chapter helps to debunk deficit myths about young bilingual children's code-switching and reveals the complexity involved in bilingual/tricultural children's identity construction and responses to literature.

Joel Dworin describes a primary-age Spanish English, Mexican American child's biliterate performance in Spanish and English. His chapter shows how the teacher helps to create an additive environment, in which Spanish and English literacy both are valued, and how this environment helps the child to further demonstrate his biliteracy.

Shuaib Meacham moves beyond specific cultural groups to look at a multicultural classroom in which childre
n from diverse cultural and linguistic backgrounds work together. He uses Murray's (1970) "blues idiom" and a jazz metaphor to examine the intersecting relations among cultural norms, gender, reading ability, and small group work. Meacham shows how cultural and gendered norms, along with perceived reading ability, can influence students' enactment of their roles in small group instruction. Meacham's analysis identifies gender and cultural issues of which teachers need to be aware when they try to empower students whose voices have been silenced.

The second set of chapters addresses curricula, assessments, and materials from the perspectives of specific cultural, linguistic, and/or racial groups. Rosary Lalik, LaNette Dellinger, and Richard Druggish present case studies of three Appalachian children to illustrate the cultural relevance of a literacy curriculum on Appalachian culture that is informed by a sociocultural perspective on learning and the concept of multiliteracies (The New London Group, 1996). Their rich portrayals of the children's literacy experiences and reflections highlight aspects of Appalachian culture that often are overlooked. They also show how the curriculum integrated family and school literacy activities so students comfortably and confidently displayed their family knowledge in the school setting.

Teresa McCarty and Galena Sells Dick's chapter focuses on a different setting, the Rough Rock School in the Navajo Nation. In presenting the bilingual–bicultural literacy materials and practices that have been effective in this setting, they take a postcolonial stance that examines historically oppressive practices. They illustrate how teachers from the Navajo Nation became empowered to develop their own assessments and curriculum through critical literacy and collaborative participation in socially meaningful events, such as summer literature camps for the elders, teachers, parents, and children, and study groups for the teachers. With this empowerment came the opportunity to co-construct knowledge and transform attitudes.

In a chapter that combines ethnographic and survey findings, Lee Gunderson and Jim Anderson report immigrant parents' reactions to the whole-language literacy curriculum and assessment practices being used in British Columbia, Canada. They show how a particular curriculum can reflect the values of the larger community, but be in conflict with the values of smaller communities. In this case, immigrant parents from Hong

Kong, Taiwan, and the Punjab in India are more comfortable with a transmission view of learning and literacy than with a sociocultural view. How to resolve the problem is not so clear.

Rosalinda B. Barrera, Ruth E. Quiroa, and Rebeca Valdivia examine the increased presence of Spanish in Latino picture storybooks, which are written in English. They conduct a literary analysis of three popular Latino picture storybooks to ascertain how well the authors have addressed the needs of two audiences: bilingual–bicultural Spanish–English readers and monolingual–monocultural English readers. Although they conclude that the use of Spanish in English books can enhance Latino characterization and settings, they warn that how Spanish is used can be problematic, especially from the perspective of Spanish-language readers. They look forward to the day when Spanish will be used effectively to strengthen the literary quality of Latino children's books in English.

The last group of chapters focuses on teachers and teacher education efforts related to multicultural literacies. Sally Oran's chapter looks at how a teacher–researcher collaboration, which involved the sharing of letters between Anglo, monolingual, pre-service teachers and predominantly Navajo, bilingual students, resulted in mutual learning and the exemplification of "third-space" theory and pedagogy (Gutiérrez, Baquedano-López, & Turner, 1997). She reports that the pre-service teachers not only were confronted with new ideas about how culture influences teaching, but also were forced to reflect on how their participation in the dominant, monolingual culture privileged their writing performance compared with that of the Navajo students.

Diane Truscott and Susan Watts examine the type of English-as-a-second-language (ESL) literacy instruction provided in an instructional setting often ignored, the all-English classroom. First, they present a model of effective ESL literacy practices. Next, they use this model to evaluate how general teachers instruct ESL students. Their results emphasize the importance of providing general classroom teachers with additional professional development in ESL literacy instruction.

Robert Rueda and Erminda García explore how well a researcher–teacher collaboration empowered bilingual teachers to implement responsive teaching, a literacy approach informed by a sociocultural perspective. They define responsive teaching as teachers' use of ongoing classroom assessments to identify individual student needs and their use of this information to change or modify their literacy instruction accordingly. Rueda and García contend that the teachers' beliefs about bilingualism, literacy, and assessment influenced how well they were able to implement responsive teaching. Their findings highlight important issues that teacher educators and researchers should take into account when they attempt to implement multicultural literacy approaches.

Margaret A. Moore-Hart, Barbara J. Diamond, and John R. Knapp describe and evaluate teachers' implementation of a multicultural literacy program with fourth- and fifth-grade students. Although the use of multicultural literature and literature-based instruction often has been proposed, very rarely have researchers actually tested the effectiveness of such a program in terms of students' reading and vocabulary test performance. In this case, the authors not only describe the program and discuss the efficacy of the professional development component, but they also compare the cultural attitudes as well as the reading and vocabulary test performance of students who participated in the program with those who did not.

The volume concludes with a chapter written by Frances Levin, Michael Smith, and Dorothy Strickland. Their investigation of a reader response approach, which involved getting pre-service and in-service teachers to read multicultural literature and discuss it in small groups, shows the difficulty of getting teachers to change hegemonic attitudes when no direction or confrontation occurs. Although both sets of teachers reported that they furthered their cultural awareness and benefited from the study group formats much more than by participating in other types of professional development activities, they really did not develop "ethical respect" (Downie & Tefler, 1970). The authors wonder whether the emphasis within reader response on the reader's personal experiences might have interfered with the teachers' ability to give "equal worth" to individuals from backgrounds different from their own, put aside their own biases, and/or recognize how society's rules and norms differentially affect diverse groups.

Collectively, the chapters in this volume reflect the different ways in which the field of multicultural literacies has been interpreted. The authors are scholars who actively have examined, and continue to examine, the intersection of difference and literacy as praxis. By bringing together the voices of researchers and teacher educators who work in the field of multicultural literacies, we maximize the opportunity for their voices, and those of their participants, to be heard. As many of the authors indicate, there still is much work to be done in the field of multicultural literacies. We hope that readers will build on the experiences and findings that we have presented so that the field of multicultural literacies will have a greater impact on literacy research, policy, and practice.

REFERENCES

Au, K. H. (1998). Social constructivism and the school literacy learning of students of diverse backgrounds. *Journal of Literacy Research, 30*(20), 297–319.

Au, K. H. (2000). A multicultural perspective on policies for improving literacy achievement: Equity and excellence. In M. Kamil, P. Mosenthal, P. D. Pearson, & R. Barr (Eds.), *Handbook of reading research* (Vol. III, pp. 835–851). Mahwah, NJ: Lawrence Erlbaum.

Banks, J. A. (1997). Approaches to multicultural curriculum reform. In J. A. Banks & C. M. Banks (Eds.), *Multicultural education: Issues and perspectives* (3rd ed., pp. 229–250). Boston: Allyn & Bacon.

Barrera, R. B. (1992). The cultural gap in literature-based literacy instruction. *Education and Urban Society, 24*(2), 227–243.

Courts, P. L. (1997). *Multicultural literacies: Dialect, discourse, and diversity.* New York: Peter Lang.

Downie, R. S., & Tefler, E. (1970). *Respect for persons.* New York: Schocken Books.

Freire, P. (1970). *Pedagogy of the oppressed.* New York: Continuum.

Freire, P., & Macedo, D. (1987). *Literacy: Reading the word and the world.* Westport, CT: Bergin & Garvey.

García, G. E., & Willis, A. I. (2001). Frameworks for understanding multicultural literacies. In P. R. Schmidt & P. B. Mosenthal (Eds.), *Reconceptualizing literacy in the new age of multiculturalism and pluralism* (pp. 3–31). Greenwich, CT: Information Age Publishing.

García, G. E., Willis, A. I., & Harris, V. J. (1998). Introduction: Appropriating and creating space for difference in literacy research. *Journal of Literacy Research, 30*(2), 181–186.

Gee, J. P. (1999). Critical issues: Reading and the New Literacy Studies: Reframing the National Academy of Sciences report on reading. *Journal of Literacy Research, 333,* 355–374.

Giroux, H. (1993). Literacy and the politics of difference. In C. Lankshear & P. L. McLaren (Eds.), *Critical literacy: Politics, praxis, and the postmodern* (pp. 367–377). Albany, NY: State University of New York Press.

Gutiérrez, K., Baquedano-López, P., & Turner, M. G. (1997). Putting language back into language arts: When the radical middle meets the third space. *Language Arts, 74,* 368–378.

Harris, V. J., (1993). Multicultural literacy and literature: The teacher's perspective. In S. Miller & B. McCoskell (Eds.), *Making space for difference* (pp. 187–295). Albany, NY: State University of New York Press.

Harris, V. J., & Willis, A. I. (2002). Multiculturalism, literature, and the curriculum. In J. Flood & D. Lapp (Eds.), *Handbook of research on teaching in the English language arts* (Vol. 2). New York: Longman.

Hernandez, H. (1989). *Multicultural education: A teacher's guide to content and process.* New York: Merrill.

John-Steiner, V., Panofsky, C. P., & Smith, L. W. (1994). Introduction. In V. John-Steiner, C. P. Panofsky, & L. W. Smith (Eds.), *Sociocultural approaches to language and literacy: An Interactionist perspective* (pp. 1–33). New York: Cambridge University Press.

Lankshear, C., & McLaren, P. L. (1993). Introduction. In C. Lankshear & P. L. McLaren (Eds.), *Critical literacy: Politics, praxis, and the postmodern* (pp. 1–56). Albany, NY: State University of New York Press.

Mertens, D. M. (1998). *Research methods in education and psychology: Integrating diversity with quantitative and qualitative approaches* Thousand Oaks, CA: Sage.

Moll, L. C. (1990). *Vygotsky and education: Instructional implications and applications of sociohistorical psychology.* Cambridge, England: Cambridge University Press.

Moll, L. C., & González, N. (1994). Critical issues: Lessons from research with language-minority children. *Journal of Reading Behavior: A Journal of Literacy, 26*(4), 439–456.

Murray, A. (1970). *The omni Americans: Some alternatives to the folklore of white supremacy.* New York: Vintage Books.

Schulman, L. (1986). Paradigms and research programs in the study of teaching: A contemporary perspective. In M. C. Wittrock (Ed.), *Handbook of research on teaching* (3rd ed., pp. 3–36). New York: Macmillan.

Sleeter, C. E., & Grant, C. A. (1987). An analysis of multicultural education in the United States. *Harvard Educational Review, 57,* 421–444.

Tharp, R. G., & Gallimore, R. (1988). *Rousing minds to life: Teaching, learning, and schooling in social context.* Cambridge, England: Cambridge University Press.

The New London Group. (1996). A pedagogy of multiliteracies: Designing social futures. *Harvard Educational Review, 66*(1), 60–92.

Tollefson, J. W. (1991). *Planning language, planning inequality: Language policy in the community.* New York: Longman.

Trueba, H. T., Jacobs, L., & Kirton, E. (1990). *Cultural conflict and adaptation: The case of Hmong children in American society.* New York: The Falmer Press.

U.S. Census Bureau. (2000). *Projections of the resident population by race, Hispanic origin, and nativity: Middle series, 2016 to 2020* [On-line]. Available: www.census.gov/population/www/projections/nation/summary/np-T5-e.pdf. Accessed: 12/13/01.

Weil, D. (1998). *Towards a critical multicultural literacy: Theory and practice for education for liberation.* New York: Peter Lang.

Wertsch, J. V. (Ed.). (1985). *Culture, communication, and cognition: Vygotskian perspectives.* Cambridge, England: Cambridge University Press.

Willis, A. I., & Harris, V. J. (1997). Expanding the boundaries: A reaction to the First-Grade Studies. *Reading Research Quarterly, 32,* 439–445.

Willis, A. I., & Harris, V. J. (2000). Political acts: Literacy learning and teaching. *Reading Research Quarterly, 35*(1), 72–88.

1

Finding Esmerelda's Shoes: A Case Study of a Young Bilingual Child's Responses to Literature

Eurydice Bouchereau Bauer
University of Illinois at Urbana–Champaign

Reader response to literature is a well-studied phenomenon. Research studies in this area have delineated five theoretical perspectives on reader response (Beach, 1993): textual responses (Eco, 1990; Rabinowitz, 1987), experiential responses (Hoffner & Cantor, 1991; Langer, 1992; Rosenblatt, 1983), psychological responses (Appleyard, 1990), social responses (Beach & Brown, 1986; Fish, 1980), and cultural responses (Giroux & Simon, 1989; Schweickart, 1986).

Reader response in the classroom typically privileges literary theorists such as Rosenblatt (1938, 1983). From this perspective, meaning does not reside in the text or with the author, but emerges from the reader's transaction with the text. More recently, researchers interested in Vygotsky's sociocultural theory have investigated how various contexts (social, cultural, and linguistic) help to shape the reader's responses (Harris & Rosales, 1998; Willis, 1997). From this sociocultural perspective, it is important to understand the readers' position culturally and historically in order to understand their responses to text (Brock & Gavelek, 1998).

Most studies examining reader response have focused on school-age children and adults rather than preschoolers. Little research has been done on the responses of preschool bilinguals. Studies on monolinguals suggest that very young children's responses to literature are shaped by their experiences with literature. Specifically, adults shape the developing literacy of children through their interactions during read-alouds (Heath, 1983; Martinez, 1983; Roser & Martinez, 1985; Sulzby, 1985). Parents shape children's responses through the strategies they use. According to Pelligrini, Perlmutter, Galda and Brody (1990), parents' strategies are linked to the type of text (narrative or expository) being read.

Although little is known about the type of responses that preschoolers give to literature, a great deal is known about other aspects of their early literacy development. Researchers agree that in the process of becoming readers and writers, preschoolers practice what it is to be literate (Sulzby, 1991). Specifically, they engage in emergent readings of favorite books, during which they turn pages, attend to pictures, and "retell" remembered versions of the text (Cochran-Smith, 1984). These emergent readers use strategies that are influenced by factors such as personal experience (Neuman & Roskos, 1992), amount of exposure to text readings (Sulzby, 1985), and textual factors: predictability, complexity, and genre (Martinez & Teale, 1988; Pappas & Brown, 1989). Elster (1994) found that preschoolers use strategies in their reading, which involve importing information from various sources: pictures, experience, previous readings, and other texts. Importations refer to "propositions related to, but not a paraphrase or rendition of, the text-explicit content of books being read" (Elster, 1998, p. 234).Thus, students' importations may provide a window into connections they make between a specific aspect of the text and their world experiences.

The term *genre*, as it is used in the response literature, refers to specific categories used to classify texts (Cullinan & Galda, 1998): poetry and verse, folklore, fantasy, science fiction, realistic fiction, historical fiction, biography, and nonfiction. Children's literature also can be divided by literary form (narratives and nonnarratives) and by format (i.e., picture books). Researchers who have investigated children's preference for narrative versus nonnarrative texts have found that grade school children typically prefer narrative texts (Baker & Stein, 1981). This preference seems to be influenced by children's greater experience with narrative texts (Baker & Stein, 1981; Baumann, 1981).

Some researchers have investigated the types of narratives that children prefer. Robinson, Larsen, Haupt, and Mohlman (1997) found that the genre and subgenre of books (alphabet or number, information, realistic fiction, traditional fantasy, and modern fantasy) influenced preschoolers' and kindergartners' selection and reselection of those texts for reading. Children in their study repeatedly selected traditional and modern fantasy books over other genres and subgenres (alphabet or number, information, and realistic fiction books). The subgenre of alphabet or number books and the genre of informational books were the least selected by the students.

Crago (1993) provided in part a possible explanation for the importance of fantasy to preschoolers. According to Crago, the ways that very young children respond to fantasy books are linked to their developmental need for fantasy play such as "pretending." Therefore, preschoolers' preference for the genre of fantasy is not arbitrary. In contrast to the study by Robinson et al. (1997), Lehr (1988) investigated the responses of kindergartners to realistic fiction and folktales and found that students had a better sense of theme for the genre of realistic fiction. Lehr concluded that realistic fiction mirrors experiences familiar to the students, which explains their better-developed sense of theme within that genre.

Crago's (1993) documentation of her daughter's emerging understanding of the fantastic during the reading of various fantasy stories provides a child-centered perspective on the early development of a specific reader's response within the genre of fantasy. Few studies to date take this type of detailed perspective on reader response for monolinguals or bilinguals. What is clearly missing in the response literature is a better understanding of the type of responses that preschoolers (monolinguals and bilinguals) exhibit during their interactions with different types of storybooks. To date, no research studies exist that clearly address the responses of preschool bilinguals. Bilinguals bring with them their languages, which are embedded in their social and cultural experiences. The way in which the linguistic and cultural aspects of the reader influence their responses needs to be well understood as we attempt to define further the transaction between the reader and the text. This is especially important because schools are charged with meeting the early literacy needs of a growing number of bilingual students. Early literacy educators must have a clear understanding of reader response in general, and of bilinguals' reading responses to face the challenge of educating all our children.

The current study documented the responses of a bilingual preschooler to specific picture books. The format of the picture books was central to the investigation (realistic fiction, fantasy, and predictable books). In particular, the study sought to understand what bilinguals bring to the story reading event. In addition, the study investigated whether the language in which the books are read to the child influences the responses given to the texts.

METHODS

Context of the Study

The following case study focuses on the literature responses of a 2-year-old, Elena, who was raised as an English and German bilingual from birth. This study is part of a larger ongoing study designed to capture Elena's interactions with English and German speakers during literacy, play, and other activities. The reported findings are based on shared readings with Elena from the age of 2 years to the age of 2 years and 8 months.

Language Context. Since Elena's birth, her mother, the researcher, has read to her in English. Her father, a native German speaker, has read to her in German. Both of her parents follow the *une personne une langue* (one person one language) rule (Ronjat, 1913). Elena's mother speaks to her exclusively in English, and her father speaks to her exclusively in German. Elena is aware of the fact that her mother understands the German spoken in the home. In addition to her parents, Elena's daycare provider, who is also a native German speaker, also reads to her in German. All of the adults communicate to each other in English.

Elena is encouraged to speak only in English with her mother and only in German with her father and *au pair.* Although Elena is addressed in English or German, she is exposed to other languages. Elena's mother was born in Haiti and speaks French and French creole. Elena is never addressed in the French or French Creole, but she is aware of these languages. That is, she knows that grandma (Elena's maternal grandmother) and her mom often speak in one of these languages. In addition, Elena's dad also speaks French, and on rare occasions speaks it to Elena's maternal grandmother.

Materials and Procedures

Responses to three books are the focus of these analyses. The three books were chosen from a corpus of 49 books read to Elena. The three books chosen for this study, *Brown Bear, Brown Bear, What Do You See?* (Martin, 1970), *Where the Wild Things Are* (Sendak, 1963), and *Black, White, Just White* (Davol, 1993) emerged as favorites that Elena requested frequently during the 8-month period. In addition, the three books were chosen because they allowed for examination of Elena's responses across different types of picture books. The books were read to her either before her naptime or before her bedtime. Each session was videotaped.

The book *Brown Bear, Brown Bear, What Do You See?* is a highly predictable and structured picture book. A simple pattern is established early in the text and repeated throughout the book. In each case, an animal is named and asked what it sees. The animal provides an answer, and then the animal seen by the first animal is asked the same question. For example, the book begins with "Brown bear, brown bear, what do you see? I see a red bird looking at me." This is followed by, "Red bird, red bird, what do you see? I see a yellow duck looking at me." This pattern is followed throughout the story. Therefore, once a child recognizes and understands the pattern, it is very easy for the child to follow along or join in the reading. The pictures support the text and provide a scaffold that also helps the child to predict the text; if a child is unsure of which animal should follow in a sequence, he or she simply has to turn the page and look at the picture to finish the phrase.

The book *Where the Wild Things Are* is a modern fantasy picture storybook. This book tells the story of a young boy, Max, who misbehaves and then is sent off to his room without his supper. While in his room, Max imagines himself taking a journey to the land "where the wild things are." In this faraway place, Max is able to conquer the wild things and becomes their ruler. For a short time, Max is very happy. However, he realizes that he misses being at home and decides to journey home. The illustrations in this text provide additional information to the story. In the middle of the book, for example, only illustrations are used to depict Max and the actions of the wild things during the wild rumpus in this fantasy land. The story is told in short poetic language that easily captures the reader's interest.

The book *Black, White, Just Right* is a realistic fiction picture storybook about a biracial family. This book follows a set pattern, but is not as predictable as *Brown Bear, Brown Bear, What Do You See?* The story is told in the first person by a young biracial girl who describes her family and their interests. Throughout the book, the child refers to her parents as mama and papa. The format used always presents the mother, father, and child. For example, the book begins by describing the mother's features followed by the father's, then their daughter's. The events and descriptions presented could be typical of any family. That is, the mother likes ballet, kittens, African art, and vegetables. The father likes rap, Saint Bernards, modern art, and barbecued ribs. Their daughter likes a variety of music, all kinds of animals, Egyptian tombs, and many types of foods. Although the content is familiar, the people in the story are unique. The family is composed of the mother, an African American, the father, a European American, and their daughter. The pictures are colorful and provide a simple but candid look at this family.

As shown in Table 1.1, each of the three books was read at least four times to Elena in both German and English. All of the books were introduced to her in English by her mother. Elena has copies of *Brown Bear, Brown Bear, What Do You See?* in both German and English. The other

TABLE 1.1
Percentage of Importations per Reading Events

Book Title	Language	No. of Readings	Average No. of Importations per Reading
BWJR	English	8	5.12
	German	4	6
WTWTA	English	8	0.75
	German	6	0.5
BBBB	English	7	1
	German	7	0.71

BWJR, *Black, White, Just Right*; WTWTA, *Where the Wild Things Are*; BBBB, *Brown Bear, Brown Bear, What Do You See?*

two books have English texts that were translated into German by the German readers as they read them. The texts as translated by the German readers were compared to see how much the readings differed from each other. Few differences were found across the readings after the second reading. It appears that Elena's father and her day-care provider memorized their translated texts and repeated them each time they read to her.

Analysis

The reading events in both German and English were transcribed by a research assistant, a native German speaker. Additionally, the German transcriptions were translated into English by the German research assistant for side-by-side comparisons of the reading events. Both the German and English reading events were coded for incidences of *importations*, comments made by Elena that went beyond repeating or paraphrasing what was in the text. The coding of the importations allowed for a closer examination concerning the type of personal connections that Elena made during each of the reading events. The importations were analyzed for their source according to Elster's (1995) categories: pictures, personal experience, previous read-alouds, and other texts.

RESULTS

Two themes emerged from the data. Both themes centered around the format of the books. The patterns that emerged across the texts held regardless of the language in which the books were read. Elena's responses to the texts read to her were limited because of her young age. It is un-likely that a child younger than 3 years of age will provide extensive re-sponses to a given text.

In this section of the chapter, excerpts from book interactions are used to illustrate certain points. The following initials are used to identify the individuals involved in the discussion: E, Elena; D, dad; M, mom; and A, *au pair*). Descriptions of adult and child actions appear in parentheses.

High Structure: Limited Importations

Echo Responses. Elena used few or no importations when she lis-tened to structurally predictable text. *Brown Bear, Brown Bear, What Do You See?* provided Elena with an opportunity to participate actively in partner reading with the reader. Most of her responses centered around helping the reader "read" the text, which limited her importations. For example, she would often say the repeated phrases as the reader read them, or she would echo them. Sometimes, anticipating what was to come in the text, she would say it before the reader. In the following ex-ample, Elena responded to her father's pauses in the reading as an invita-tion to say part of the phrase:

German Dialogue	*English Translation*
D: "Brauner Bär, brauner Bär, was siehst du?" (pauses)	D: "Brown bear, brown bear, what do you see?"
E: "Baune Bä."	E: "Brown bear."
D: "Brauner Bär, was siehst du?"	D: "Brown bear, what do you see?"
D: Ich sehen einen	D: "I see a . . ."
E: "Rote Voge."	E: "Red bird."
D: "Roten Vogel, der mich anschaut."	D: "Red bird looking at me."

Intertextual Links

When reading this predictable text, Elena did not engage the readers in discussions about the book, nor did she try to introduce any of her life experiences into the readings. On several occasions, Elena made intertextual links between the book *Brown Bear, Brown Bear, What Do You See?* and another similar book *Polar Bear, Polar Bear, What Do You Hear?* Both books follow the same melody and pattern. While reading *Brown Bear, Brown Bear, What Do You See?* with her mother, Elena imported (Elster, 1995) the repeated phrase from the book *Polar Bear, Polar Bear, What Do You Hear?* This importation was found in both the English and German transcripts.

German Dialogue	*English Translation*
D: "Gelbe Gans, gelbe Gans, was siehst du?"	D: "Yellow duck, yellow duck, what do you see?"
D: "Ich sehe . . . Was sieht die gelbe Gans?"	D: "I see . . . What does the yellow duck see?"
E: "Gebe Gans what do you hear?"	E: "Yellow duck what do you hear?"
D: "Was sieht die gelbe Gans?"	D: "What does the yellow duck see?"
E: "Gebe Gans, what do you hör?"	E: "Yellow duck, what do you hear?"
D: "Sieht ein blaues Pferd."	D: "It sees a blue horse."

English Dialogue
M: "Red bird, red bird, what do you see?"
M: "I see a . . . What does he see?"
E: "Red bird, what do you hear?"
M: "What does the red bird see?"
E: "I hear a yellow duck."
M: "I see a yellow duck looking at me."

It should be noted that Elena responded to the first question in both ex-amples by importing the phrase "what do you hear" from the *Polar Bear, Polar Bear, What Do You Hear* book. When she was questioned a second time by her mother, she answered the question, but kept the imported phrase. This seems to suggest that she was not attending to the meaning cue put forth by her mother and father, but was attending to the formu-laic phrases of the text.

Meaningful Prose: High Importations

Importations occurred most when the text was not highly predictable and the genre of the story was most similar to her life (i.e., realistic fiction). Realistic fiction created an entrée for Elena to introduce her comparable life experiences into the text. *Black, White, Just Right*, a book about a bira-cial family with a composition similar that of Elena's family, in which the mother is African American, the father European, and the child biracial, led to more importations (Elster, 1995) within individual readings and across readings (Table 1.1).

Experience-Driven Responses.   Many of Elena's importations were tied to the illustrations, but represented her personal experiences. One type of importation was a deliberate attempt to sort out her family structure by using the pictures in the book. For example, the dedication page in the book has a picture of the author (a European American woman) standing between her two grandchildren (a girl and a boy). Elena noticed the two children, but instead of making a direct connection between the children and herself, she connected the illustration to another family member. That is she linked her mother's complexion to that of the author's granddaughter:

E: "Dis (this) mommy!" (looking at the little girl)
M: "Who, the little girl?"
E: "Dis (this) mommy!"
M: (Laughs)
E: "Dis (this) mommy, dis!"
M: "You think she looks like me? We have the same coloring."

Elena's attention to the dedication page is not surprising. Whenever her mother read with her, she pointed out that the book was dedicated to the author's grandchildren. Elena's connection between the picture on the dedication page and her own family is an extension of the routine established by her mother.

Other routines during the reading of *Black, White, Just Right* clarified the way that Elena was approaching the text. Before reading the book to Elena, her mother would turn to the first page of the story and ask her to label the characters in the illustrations. This activity was first initiated by Elena and later supported by her mother. Often, when Elena's mother pointed to the woman, Elena said, "Dat (that is) mommy." When she pointed to the father, Elena said, "Daddy." When she pointed to the little girl, Elena said, "Dis (this is) Lena!" Although Elena recognized that there were parent characters in the story, she clearly was identifying with the little girl in the story.

The format of the story supported and perhaps heightened Elena's interest in the characters by introducing new information about them in a set pattern. For example, the book described the characters' physical attributes in the following way:

> Black is the color of Mama's hair, crinkling, curling around her face. Papa's hair is popcorn colored, short and straight and silky-smooth. My hair? Halfway in between a dark brown ponytail tied tight. Three in the mirror—we look just right!

This format made it very easy for Elena to separate the characters and their attributes.

Elena's strong connection with the text was further revealed during discussions around the topic "Esmerelda shoes." Elena had a pair of tennis shoes with a picture of the Disney character, Esmerelda, on them. The character was brown-skinned with dark black hair. This pair of shoes was her most prized possession. From Elena's perspective, an illustration in the book, a mural of brown-skinned women in an old Egyptian tomb, resembled the Esmerelda picture on her shoes. It did not matter who was reading the book; the reader was always stopped on that page. For example, during a reading with her mother, Elena stopped her to show her the connection she was making.

Text:	"Mama stares at African masks, curved drums, carved figures made of wood. Papa goes for modern art, all squiggles, squares, and stretched out shapes. My choice"
E:	"Ma shoes."
M:	"Yeah."
E:	"Ma shoes!!"
M:	"Yeah, she reminds you of the girl on your shoes."
E:	"Uh hum."

Again, this example highlights Elena's attempt to identify with the girl in the story. Her choice, like that of the protagonist in the story, is for the Esmerelda/Egyptian-like women.

Picture-Driven Connections.   Some of Elena's importations were triggered by illustrations that reminded her of specific experiences with her family. Near the end of the book, there is a picture of the father carrying the little girl on his shoulder. During reading sessions, Elena talked about her own experience with her dad carrying her on his shoulder.

E: "Like Mein dahdy." (like my daddy)

M: "Did your daddy put you on his shoulder?"
E: "Ja, an hoch." (yes, and high)
M: "Were you feeling really tall?"
E: "Ja." (yes)

Wherever Elena found a personal connection to be made with the text, she made it and then engaged the reader in a discussion centered around the related events. As with the preceding example, when Elena listened to the story *Black, White, Just Right*, she had a tendency to use her German with her mom when she discussed her dad. A similar pattern was not found when Elena read with the German readers. She did not comment about her experiences with her mom during those readings.

Descriptive Text Responses. Although Elena made a number of personal connections with the book *Black, White, Just Right*, she did not make the same type of connection or as many connections with the fantasy book *Where the Wild Things Are*. Her responses during the readings of *Where the Wild Things Are* were tied to the illustrations and reflect mostly her observation of what was taking place in the story. Some of her comments described what the characters were doing. For example, during one of the reading sessions, she pointed to one of the wild things and said, "He scares you." This comment was directed to the main character, Max. In addition to comments that situated her as an observer, she also pointed out behaviors similar to her own. For example, as part of the reading routine, the readers would describe the illustrations during the wild rumpus. For example, during a reading with the *au pair*, she read the illustration-only pages in the following way:

> Oh Lena, guck mal wie sie tanzen! Und den Mond anbrüllen! Und an den Bäumen hängen und mit den Füßen strampeln und einen Marsch machen, bei dem Max auf dem Rücken sitzt auf einem der wilden Tiere.

> Oh Lena, look how they are dancing. And yelling at the moon. And hang in the trees. And kick with their feet. And are going on a march, during which Max is sitting on the back of one of the wild animals.

There was no text on these pages, so the reader's descriptions of the pictures kept the flow of the story moving forward. On one of the wordless pages, Max, the main character, is shown swinging in a tree. Regardless of the reader, whenever this page was described, Elena would say, "In mine (my) tree swing." According to Elena, she too enjoys swinging, especially on her jungle gym.

Elena's other comments during the readings of *Where the Wild Things Are* tended to redirect the reader's attention to a specific detail in the illustrations. For example, she would say things like "look at he (his) eyes," or "he funny" while pointing to one of the wild things. Although she was interested in the illustrations, she did not want to engage the readers in a discussion about them. If the reader attempted to sustain a discussion about the illustrations, she would often say, "Wead" (read). Although this text was read to Elena often in both German and English, her level of engagement with the readers and the text was far less than with *Black, White, Just Right.*

Responses Across the Text

The three books were of different interest to Elena, and she responded accordingly. The importance Elena gave a particular book was tied in part to the format and content of the text.

It appears that Elena approached the predictable text *Brown Bear, Brown Bear, What Do You See?* as an opportunity to practice sounding like a reader in English and German. The repetitive pattern, the rhyming, and the simple language provided a level of scaffolding that made it very easy for her to memorize the text. After a couple of readings in the two languages, Elena could participate in the "reading" of the book. Elena was possibly drawn to this book because of its wonderful rhythm. However, the rhythm and pattern of the text also limited Elena's responses. Elena never responded to the content of the book. That is, she never commented about the habitat of these animals or tried to link the book animals with those she had seen in her environment. Nor did she talk about what the animals in her environment might see. Another explanation is that Elena did not make personal connections because the adult readers did not encourage this kind of behavior. It is also possible that there simply was not enough content inviting her to make a deep connection with the text. Therefore, this text structure limited her personal responses, but provided her with a format that helped her to practice her reading in both of her languages.

Elena's responses to the fantasy text, *Where the Wild Things Are*, was qualitatively different from her responses to the predictable text. When Elena listened to *Where the Wild Things Are*, she did not try to read the text with the reader as she did with *Brown Bear, Brown Bear, What Do You See?* Instead, she listened to the reader and responded to the content of the story. It is not clear from this data whether the prose format made it easier for her to stay focused on the storyline and to import relevant information to the readings. Nevertheless, most of her importations were tied to illustrations and did not reflect a deep personal connection. Elena could identify and respond to some of the things that Max did, but did not see herself as Max. Therefore, her role was that of the observer pointing out important happenings to the reader.

Realistic fiction provided Elena with the greatest opportunity for responding in different ways. *Black, White, Just Right* allowed Elena to bring her personal life into the story, and to act as commentator-observer. The format of the story allowed Elena to position herself in the center of the story. Because the story is told in the first person by the child, and because her name is never mentioned, Elena could easily take on the perspective of the storyteller. For example, Elena's comments such as "dat's me," "like me," or "like my mommy and daddy" indicate that she was perhaps embedding her life in the fabric of the story. The family structure depicted in the story is one very familiar to Elena. The format and the content of the book transformed the reading experience for Elena into a discussion of her life. This may explain Elena's active role in seeking opportunities for discussions throughout the readings. It appears that realistic fiction affirmed her personal experience and allowed her to examine her place in her family. As a result, Elena talked more and responded in a variety of ways to the text.

CONCLUSION

The issue of a bilingual reader's responses is one that cannot be addressed without raising the question of language. To understand the meaning behind bilinguals' responses, it is important to recognize that they have two languages within which to respond to literature. More importantly, their languages may play a role in shaping their responses. The following section provides final remarks on Elena's responses and their link to the current literature. First, the discussion focuses on three categories of responses. This is followed by a discussion on the importance of these findings to educators.

Reader-Shaped Responses

The response literature on preschoolers suggests that children's responses are shaped by the reader (Martinez, 1983; Roser & Martinez, 1985; Sulzby, 1985). This study seems to support that finding. Elena exhibited certain behaviors similar to those discussed in the cited studies. For example, Elena's attention to the dedication page in *Black, White, Just Right* was a direct result of her mother pointing out to her the author's note. Subsequently, as Elena became comfortable with the book and freely interacted with the readers, she also focused on the dedication page. Although there is some overlap with previous research, there were differences between what was modeled and Elena's enactment of that routine. As shown in the Results section, Elena adapted the routine interaction surrounding the introduction by inserting her world knowledge into the interaction. In essence, Elena added her own meaning to the message that the author wanted to convey. It is possible that Elena's high interest and engagement with *Black, White, Just Right* created a comfort zone that allowed her to move freely beyond adult-established routines.

Language-Driven Responses

Although some preschoolers' responses may be shaped by the reader's comments, the responses of bilinguals also may be shaped by a meshing of the experience to which the child is responding, the person the child associates with that experience, and the language of that individual. This certainly appears to have been the case with Elena when she was discussing *Black, White, Just Right*. As recalled, Elena had a tendency to discuss in German with her mother her personal experience of riding on her dad's shoulder. Elena's use of German with her mother may reflect the fact that Elena knows that her mother will understand her. However, this raises the issue of whether experiences for bilinguals are recalled within the language wherein it occurred. That is not to say that the child does not have the words to describe the experience in the other language. Certainly, Elena had the English words to describe to her mother her experience with her dad. What seems to be important is that her response revolved around a "daddy experience," which to her may also have meant a "German experience."

Although the preceding discussion on Elena's German response in an English reading context raises the issue of how responses occur for bilinguals, it is important to note that Elena did not provide a parallel example with the German readers. That is to say, she did not discuss specific "mother experiences" with the German readers. Her discussions with them focused on what she could do that was similar to the protagonist's actions. Researchers have raised the issue of topic-specific code-switching in oral communication (Boeschoten & Verhoeven, 1987; Stavans, 1992). It is possible that a similar phenomenon takes place during interaction with print. This certainly is a point that should be investigated further by researchers.

All Narratives Are Not the Same

Elena responded differently to the three narrative texts read to her. Elena imported very little during the repeated readings of *Brown Bear, Brown Bear, What Do You See?* She imported some with the book *Where the Wild Things Are*, and a great deal with the realistic fiction *Black, White, Just Right*. This case study seems to support Lehr's (1988) contention that realistic fiction mirrors the experiences most similar to those of the emergent readers, which may create a unique link for understanding realistic text. It is possible that Elena's comfort with this realistic fiction led her to import more relevant information through the pictures and from her personal experience. It is not clear whether Elena's importations increased her engagement with the text, or whether her level of engagement increased her importations. What is clear is that Elena's importations provided a window into what she found to be important during the readings. Understanding what preshoolers view to be important during reading events may lead to a deeper appreciation for the way they create meaning.

Importance to Educators

Elena's response patterns have raised questions regarding the texts used with young children, particularly with bilinguals. Often in the early literacy literature, teachers are advised to make books available to children in an attempt to shape their literacy experiences positively. The assumption is that age-appropriate books, whatever the form, will have a positive impact on students. This study does not dispute that statement, but makes clearer the ways in which certain books can influence preschoolers.

Findings from this study suggest that educators must provide a variety of texts to the young reader, and that realistic fiction that is personally relevant may be particularly desirable to foster meaningful engagement with books. This has special significance to preschool bilinguals. Reading books to preschool bilinguals that allow them greater opportunity to see themselves may change their level of engagement with the text and afford them different opportunities to interact around print. This level of engagement is important for all students, but it is especially important for bilinguals. Findings from studies on language minorities in this country suggest that they often are left out of the literacy club. Finding text that invites students to respond in various ways will assist them in developing greater interest in what books have to offer.

REFERENCES

Appleyard, J. (1990). *Becoming a reader: The experience of fiction from adolescent to adulthood.* New York: Cambridge University Press.

Baker, L., & Stein, N. (1981). The development of prose comprehension skills. In C. Santa & B. Hayes (Eds.), *Children's prose comprehension research and practice* (pp. 7–43). Newark, DE: International Reading Association.

Baumann, J. (1981). *Children's ability to comprehend main ideas after reading expository prose.* Paper presented at the annual meeting at the National Reading Conference, Dallas, TX.

Beach, R. (1993). *Reader-response theories.* Urbana, IL: NCTE.

Beach, R., & Brown, R. (1986). Discourse conventions and literary inferences. In R. Tierney, P. Anders, & J. Mitchell (Eds.), *Understanding readers' understanding* (pp. 147–174). Hillsdale, NJ: Lawrence Erlbaum Associates.

Brock, C., & Gavelek, J. (1998). Fostering children's engagement with texts: A sociocultural perspective. In T. Raphael & K. Au (Eds.), *Literature-based instruction: Reshaping the curriculum* (pp. 71–94). Norwood, MA: Christopher-Gordon.

Cochran-Smith, M. (1984). *The making of a reader.* Norwood, NJ: Ablex.

Crago, M. (1993). Creating and comprehending the fantastic: A case study of a child from twenty to thirty-five months. *Children's Literature in Education, 24*(3), 209–222.

Cullinan, B., & Galda, L. (1998). *Literature and the child.* Orlando, FL: Harcourt Brace & Company.

Eco, U. (1990). *The limits of interpretation.* Bloomington, IN: Indiana University Press.

Elster, C. (1994). Patterns within preschoolers' emergent readings. *Reading Research Quarterly, 29*(4), 402–418.

Elster, C. (1995). Importations in preschoolers' emergent reading. *Journal of Reading Behavior, 27*(1), 65–84.

Elster, C. (1998). *Knowledge-based importations in shared and emergent readings: Evidence of contextual constraints on reading.* Paper presented at the forty-seventh annual meeting at the National Reading Conference, Scottsdale, AZ.

Fish, S. (1980). *Is there a text in this class? The authority of interpretive communities.* Cambridge, MA: Harvard University Press.

Giroux, H., & Simon, R. (1989). Popular culture and critical pedagogy: Everyday life as a basis for curriculum knowledge. In H. Giroux & P. McLaren (Eds.), *Critical pedagogy: The state, and cultural struggle.* Albany, NY: State University of New York Press.

Harris, V., & Rosales, M. (1998). Biracial and multicultural identity: Dilemmas for children's literature. In T. Raphael & K. Au (Eds.), *Literature-based instruction: Reshaping the curriculum.* Norwood, MA: Christopher-Gordon.

Heath, S. (1983). *Ways with words.* New York: Cambridge University Press.

Hoffner, C., & Cantor, J. (1991). Perceiving and responding to mass media characters. In J. Bryant & D. Zillmann (Eds.), *Responding to the screen: Reception and reaction processes.* Hillsdale, NJ: Lawrence Erlbaum Associates.

Hunt, R., & Vipond, D. (1985). Crash-testing a transactional model of literacy learning. *Reader, 14*, 23–39.

Langer, J. (1992). *Literature instruction: A focus on student response*. Urbana, IL: NCTE.

Lehr, S. (1988). The child's developing sense of theme as a response to literature. *Reading Research Quarterly, 23*, 337–357.

Martinez, M. (1983). Young children's verbal responses to literature in parent–child story-time interactions (doctoral dissertation, University of Texas at Austin). *Dissertation Abstracts International, 44*, 1044A.

Martinez, M., & Teale, W. (1988). Reading in a kindergarten library. *The Reading Teacher, 41*, 568–572.

Neuman, S., & Roskos, K. (1992). Literacy objects as cultural tools: Effects on children's literacy behaviors in play. *Reading Research Quarterly, 27*, 202–225.

Pappas, S., & Brown, E. (1989). Using turns at story reading as scaffolding for learning. *Theory Into Practice, 28*, 105–113.

Pelligrini, A. D., Perlmutter, J., Galda, L., & Brody, G. (1990). Joint reading between black Head Start children and their mothers. *Child Development, 61*, 443–453.

Rabinowitz, P. (1987). *Before reading: Narrative conventions and the politics of interpretation*. Ithaca, NY: Cornell University Press.

Robinson, C., Larson, J., Haupt, J., & Mohlman, J. (1997). Picture book selection behaviors of emergent readers: Influence of genre, familiarity, and book attributes. *Reading Research and Instruction, 36*, 287–304.

Ronjat, J. (1913). *Le Developpment Du Langage*. Paris: Champion.

Rosenblatt, L. (1938). *Literature as exploration*. New York: Noble & Noble.

Roser, N., & Martinez, M. (1985). Roles adults play in preschoolers' response to literature. *Language Arts, 62*(5), 185–190.

Schweickart, P. (1986). Reading ourselves: Toward a feminist theory of reading. In E. Flynn & P. Schweickart (Eds.), *Gender and reading: Essays on readers, texts, and contexts*. Baltimore, MD: John Hopkins University Press.

Sulzby, E. (1985). Children's emergent reading of favorite story books. *Reading Research Quarterly, 20*, 458–481.

Sulzby, E. (1991). Assessment of emergent literacy: Storybook reading. *The Reading Teacher, 44*(7), 498–500.

Willis, A. I. (1997). Exploring multicultural literature as cultural production. In T. Rogers & A. Soter (Eds.), *Reading across cultures: Teaching literature in a diverse society* (pp. 135–160). New York: Teachers College Press Columbia University.

WORKS CITED

Davol, M. (1993). *Black, white, just right*. Morton Grove, IL: Albert Whitman.

Martin, B. (1970). *Brown bear, brown bear, what do you see?* New York: Henry Holt & Co.

Sendak, M. (1963). *Where the wild things are*. New York: Scholastic.

2

Examining Children's Biliteracy in the Classroom

Joel Dworin
The University of Texas at Austin

Biliteracy is an important area of study that promises much in terms of helping us to better understand children's language and literacy development, yet it has received relatively little attention from researchers and scholars. *Biliteracy* is a term used to describe children's literate competencies in two languages, developed to varying degrees, either simultaneously or successively. In the United States, one of the few settings in which to study biliteracy is among Latina/o children in bilingual education programs.[1] These children comprise approximately 75% of all students in such programs (August & Hakuta, 1997).

Although one might expect to find research on biliteracy in areas such as bilingual education or second language learning, a review of the literature in these areas indicates that this is not the case. Ironically, even in the field of literacy research, where the relationship of different "literacies" to social contexts and cultural practices has become a prominent feature of study (John-Steiner, Panofsky & Smith, 1994; Scribner &

---

[1]This is not to suggest that children develop literacy or biliteracy solely in classrooms, but that the phenomenon of biliteracy is most visible for study in bilingual classrooms (Moll & Dworin, 1996). At the same time, although biliteracy is not fostered and not an instructional goal in most bilingual classrooms, it is a common "by-product" of languages-in-contact that may be observed among "language-minority" students. However, given the compensatory "Americanizing" character of most bilingual programs, in which proficiency in English is the main goal, students do not typically develop their biliteracy beyond incipient levels in schools without deliberate instructional support.

Cole, 1981), the topic of biliteracy has not received much attention. This neglect continues even though bilingualism is such a common phenomenon worldwide and obviously relevant to the study of how literacy is constituted in different contexts. (Sample studies of biliteracy include Bialystok, 1997; Ferdman, Weber, & Ramírez, 1994; Jiménez, García, & Pearson, 1996; Moll & Dworin, 1996; and Walsh, 1994.)

The same situation holds even for the study of bilingualism, a field that has tended to ignore the study of literacy. As Valdés (1992) noted: "In general, the research on bilingualism has concerned itself primarily with the study of the spoken language. Most studies have focused on bilingualism as opposed to biliteracy" (p. 5). None of the early work in bilingualism (Haugen, 1950; Leopold, 1939–1949; Weinreich, 1953) examined issues of biliteracy, and neither of two influential books, one on bilingualism (Hakuta, 1986) and the other on second language acquisition (Bialystok & Hakuta, 1994), addresses biliteracy to any extent.[2]

In this chapter, I discuss biliteracy, using selected examples from a case study of Daniel, a 7-year-old Mexican American student who was becoming biliterate in Spanish and English. First, I introduce biliteracy as a topic of study, identify its significance in education, and outline the theoretical foundations that informed this work. Next, I describe relevant aspects of the classroom setting, the teacher, and the students to provide an orientation to the specific qualities of the classroom. This section is followed by a discussion of selected examples from Daniel's case study to provide some insights into his biliteracy development.

SIGNIFICANCE OF BILITERACY

One of the most significant implications of biliteracy lies with its potential intellectual consequences, particularly students' ability to establish mediated relationships between symbol systems and the social world to create knowledge and transform it for meaningful purposes. Students' biliterate abilities, therefore, represent key linguistic and cultural tools

[2]However, a growing body of research is concerned with bilingual education in U.S. classrooms, and the current study has been informed by many of these studies, particularly those that used qualitative methods to study classroom life (Díaz, Moll, & Mehan, 1986; Montiel, 1992; Quintero, 1986; Whitmore & Crowell, 1994). In addition, there are many studies of bilingual children's reading (Barrera, 1983; Faltis, 1986; Hudelson, 1981a; Jiménez et al., 1996; among others) as well as studies of bilinguals and writing (Ammon, 1985; Hudelson, 1988, 1981b; Johnson & Roen, 1989; Lanauze & Snow, 1989; Maguire, 1987; among others). These and other studies have been an important source for understanding both theoretical perspectives of and pedagogical practices in bilingual classrooms.

that may greatly assist their intellectual development in ways not readily available in monolingual English classrooms. Unlike monolinguals, these children can transact with two literate worlds, thus amplifying their resources for thinking and learning (Moll & Dworin, 1996).

There is also the relatively unexplored area of the cognitive consequences of biliteracy. Studies by Díaz (1983), among others (Bild & Swain, 1989; Díaz & Klinger, 1991; Hakuta, 1986; Hakuta & Díaz, 1985; Malakoff & Hakuta, 1991; Reynolds, 1991), suggest that there are differences in cognitive processes between monolingual and bilingual students, and that bilinguals may have significant cognitive advantages over monolinguals. Although considerable research has been done in this area (see e.g., Bialystok, 1991), less work has been done on biliteracy per se and the cognitive advantages that may result, especially from its use in classrooms. This may be the result of several factors, among them the hegemony of English in U.S. society and its predominance as the language of literacy in the schools. Other likely factors impeding such research include the general lack of importance given by the dominant culture to biliteracy and its development and the frequent focus on students' English proficiency as the main goal of most bilingual educational programs in this country.

Biliteracy is an important component for the development of a culturally relevant pedagogy for Latina/o children. Biliterate students are able to access a broader range of cultural resources in two languages, including, but not limited to, mass media, the Internet, library resources, and the many forms of popular texts, as well as other Spanish- or English-speaking children and adults who reside outside their immediate area. Thus, their worlds can expand to include not only the United States, but also Latin America and countries of other Spanish-speaking people, creating intellectual linkages to a legacy of Spanish discourses, literatures, and literacies.[3] Literacy in the two languages could mediate innumerable classroom projects as part of a culturally relevant pedagogy (Ladson-Billings, 1995; Moll, Vélez-Ibáñez, & Greenberg, with Andrade, R., Dworin, J., Saavedra, E., & Whitmore, K., 1990), precisely because students' biliteracy and bilingualism are the vital tools of inquiry within these cultural contexts. Teachers also could promote similar objectives through classroom studies in their lo-

---

[3]A personal comment by Ferdman (1990) is relevant in this regard. He described the mediating role of biliteracy and its importance to his ethnic identity in transactions with texts as an adult biliterate: "When I want to read a Latin American author, I will do so in Spanish, my native tongue, rather than in an English translation. My choice is based not only on a desire to read the original, but also to reaffirm my connection with Latin American symbols and texts. In spite of ostensibly similar content, I experience the images and meanings differently in the two languages" (p. 196).

cal communities as well, using students' cultural backgrounds in different, yet perhaps even more significant ways (Moll, Tapia, & Whitmore, 1993). In short, biliteracy might be fully used for academic purposes that expand learning possibilities by building on the languages and cultures that these students bring to their classrooms.

Finally, there is potential for "language majority" (monolingual English or Anglophone) students to become biliterate within school contexts. However, this might be a more challenging undertaking for at least two reasons. First, providing sufficient support for the biliteracy development of these children within and outside classrooms is difficult, given the hegemony of English in U.S. society (Shannon, 1995; Walsh, 1991). Second, elective bilingualism tends to be an individual, rather than a group, process (Valdés, 1992; Valdés & Figueroa, 1994). Biliteracy development for Anglophone students is possible, nonetheless, and does occur in bilingual settings. However, relatively little research attention has been given to this topic, especially in qualitative research. In general, then, further research is needed in all the areas outlined earlier to help advance an understanding of the potential intellectual, cognitive, and cultural consequences of biliteracy in classroom settings.

The examples provided in this chapter are from a study in which I examined English–Spanish biliteracy development among students in a bilingual, combination grade 2–3 grade classroom for one school year (Dworin, 1996). The study used a number of qualitative methods, especially a case study approach, to allow for an in-depth examination of specific children's English–Spanish biliteracy development and the respective supporting contexts. Three case studies of students provided insights into significant aspects of each student's developing biliteracy and demonstrated that there are multiple paths to English–Spanish biliteracy (Barrera, 1983; Edelsky, 1986, 1991; Goodman, Goodman, & Flores, 1979; Moll & Dworin, 1996). The results of this inquiry suggest that biliteracy development in classrooms is feasible, but that teachers must create "additive" conditions, encouraging students to use and develop their Spanish along with their English (Landry & Allard, 1991), and attempt to make both languages relatively "unmarked" in the classroom, that is, comparable in status.

THEORETICAL FRAMEWORK

A key assumption of the study, and one that distinguishes it from most studies of bilingual classrooms, is that biliteracy is a special form of literacy needing to be understood as distinct from that of monolinguals. The bilingual person may experience a wider range and variety of literacy practices than the monolingual person because of participation in different social networks, for example, those that could amplify the potential consequences of literacy beyond what can be accomplished by the monolingual person in one language or the other (Moll & Dworin, 1996). Valdés (1992), among others (Moll & Dworin, 1996; Walsh, 1991), also subscribes to the view that the study of bilinguals and biliteracy requires a different research lens. She calls for a rethinking of assumptions about first and second language writing in English and emphasizes the need to develop research that views these practices from a "bilingual perspective."

Much of the work on bilingual education, however, suffers from applying to bilingual situations research and instructional practices drawn from work conducted with English monolinguals with little appreciation that there may be important differences (Moll & Dworin, 1996; Valdés, 1992, 1997). Grosjean (1989), for example, has discussed this monolingual view of bilingualism and its negative consequences. Much, if not all of his discussion also applies to biliteracy and biliterates. The key point is that a monolingual perspective does not suffice for understanding bilinguals and bilingualism, or biliteracy, yet this is the guiding perspective for much of the research in this area (Dodson, 1985; Moll & Dworin, 1996; Valdés, 1992; Walsh, 1991).

METHODS

Data collection took place in the classroom and school over a period of 9 months, or one academic year. The primary data sources consisted of participant observations, field notes, interviews, student reading and writing samples, and informal conversations with the teacher and students. I spent more than 350 hours in the school. The participant observations were conducted approximately twice per week throughout the school year, and each visit lasted from 5 to 6 hours. I used a case study approach to document specific students' dual language and literacy development in the classroom (Merriam, 1988; Spradley, 1980; Yin, 1984).

Field notes from participant observations were coded and analyzed for themes. Emerging patterns in the data provided direction for further data gathering. Several methods of analysis for constructing case studies of the focal students were used, among them miscue analysis of reading samples and holistic analysis of selected writing samples. Steps in the analytical process included coding transcribed interviews for content, examining coded field notes describing focal students in classroom activities, and coding by themes or topics the transcribed cassette recordings of informal conversations with the students and teacher.

The Teacher

When I began the study, Kathy, a certified bilingual teacher who held a bachelor's degree in elementary education, had been teaching for 12 years. (She would later receive her master's degree in language, reading, and culture in December 1998). She had learned Spanish in Mexico and in Tucson, Arizona, her hometown. Well-respected by her peers and others in the profession, Kathy had given professional presentations on numerous occasions for school district in-services, national workshops, and conferences.

Kathy reported that she had been developing as a teacher and was more confident at the time of the study than in previous years. She subscribed to a holistic philosophy of instruction that views understanding children and the knowledge they bring to school as extremely important to good teaching and critical to learning. In her classroom, children learned to work collaboratively as a community of learners, and being a good student included positive working relationships with other students.

The Students

Each classroom in this K–3 primary school was known by a teacher-designated name. The classroom in which this study took place was known as the "Tree Room." At the beginning of the school year, there were 27 students in the class, 14 second and 13 third graders. Twenty of these children were from neighborhoods near the school. The rest were from different parts of the city and attended 22nd Street Primary Magnet School voluntarily as part of the school district's desegregation program. All but one of the second graders had attended 22nd Street the previous year, and most of the third graders had been there in second grade. Of the 27 students in the Tree Room, 12 were girls (7 in second grade, 5 in third grade) and 15 were boys (6 in second grade, 9 in third grade). There were 18 Mexican American/Chicano, 8 Anglo, and 1 African American students in the class.

There was a diverse range in the children's language and literacy abilities at the beginning of the school year. Ten of the children spoke only English, and 12 used only English for reading and writing. One of the students was Spanish monolingual in speaking, reading, and writing. Of the Mexican American/Chicano students, three were English dominant in speaking, reading, and writing, but they also spoke Spanish. The rest were to varying degrees bilingual speakers of English and Spanish, with a broad range of reading and writing abilities in the two languages. Two or three of the Anglo students knew a little Spanish and understood some phrases used on the playground. Most significant for biliteracy development, 16 of the students were bilingual English and Spanish.

The 22nd Street bilingual program had characteristics of a maintenance-type program. Spanish was used as the co-language of the classroom, and students were not pressured to learn English at the expense of Spanish. In other words, it was not a "subtractive" program (Kjolseth, 1982; Lambert, 1974) in which the goal was to replace Spanish with English as the sole language of instruction.

Both the monolingualism of the English students and the bilingualism of most of the native Spanish speakers represented key resources for bilingual and biliteracy development. These language resources created positive conditions for biliteracy development not only among the native Spanish-speaking students, but among the monolingual English speakers as well. Given the collaborative approach to learning in this classroom, the students themselves became primary resources for their learning. Language and literacy were appropriated mostly through social rather than solitary contexts, and sharing ideas through talking, reading, and writing was expected and encouraged by the teacher (Wells & Chang-Wells, 1992).

DANIEL: A BILINGUAL SECOND GRADER BECOMING BILITERATE

During the first month of school, when Kathy discussed the literacy development of her students with me, Daniel was one of the children she described as "bilingual and becoming biliterate." He and his family lived in one of the neighborhoods immediately adjacent to his school, which he had attended the previous year. Daniel was a good student, well liked by his classmates. He had a good sense of humor and was very articulate. He also tended to be something of a perfectionist, and because of this, could be very self-critical at times.

In this section, I discuss Daniel's biliteracy, specifically his reading, by presenting examples in English and Spanish and identifying some of the supports for his literacy development in the two languages. The focus is on the teacher's mediational role, the importance of Daniel's view of himself as a bilingual person, and how these two aspects facilitated his biliteracy development.

The Teacher's Mediational Role

In September, Kathy assessed the oral reading of each of her students using the "running record" technique (Clay, 1988). On the day she assessed
Daniel, I had a discussion with her about his reading. She shared with me
some thoughts about the reading session:

> Then I have these books, you know, the kind with real predictable text,
> but I wanted to see if he could handle something harder. I had him read *El
> Ratoncito del Campo y el Ratoncito de la Ciudad* (The Little Mouse From the
> Country and the Little Mouse From the City). You know, it's an extended
> piece of text, it's got a lot of words. So, I wanted to see if he could do it.

Kathy then described her session with Daniel, revealing her role in
helping him use some specific reading strategies. With a little assistance
from his teacher, mostly in the form of encouragement, Daniel was able
to read the entire book. Kathy elaborated:

> But I showed him this book and I said, "You know, when you're looking at
> a book, there's nothing wrong with first just looking at the pictures and us-
> ing picture clues." I said, "I still use picture clues when I read." So I
> showed this to him and said, "You know, Daniel, I bet you could read this
> [the *El Ratoncito* book] to me." And so he kinda looked at me like I was
> nuts. I asked him to look at the pictures and then I left the room. When I
> came back, he was just, like, frozen on the first page. And I said to him,
> "¿Quieres empezar, mi'jo?" ("Do you want to begin, my son?"). He looked
> at me. So I asked him, "¿Por qúe no empiezo contigo?" ("Why don't I be-
> gin with you?"). He felt a lot better. So I showed him the title, and we read
> it together. "Yo te voy a ayudar con la primera página." ("I am going to
> help you with the first page"). And we started reading, but actually I
> stopped after the first sentence. And so he read the entire book, doing real
> interesting things, you know, [such as] looking at the pictures. I was really
> pleased because it was a long piece of reading for him.

As part of this assessment, Kathy also asked Daniel several questions
about the story immediately after he had finished reading it in order to
get a basic sense of his understanding of the text. Kathy told me that
Daniel "got the gist of it" and was able to articulate the overall theme or
"message" of *El Ratoncito*: You should be happy with what you have.
Kathy was pleased. She noted that although Daniel was a little tense during this process, he was not afraid to take on the challenge of reading difficult text.

In this instance, Kathy wanted to see how Daniel would transact with text that might be just a bit difficult for him, but for which she would provide support and mediate. This is an example of reading in the "zone of proximal development" (Vygotsky, 1978), in which activity that is assisted and supported by another eventually becomes learned and then can be accomplished independently. Therefore, early in the school year, Daniel demonstrated to his teacher that he was a proficient reader in Spanish and also a "risk-taker" who was willing to read longer, more complex text in his native language.

Daniel's View of His Literacy Abilities

Also at the beginning of the school year, I asked Daniel about his reading in two languages. He stated that he read equally in both Spanish and English. He said Spanish was his first language, and then added, "but I was born with a little bit of English." Although Daniel reported that he spoke, read, and wrote English and Spanish, he further qualified this by commenting on language use in his home by him and his parents. He said he spoke Spanish at home but read mostly English. His father spoke English and Spanish, and his mother spoke Spanish but was learning English.

Daniel viewed himself as a capable reader in English and Spanish. This kind of confidence, or affective stance, is important for reading. It is especially crucial for bilingual children, given their potential for literate development in two languages. An example of this confidence was demonstrated in August, when Daniel initiated arrangements with his first-grade teacher of the previous year for him to read a story aloud to her class. What he chose to read was a humorous book in English that he thought the students might enjoy, *The Dumb Bunnies* by Sue Denim (1994). In this instance, Daniel showed he was willing to take risks by reading to a younger audience in his developing second language.

Daniel seemed to be quite aware of his repertoire of reading strategies, and was able to discuss them easily with me. He did not distinguish between reading in Spanish or English when talking about strategies. This lack of distinction is significant because it suggests that reading is a unitary process, one that is essentially the same, regardless of language (Goodman, 1996). Otherwise, Daniel may have described his Spanish reading strategies in ways distinct from his English reading strategies (see Jiménez et al., 1996). It also suggests the "interconnected" nature of biliteracy development. That is, biliterates (and bilinguals) are not "monolinguals with two languages" (Grosjean, 1989), but rather distinct entities whose use of two languages is perhaps much more interdependent, given certain conditions, than previously understood.

In an interview with Daniel later in the school year, I asked him a number of questions about his reading strategies, using Burke's Reading Interview (Goodman, Watson, & Burke, 1987). His responses provided further evidence that he was a capable reader who consciously used strategies to create meaning in transactions with text. The following is an excerpt from that interview.

R: "Daniel, when you're reading and you come to something you don't know, what do you do?"

D: "Well, I skip it and once I read the whole word—the whole line, and then I go—and then I come back to it and try and read it."

R: "Do you ever do anything else?"

D: "Uh, sometimes."

R: "Yeah? What else would you do?"

D: "Well, I'll try and read it or look at the picture and see what they're talking about."

Reading in English

On a number of occasions during the course of the study, Daniel read self-selected books and discussed them with me after finishing them. During one such session at the beginning of March, I asked Daniel to select a book (or books) that he wanted to read. These were from a group of books in English that his teacher recommended for native Spanish readers because they are relatively easy to read and also deal with everyday themes that the children might enjoy. He chose two books by Lorraine Wilson, *The Day I Lost My Bus Pass* (1987b) and *The Costume Party* (1987a).

We sat at the small round table in the area behind the loft. I asked him to read aloud "as if I were not there" to assist him with his reading. I helped Daniel only if he appeared to be having a great deal of difficulty, typically when he became silent for a long time. In these situations, I sometimes told him what an individual word was, or assisted him in figuring out the word through suggestions or clues. When he was finished reading each story, I asked him to retell the story to me. Then I asked him questions about what he had just read to gain a sense of his reading comprehension.

To analyze Daniel's reading of these two books, I used a method modified from miscue analysis (because of the relatively small number of words in the texts) that afforded me insights into his reading strategies (Goodman et al., 1987). In general, Daniel demonstrated that he was a proficient reader in English and very capable in his transactions with English text. The following examples are from his reading of *The Day I Lost My Pass*, a 131-word text. Daniel's changes to the text are in boldface type.

Text as written:
          When I get on the bus, I show
          my bus pass to the driver.

Text as read by Daniel:
          When I **got** on the bus, I **showed**
          my bus pass to the driver.

In this example, although Daniel's miscues altered the grammar and meaning of the text somewhat, the changes made in *get* and *show* showed strengths on the part of the reader, not deficits. First of all, Daniel maintained the base meaning of the miscued verbs although he altered the tense, and then he displayed enough sense of English grammar to make the second miscue conform in tense to the preceding one.

Daniel had a number of different reading strategies and used them with finesse. Self-correction was one of them. This is an important strategy used by proficient readers that provides powerful insights into their concern for meaning and effectiveness in creating meaning. The following two examples of Daniel's self-correcting ability are also from his reading of *The Day I Lost My Pass*.

Text as written:
     I had to walk all the way home.

Text as read by Daniel:
     I had to (three times) **wait** (then corrected to **walk**) all the way home.

Text as written:
     I've been worried about you.

Text as read by Daniel read:
     I'm been (then corrected as follows, with miscue **worrying**)
     I've been **worrying** about you.

Goodman et al. (1987) have written about the significance of miscues like the preceding that Daniel made in English reading:

When miscues result in sentences that are syntactically unacceptable and readers correct such miscues, this shows that readers are concerned with the linguistic structure of their reading and that they are concerned that their reading sound like language. (p. 72)

DANIEL'S WRITING DEVELOPMENT
IN TWO LANGUAGES

Whereas Daniel was a capable reader in both languages, most of his writing in class was in Spanish. For example, of the 31 writing samples that I was able to collect during the study, 7 were in English, 20 were in Spanish, and 4 were in Spanish with some English. Of these, 19 were letters, 5 were reports, and the others included homework, stories, and a poem.

In his first writing assignment of the school year (in August), Daniel wrote a letter to his teacher in Spanish, limiting it to his activities during the summer vacation. Immediately after finishing the first letter, he began to write another letter on the same topic, in English (Fig. 2.1). Although Daniel wrote only one line in his unfinished English letter, it provided evidence that he was becoming a writer in both languages.

An important class routine that Kathy used to facilitate children's biliteracy development was the Child of the Week, also known as the "Tree"mendous Person of the Week. This activity was designed to help the children learn to use oral and written language and to build the classroom community. This context supported their developing literacies because letter writing is an "intermediate" form of literacy for children (Newkirk, 1989) that serves an "interactional function" (Halliday, 1975), and one that offers accessible ways of communicating in writing.

Daniel wrote a "Tree"mendous Person letter to his classmate Sean at midyear, namely, in January (Fig. 2.2). This letter demonstrates Daniel's deliberate effort to communicate in English, apparently because he knew Sean did not read Spanish very well. It also provides evidence of Daniel's developing ability to write in English. The letter is fairly short (39 words). It includes two comments about Sean and three questions for him. The first sentence seems to reflect Daniel's observation that Sean is a well-behaved student who does not talk with his friends in the classroom when it is inappropriate for him to do so. The final sentence appears to extend this complimentary theme. Daniel's three questions about whether Sean likes hot dogs, the Tree Room, and the Pizza Hut indicate curiosity about a classmate who had made a presentation about himself and his family. Although some punctuation, spelling, and syntactic errors are reflected in the letter, it certainly is understandable and demonstrates Daniel's confidence and ability to write in English.

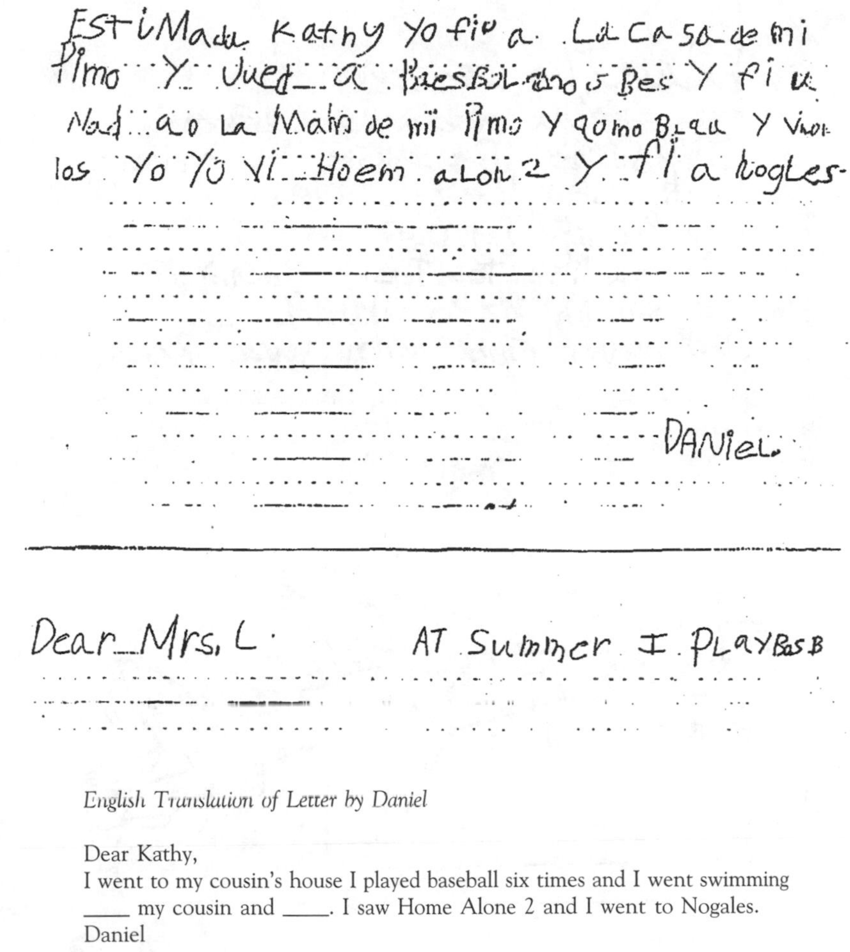

EstiMada Kathy Yo fiv a. La Casa de mi Pimo Y Vueg a PiesBol ano s Bes Y fi u Nad ao La Matn de mi Pimo Y qomo Blu Y vino los Yo Yo Vi Hoem aLon 2 Y fl a Nogles.

DANIEL

Dear Mrs. L. AT Summer I PLayBsB

English Translation of Letter by Daniel

Dear Kathy,
I went to my cousin's house I played baseball six times and I went swimming
____ my cousin and ____. I saw Home Alone 2 and I went to Nogales.
Daniel

FIG. 2.1. Spanish letter and unfinished English letter from Daniel to Mrs. L.

During the second half of the school year, in early March, Daniel wrote a letter written to another classmate, Roberto (Fig. 2.3). In the two preceding letters, we can see growth and development in Daniel's writing, as compared with his first Spanish and English letters to his teacher, written in August. His March letter in Spanish to Roberto is more than twice as long (85 words) as his August letter in Spanish to his teacher (41 words). Although he code-switched into English in one sentence, 90% of the March letter is in Spanish. His January letter in English to Sean is five times longer than his incomplete English letter to his teacher at the beginning of the school year. In both letters, there are

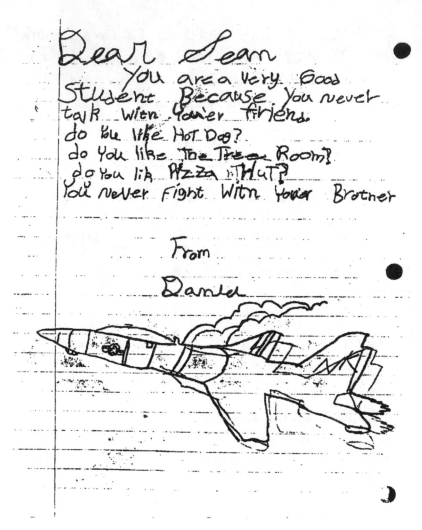

FIG. 2.2.   "Tree"mendous Person letter from Daniel to his classmate Sean.

punctuation and spelling miscues. However, the purpose of these letters was mainly to communicate with peers. The focus was not on writing conventions.

The final example of his writing is a game review that Daniel wrote in English in April (Fig. 2.4). It was published along with other reviews by the class and displayed for customers' viewing at a local store for children that donated several games to the students for a class project.

Daniel's review of the Happy Traveler game is in English and contains 88 words. With only a few punctuation exceptions, it is written conven-

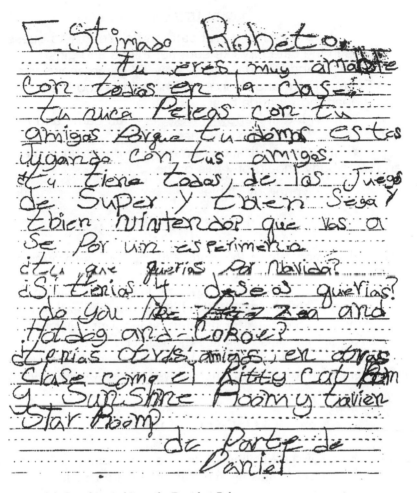

English Translation of Letter by Daniel to Roberto

Dear Roberto,

You are very kind with everyone in the class. You never fight with your friends because you are gentle when playing with your friends. Do you have all of the Super Games and also Sega? And also Nintendo? What are you going to do for an experiment? What did you want for Christmas? If you had four wishes, what would you want? Do you like Pizza and Hot dogs and Coke? Did you have other friends in other classes like the Kitty Cat Room and Sunshine Room and also Star Room?

By Daniel

FIG. 2.3. Letter from Daniel to Roberto.

43

Happy Traveler

It's a classifying and card game. You try to guess what fits in the category like summer things and girls' names- Kyla and Brenda. Old or new TV game shows like The Price is Right and Jeopardy. Things in a zoo like a lion and a bear and a panda bear.

I think that Happy Traveler is a fun game and a going game. You can go anywhere with it.

It's a memorization game and a guessing game, and everybody should buy this game.

Written by Daniel

FIG. 2.4.   Game review by Daniel.

tionally and appropriately for the genre. Although only a few examples of Daniel's writing were examined in this article, they demonstrate development in his writing. He wrote increasingly longer and somewhat more complex pieces in both languages. He chose to write the games review in English rather than Spanish, demonstrating his incipient biliteracy to a relatively broad audience and informing them about a game he enjoyed. By the end of second grade, Daniel was becoming biliterate, and thus more able to interact with two written language systems for a variety of purposes.

CLOSING REMARKS

In this chapter, I discussed biliteracy development because of its potential as a tool for students' thinking and learning in two languages in classroom settings. Selected examples from Daniel were discussed. He was a student who did not seem to think that his bilingual and biliterate abilities were unusual or anything but natural. In the context of his classroom and home, this certainly was the case. He used his bilingualism to communicate with his teacher and other students in his class and school. Daniel enjoyed reading in English and Spanish and used his repertoire of reading strategies to create meaning when transacting with texts in two languages. He found writing to be somewhat difficult, depending on his purposes and audience. He tended to be a perfectionist, so he wrote slowly and carefully. He wrote more often in Spanish than in English and read more than he wrote. Daniel was only 7 years old when I worked with him, yet he was already becoming biliterate. He therefore could access the two literate worlds available to him in his classroom and beyond.

REFERENCES

Ammon, P. (1985). Helping children learn to write in English as a second language: Some observations and some hypotheses. In S. Freedman (Ed.), *The acquisition of written language: response and revision* (pp. 65–84). Norwood, NJ: Ablex.

August, D., & Hakuta, K. (Eds.). (1997). *Improving schooling for language-minority children: A research agenda.* Committee on Developing a Research Agenda on the Education of Limited-English-Proficient and Bilingual Students. National Research Council, Institute of Medicine, Washington, DC: National Academy Press.

Barrera, R. B. (1983). Bilingual reading in the primary grades: Some questions about questionable views and practices. In T. H. Escobedo (Ed.), *Early childhood bilingual education: A Hispanic perspective* (pp. 164–184). New York: Teachers College Press.

Bialystok, E. (1997). Effects of bilingualism and biliteracy on children's emerging concepts of print. *Developmental Psychology, 33*(3), 429–440.

Bialystok, E. (Ed.). (1991). *Language processing in bilingual children.* Cambridge: Cambridge University Press.

Bialystok, E., & Hakuta, K. (1994). *In other words: The science and psychology of second-language acquisition.* New York: Basic Books.

Bild, E. R., & Owain, M. (1989). Minority language students in a French immersion programme: Their French proficiency. *Journal of Multilingual and Multicultural Development, 10,* 255–274.

Clay, M. M. (1988). *The early detection of reading difficulties* (3rd ed.). Aukland: Heinemann.

Denim, S. (1994). *The dumb bunnies.* New York: The Blue Sky Press.

Díaz, R. M. (1983). Thought and two languages: The impact of bilingualism on cognitive development. In E. W. Gordon (Ed.), *Review of research in education* (Vol. 10, pp. 23–54). Washington, DC: American Educational Research Association.

Díaz, R. M., & Klinger, C. (1991). Towards an explanatory model of the interaction between bilingualism and cognitive development. In E. Bialystok (Ed.), *Language processing in bilingual children* (pp. 167–192). Cambridge, UK: Cambridge University Press.

Díaz, S., Moll, L. C., & Mehan, H. (1986). Sociocultural resources in instruction: A context-specific approach. In California State Department of Education, *Beyond language: Social and cultural factors in schooling language minority children* (pp. 187–230). Los Angeles: California State University, Evaluation, Dissemination and Assessment Center.

Dodson, C. J. (1985). Second language acquisition and bilingual development: A theoretical framework. *Journal of Multilingual and Multicultural Development, 5*(6), 325–346.

Dworin, J. E. (1996). *Biliteracy development: The appropriation of English and Spanish literacy by second and third grade students.* Tucson, AZ: Unpublished doctoral dissertation, University of Arizona.

Edelsky, C. (1986). *Writing in a bilingual program: Había una vez.* Norwood, NJ: Ablex.

Edelsky, C. (1991). *With literacy and justice for all: Rethinking the social in language and education.* London: The Falmer Press.

Faltis, C. (1986). Initial cross-lingual reading transfer in bilingual second grade classrooms. In E. E. Garcia & B. Flores (Eds.), *Language and literacy research in bilingual education* (pp. 122–141). Tempe, AZ: Center for Bilingual Education, Arizona State University.

Ferdman, B. M. (1990). Literacy and cultural identity. *Harvard Educational Review, 60,* 181–204.

Ferdman, B. M., Weber, R., & Ramírez, A. G. (Eds.). (1994). *Literacy across languages and cultures*. Albany: State University Press of New York.

Goodman, K. (1996). *On reading*. Portsmouth, NH: Heinemann.

Goodman, K. S., Goodman, Y. M., & Flores, B. (1979). *Reading in the bilingual classroom: Literacy and biliteracy*. Rosslyn, VA: National Clearinghouse for Bilingual Education.

Goodman, Y. M., Watson, D., & Burke, C. (1987). *Reading miscue inventory: Alternative procedures*. New York: Richard C. Owen.

Grosjean, F. (1989). Neurolinguists, beware! The bilingual is not two monolinguals in one person. *Brain and Language, 36*, 3–15.

Hakuta, K. (1986). *Mirror of language: The debate over bilingualism*. New York: Basic Books.

Hakuta, K., & Díaz, R. (1985). The relationship between degree of bilingualism and cognitive ability: A critical discussion and some new longitudinal data. In K. E. Nelson (Ed.), *Children's language* (Vol. 5, pp. xx–xx). Hillsdale, NJ: Lawrence Erlbaum Associates.

Halliday, M. A. K. (1975). *Learning how to mean*. London: Edward Arnold.

Haugen, E. (1950). Problems of bilingualism. *Lingua, 2*(1), 271–290.

Hudelson, S. (Ed.). (1981a). *Learning to read in different languages*. Washington, DC: Center for Applied Linguistics.

Hudelson, S. (1981b). Kan yu ret an rayt en ingles: Children become literate in English as a second language. *TESOL Quarterly, 18*, 221–238.

Hudelson, S. (1988). Writing in a second language. *Annual Review of Applied Linguistics, 9*(1), 210–222.

Jiménez, R. T., García, G. E., & Pearson, P. D. (1996). The reading strategies of bilingual Latina/o students who are successful English readers: Opportunities and obstacles. *Reading Research Quarterly, 31*(1), 90–112.

Johnson, D. M., & Roen, D. H. (Eds.). (1989). *Richness in writing: Empowering ESL students*. New York: Longman.

John-Steiner, V., Panofsky, C. P., & Smith, L. R. (1994). *Sociocultural approaches to language and literacy: An interactionist perspective*. Cambridge: Cambridge University Press.

Kjolseth, R. (1982). Bilingual education programs in the United States: For assimilation or pluralism? In B. Spolsky (Ed.), *The language education of minority children* (pp. 94–121). Rowley, MA: Newbury House.

Ladson-Billings, G. (1995). Toward a theory of culturally relevant pedagogy. *American Educational Research Journal, 32*(3), 465–491.

Lambert, W. (1974). Culture and language as factors in learning and education. In F. E. Aboud & R. D. Meade (Eds.), *Cultural factors in learning and education*. Bellingham, WA: Western Washington State College.

Lanauze, M., & Snow, C. (1989). The relation between first- and second-language writing skills: Evidence from Puerto Rican elementary school children in bilingual programs. *Linguistics and Education, 1*(3), 323–339.

Landry, R., & Allard, R. (1991). Can schools promote additive bilingualism in minority group children? In L. M. Malave & G. DuQuette (Eds.), *Language, culture and cognition* (pp. 198–231). Clevedon, UK: Multilingual Matters.

Leopold, W. F. (1939–1949). *Speech development of a bilingual child* (Vols. 1–4). Evanston, IL: Northwestern University Press.

Maguire, M. H. (1987). Is writing a story in a second language that much more complex than in a first language? Childrens' perceptions. *Carleton Papers in Applied Language Studies, IV*, 17–65.

Malakoff, L. M., & Hakuta, K. (1991). Translation skill and metalinguistic awareness in bilinguals. In E. Bialystok (Ed.), *Language processing in bilingual children* (pp. 141–166). Cambridge, UK: Cambridge University Press.

Merriam, S. B. (1988). *Case study research in education.* San Francisco: Jossey Bass.

Moll, L. C., & Dworin, J. E. (1996). Biliteracy development in classrooms: Social dynamics and cultural possibilities. In D. Hicks (Ed.), *Child discourse and social learning: An interdisciplinary perspective* (pp. 221–246). Cambridge, UK: Cambridge University Press.

Moll, L. C., Tapia, J., & Whitmore, K. (1993). Living knowledge: The social distribution of cultural resources for thinking. In G. Salomon (Ed.), *Distributed cognitions.* Cambridge, UK: Cambridge University Press.

Moll, L. C., Vélez-Ibáñez, C., Greenberg, J., with Andrade, R., Dworin, J., Saavedra, E., & Whitmore, K. (1990). *Community knowledge and classroom practice: Combining resources for literacy instruction.* (IARP Sub-contract No. L-10. Office of Bilingual Education and Minority Language Affairs). Tucson, AZ: University of Arizona, College of Education and Bureau of Applied Research in Anthropology.

Montiel, Y. T. (1992). *Spanish-speaking children's emergent literacy during first and second grades: Three case studies.* Tempe, AZ: Unpublished doctoral dissertation, Arizona State University.

Newkirk, T. (1989) *More than stories: The range of children's writing.* Portsmouth, NH: Heinemann.

Quintero, E. P. (1986). *Sociocultural context and its relation to literacy development in bilingual preschoolers.* Las Cruces, NM: Unpublished doctoral dissertation, New Mexico State University.

Reynolds, A. G. (1991). The cognitive consequences of bilingualism. In A. G. Reynolds (Ed.), *Bilingualism, multiculturalism, and second language learning* (pp. 145–182). Hillsdale, NJ: Lawrence Erlbaum Associates.

Scribner, S., & Cole, M. (1981). *The psychology of literacy.* Cambridge, MA: Harvard University Press.

Shannon, S. M. (1995). The hegemony of English: A case study of one bilingual classroom as site of resistance. *Linguistics and Education, 7,* 175–200.

Spradley, J. P. (1980). *Participant observation.* New York: Holt, Rinehart & Winston.

Valdés, G. (1992). Bilingual minorities and language issues in writing: Toward profession-wide responses to a new challenge. *Written Communication, 9*(1), 85–136.

Valdés, G. (1997). Dual-language immersion programs: A cautionary note concerning the education of language-minority students. *Harvard Educational Review, 67*(3), 391–429.

Valdés, G., & Figueroa, R. A. (1994). *Bilingualism and testing: A special case of bias.* Norwood, NJ: Ablex.

Vygotsky, L. S. (1978). *Mind in society: The development of higher psychological processes.* In M. Cole, V. John-Steiner, S. Scribner, & E. Souberman (Eds.). Cambridge, MA: Harvard University Press.

Walsh, C. E. (1991). *Pedagogy and the struggle for voice: Issues of language, power, and schooling for Puerto Ricans.* New York: Bergin & Garvey.

Walsh, C. E. (1994). Engaging students in learning: Literacy, language, and knowledge production with Latino adolescents. In D. Spener (Ed.), *Adult biliteracy in the United States* (pp. 211–237). McHenry, IL: Center for Applied Linguistics and the National Clearinghouse on Literacy Education.

Weinreich, U. (1953). *Languages in contact*. New York: Linguistic Circle of New York.

Wells, G., & Chang-Wells, G. L. (1992). *Constructing knowledge together: Classrooms as centers of inquiry and literacy*. Portsmouth, NH: Heinemann.

Whitmore, K. F., & Crowell, C. G. (1994). *Inventing a classroom: Life in a whole language learning community*. York, ME: Stenhouse Publishers.

Wilson, L. (1987a). *The costume party*. Sydney: Maurbern Pty Ltd.

Wilson, L. (1987b). *The day I lost my bus pass*. Sydney: Maurbern Pty Ltd.

Yin, R. K. (1984). *Case study research: Design and methods*. Beverly Hills: Sage Publications, Inc.

3

Headwoman's Blues: Small Group Reading and the Interactions of Culture, Gender, and Ability

Shuaib J. Meacham
University of Delaware

The grouping of students in literacy instruction has been a topic of much study and debate within educational research and practice. Ability grouping, heterogeneous grouping, and more recently, literature discussion groups and book clubs have become prominent practices in literacy research and instruction. These issues have also been examined from cultural diversity and second-language perspectives. This chapter, taken from a larger study of cultural diversity and literacy instruction, examines interactions among these grouping factors. Specifically, this chapter demonstrates how factors of ability, culture, and gender interact dynamically to effect an impact on student literacy experiences in small group instruction. The following sections briefly review the literature, describe research methods, and present the findings and conclusion.

THEMES IN THE LITERATURE ON GROUPING AND LITERACY

This brief literature review examines three primary areas of emphasis in the research on grouping and literacy instruction. This research includes studies that have examined the comparative achievement resulting from different grouping practices, studies that have looked at student and teacher conduct and group productivity, and studies that have focused on practices conducive to literacy acquisition. Studies examining the effectiveness of different grouping practices have looked at whole class, small group, and ability grouping, as well as heterogeneous grouping practices.

Lou, Spence, Pulsen, Chambers, and d'Apollonia (1996) described a recent comprehensive review of this literature. Their review focused on the comparative effectiveness of different grouping practices. The effectiveness of whole group literacy instruction was compared with that of small group instruction, whereas the effectiveness of homogeneous ability grouping was compared with that of heterogeneous grouping. Although no grouping practice was found to be uniformly superior, small group learning was more effective than whole group learning, and homogeneous ability grouping was slightly more effective than heterogeneous grouping. The authors emphasized, however, that maximum effectiveness, regardless of grouping, was achieved when instructional materials and teaching practices were adapted to instructional objectives. Berghoff and Egawa (1991) performed a comparative analysis of student learning in the variety of grouping contexts they used in their classrooms. The authors found that each grouping practice, whether whole group, small group, pairs, or independent, provided instructional advantages for the teacher and learning advantages for the students depending on why, when, and how the practices were implemented.

Several studies have examined student and teacher conduct in small group learning (Barnes, Barnes, & Clarke, 1984; Berghoff & Egawa, 1991; Cazden, 1986; MacGillivray & Hawes, 1994; McMahon & Goatley, 1995). These studies investigated the practices in which teachers and students engaged during small group instruction and evaluated their impact on the achievement of instructional objectives. MacGillivray and Hawes (1994) examined the different "roles" that students adopted in the context of "partner reading" (p. 213). They found that students adopted four types of relationships or "role sets" in peer literacy interactions: pleasure, assistance, teacher–student, and boss–employee relationships. Two of the roles, teacher–student and boss–employee, implied the presence of hierarchical relationships in student practice. This prominence of hierarchy led the researchers to suggest that even in the absence of ability grouping, students still carried out reading tasks in terms of power relationships.

Other studies have examined instructional approaches in cooperative groupings that maximize reading comprehension, meaning-making, and collaboratively negotiated understanding of text (Leal, 1993; Meloth & Deering, 1992; Tinalli & Drake, 1993). Meloth and Deering (1992) discussed the quality and frequency of various kinds of talk in cooperative learning groups as well as the level of literacy comprehension associated with various instructional strategies. In particular, they found that activity sheets used to guide interactions lead to less off-task talk and higher gains in student reading comprehension. Tinalli and Drake (1993) looked at literature groups and the manner in which children collectively negotiated the meaning of texts. In contrast to the assumption that there is a "natural" quality of child interaction with literature, they found that "think aloud" strategies, in which children are encouraged to be aware of their thought processes, enhanced the abilities of peers to negotiate the meaning and understanding of texts collectively.

Issues of race, culture, and gender diversity also have been integrated into the study of grouping and literacy instruction. Research such as that of Braddock and Dawkins (1993) and Braddock and Troyna (1992) has emphasized the negative impact of ability grouping on the learning outcomes of students from nonmainstream backgrounds. In contrast, Lee and Slaughter-Defoe (1994), Garcia (1994), and Lomawaima (1994) have discussed the cultural appropriateness of cooperative learning frameworks for the literacy achievement and overall learning of African American, Latino, and Native American students. Cherland (1992) and Evans (1996) have discussed the differing qualities of literature responses between boys and girls in literature discussion groups. In another recent study, Kreuger and Townsend (1997) found that practices in the "reading club" improved the literacy acquisition of second-language learners. Specifically, the authors found that through a recurring sequence of instructional practices, all of the children were able to read the weekly story independently by the end of the week.

Collectively, the studies cited have provided considerable insight into factors that impede or promote literacy achievement and productive student interactions in reading groups. Over time, these studies gradually have integrated more variables into the analysis of small group practices in literacy instruction. Kreuger and Townsend (1997) in particular, were able to look simultaneously at issues of grouping, literacy acquisition, and second-language acquisition. This is an important trend because most studies in this literature do not examine the interactions among multiple variables. Thus, the manner in which diversity, grouping, and student and teacher conduct as well as the ways that they may influence one another are not evident. This limitation is of considerable importance because the small group literacy instruction in an increasing number of classrooms, particularly those in major urban settings, must contend with multiple influences simultaneously. This chapter attempts to expand on recent trends and supplement traditional limitations by looking at interactions among the factors of culture, gender, and teacher practice, and their impact on small group literacy instruction.

THEORETICAL FRAMEWORK

The Blues Idiom and the Crossroads

This chapter adopts cultural theorist Albert Murray's (1970) concept of the "blues idiom" as a theoretical lense through which to make sense of literacy instruction in a multiply diverse classroom context. The blues idiom, not to be confused or equated with "twelve-bar" blues music, is a theoretical synthesis of rituals, dispositions, and attitudinal patterns implicit in African American music, art, style, language, and social interactions. Western European–based conceptions of knowledge and culture emphasize hierarchy, division, and categorization (Foucault, 1975 in Rabinow, 1984; West, 1982). The blues idiom was selected because it embodies a worldview that more closely approximates the relations between knowledge and culture found in a culturally diverse classroom. Specifically, the blues idiom implies an ethos in which intersections, connections, and interactions across categories are considered the norm (Gates, 1988). However, before describing the specific features of the blues idiom, it is necessary to discuss a larger process undergirding the blues cosmology, specifically that of the "crossroads."

Described as a foundational concept in many African cosmological systems (Gates, 1988; Thompson, 1984), the crossroads represents a definitive personal and cultural moment during which a sense of norm is disrupted. Gates (1988) also suggested that the crossroads is that point at which one's previous level of conceptual understanding is no longer sufficient to meet current challenges. Specific to the contingencies of cultural diversity, the crossroads also is represented in spatial terms. Thompson (1984) described the crossroads according to the following spatial parameters:

> A fork in the road (or even a forked branch), . . . [a] crucially important symbol of passage and communication between worlds, . . . the point of intersection between the ancestors and the living. (p. 109)

As Thompson (1984) suggested, the crossroads is a place where worlds come together, the point at which differences intersect. Often, it is this intersection of different worlds that precipitates the disruption of norms.

Break, Improvisation, and Affirmation

Murray (1970) suggested that many aspects of African American culture, particularly the music of jazz, constitutes a ritualization of the crossroads experience. According to Murray (1970), jazz ritualizes an experiential norm (p. 70) for African American people, the disruption and improvisational response of which has been a definitive cultural experience.

The blues idiom ritualizes the crossroads experience in three intercon-nected phases. The first phase is that of "the break." The break is the rit-ualization of the crisis, that point of intersection at which a singular sense of norm is disrupted. The break corresponds to that moment in a jazz composition when the rhythmic and melodic structures are disrupted, leaving the soloist with a comparatively empty sonic landscape. This is the moment at which improvisation, the second phase of the blues idiom, begins. Improvisation, however, is not to be confused with an "anything goes" or a "winging it" mentality. Improvisation, in fact, requires the solo-ist to call on her or his already known repertoire of skills and knowledge and adapt it to the current challenge. Because the context of improvisa-tion is the intersection of multiple worlds, improvisation frequently in-cludes the integration of multiple cultural norms.

The final phase in the blues idiom process is that of affirmation. Within affirmation, the break has been confronted, the improvisation conducted, and a new yet connected set of understandings regarding both self and circumstance is put in place. Affirmation primarily amounts to a new level of understanding from which "higher and richer levels of improvisation" (Murray, 1970, p. 59) may be conducted in the future.

With respect to the blues idiom, literacy and literacy instruction be-comes constructed as a cultural practice that invariably confronts readers with disruptions of normative assumptions. In general, Vygotsky (1986) identifies this disruption of children's "spontaneous" conceptual under-standing learned at home as a basic component of the school learning experience. Tharp and Gallimore (1991) suggested that literacy comprehen-sion is a process through which children "weave" school knowledge with the home-based understandings that they bring to school. These disruptive pro-cesses are only magnified in a context of cultural diversity, particularly in the reading of multicultural literature and expository texts. Multicultural litera-ture and expository texts necessarily confront readers with material that dis-rupts personal and cultural normative assumptions. However, to understand the concepts in this kind of literacy instruction, these disruptions must some-how be improvisationally woven into children's prior knowledge.

METHOD

The Setting

To study the interactions among multiple variables in literacy instruction with a focus on cultural diversity, a highly diverse classroom population was selected. Classroom data were taken from a combined second- and third-grade classroom wherein 11 different cultures were represented. Many of the students were in their first 4 years of residence in the United States. Thus, there literally existed an international network of influences in the classroom.

Framework for Data Collection and Analysis

In an attempt to methodologically capture the crossroads dynamics of the blues idiom, I adopted Baker's (1984) literary conception of "matrix" (p. 3) as a structural framework for data collection and analysis. In his study, Blues, Ideology and Afro-American Literature, Baker defined a matrix as "a network . . . a web of intersecting, crisscrossing impulses always in productive transit" (p. 3). Thus, methods of data collection and analysis were perceived as constructing a "network" of interconnected information sources. Therefore, the data collection drew information from multiple contexts in terms of student and teacher life experiences. Data analysis attempted to map out the contextual sources and trajectories of information while identifying when these contexts overlapped. The specifics of this process are outlined in the following sections.

Data Collection and Analysis.   The foundation of data collection involved audiotaped participant observations of classroom literacy instruction supplemented by field notes. These observations were conducted 3 days a week for 3 and 5 hours each day throughout the school year. Classroom data were supplemented by data from a variety of interconnected sources: parent interviews with 24 of the 28 student families, teacher interviews, student interviews, document collections, and observations of community cultural events in which students and their families participated.

Family interviews focused on issues such as home literacy practices and expectations, parent education experiences, and if applicable, literacy and schooling practices and expectations from the students' non–United States countries of origin. Four 90- to 120-min teacher interviews also were conducted over the course of the study. The interviews were, in fact, conversations wherein the teacher and the researcher collaboratively discussed the literacy and cultural issues examined by the study. The teacher, with more than 25 years of experience, acted as what I refer to as a cotheorist, coconstructing meaning of observed classroom activities through informal data analysis. Formal audiotaped interviews were supplemented by ongoing, informal conversations in which impressions were exchanged immediately after significant instructional events.

Document collections consisted of four document sources: student writing and classroom literacy documents, teacher–family correspondence, international documents, and cotemporaneous articles. Student writing and classroom literacy collections were composed of daily journal entries, creative and expository writing assignments, and classroom literacy worksheets. Family correspondence documents consisted of teacher newsletters and notices, which elicited parental responses regarding information related to instruction. Document collection gathered education documents via the Internet originating from the countries of origin of students not born in the United States. These sources, mainly educational policy documents from departments of education, were used to verify and elaborate on statements made in interviews regarding literacy and educational expectations in international contexts. Cotemporaneous articles were taken from local, national, and regional newspapers and periodicals collected during the period of classroom data collection. These articles were used to add depth and richness to classroom overlaps as they dealt with issues that corresponded to classroom events.

Data Analysis.   The data analysis aimed to identify "intertextual overlaps" across the variety of data collection sources. Data analysis used the constant comparative method described by Strauss (1987), with an emphasis not only on categorical distinctions, but also on contexts wherein categories crossed. Through the analysis, I initially identified distinct domains based on cultural categories such as African American, Nepalese, Indian, and Chinese, but subsequently examined instances in which these domains crossed or overlapped experiences, practices, and conceptual understandings regarding the literacy of other cultural domains. This analysis occurred in five stages.

The first stage of analysis was that of "open coding." Through open coding, I identified student–teacher, student–student, and student–researcher discussions of texts, both literary and expository, that related to the topic of culture. The coding identified the students involved, the nationalities of the students, and the text or curricular context that promoted the discussion. The open coding results were filed according to the nationality of the student or students making the statement.

Open coding was followed by a second stage of analysis, "overlap identification," which analyzed the cultural discussions found through open coding, identifying explicit and implicit relations between literacy text or instructional topic and the student's cultural background. In an explicit relation, the student verbally identified the relation. In an implicit relation, the content of the discussion was informed by the relation between the cultural content of the text or instructional topic and the student's background, but not verbally identified. These overlaps were coded in terms of the students, their nationalities, and the cultures involved in the overlap.

After the identification of overlaps, "selective coding" was conducted to identify contextual factors such as "conditions [and] consequences" (Strauss, 1987, p. 33) that may have been conducive to the emergence of cross-cultural connections. At this stage, the particular instructional context of the overlap was identified. For example, the instructional context such as reading group (ability), whole-class story reading and discussion, independent reading, or unit instruction group (mixed ability) was determined. In addition to details about the instructional context, specific characteristics of the overlap were identified. Many overlaps, for example, involved commonalities or tensions related to students' religious traditions and those overlaps represented in the text or curricular topic. Other overlaps involved issued related to gender roles, classroom rituals, and corporate influences on literacy and culture.

The fourth level of classroom data analysis examined the relations among categories and factors. This level of analysis documented the way that instructional components in various domains worked together to produce the overlapping connections and tensions.

The fifth and final stage of analysis was conducted to enhance the conceptual richness of the overlaps identified in classroom literacy instruction. This analysis involved identifying connections between overlaps identified in classroom and issues discussed in parent–teacher interviews, the running article collection, participant observation in nonschool settings, and document collections via the Internet. Data from these domains then were superimposed over the literacy instruction overlaps to which they most closely related. This enabled me to identify family practices, teacher cultural dispositions, educational experiences outside the United States, and global cultural trends that may have played a part in literacy discussions observed in the classroom.

THE HEADWOMAN AND CULTURAL WEAVING

Unit Instruction

The small group interactions of mixed ability level examined in this chapter were taken from data collected in an instructional unit focused specifically on the Iroquois nation. Within the classroom, unit instruction is

that context in which students normally worked in small groups representing mixed levels of literacy competency. This heterogeneous grouping
contrasted with morning reading groups, which were formed according to
literacy competency. An attempt was made to conceal the hierarchy by
naming the groups according to the text they were reading. Therefore,
not only did the names not designate hierarchy, but they were changed
regularly throughout the year. At this point in the year, however, the
reading groups consisted of Fried Worms as highest in literacy competency, Freckle Juice as the next group, and Garden Gates as the third in
reading level. *Blue-Tailed Horse* was the book read by the name assigned
to the students who spoke English as a second language. However, as
Berghoff and Egawa (1991) suggested, students frequently are able to
gauge the hierarchy despite attempts to conceal it.

Unit instruction begins with a whole-class 5- to 10-min presentation,
followed by small group interaction for the remainder of the 40-min period. Depending on the activity, the 40 min period was regularly extended so group work could be completed.

Curricular Weaving.   "Curricular weaving" denotes the regular instructional practice by which the classroom teacher takes topical issues
and integrates them into classroom rituals, themes, and organizational or
instructional practices. An apprentice weaver in her spare time, Gloria
frequently used weaving as a metaphor to describe her classroom practice. She regularly conceived of curricula and cultural variables as
"threads" in a woven fabric of instruction. When the threads were resonant or compatible, Gloria would weave curricular content, instructional
practices, and cultural themes together as she constructed educational
experiences for her students.

In the Iroquois unit, Gloria identified resonant threads between the
clan structure of the Iroquois and the small group instruction of the unit
class period. She wove the two threads together by having the heterogeneous literacy groups identify themselves as clans. In keeping with the Iroquois tradition, each of the clans was required to have a "headwoman"
act as the leader of the group. Thus, each of the unit instructional groups
or clans would have a girl as leader of the group. This headwoman was
charged with supervising the proper conduct of all clan activities, which
included allocating shared reading responsibilities and turn taking toward
the completion of clan assignments.

The primary outcome from the weaving of instructional and cultural
variables is that the learning becomes multifaceted. Gloria used the instructional objectives not only to increase literacy competency and stu-

dents' store of cultural knowledge, but also to complement the values of equity, service, and respect that she ritually promoted in her classroom. The Iroquois role of headwoman therefore was replicated not only to provide the children with an abstract experience of Iroquois leadership, but also to reinforce primary classroom values through an experience guided by Iroquois principles of gendered leadership. Thus, within the unit framework, the students engaged in literacy practices, learned cultural information, and reinforced values conducive to a diverse classroom environment.

"Crossing" and the Interaction of Multiple Variables

Gloria's weaving of the Iroquois clan structure with the mixed reading group instructional format created a crossing of instructional and diversity variables. Iroquois content related to culture and gender crossed literacy pedagogical variables related to mixed ability grouping. The initial outcome of the crossing was that reading group leadership became gendered, in that a girl led each group. Another outcome of Gloria's instructional weaving was that the experience of female leadership crossed the diversity of cultural dispositions related to female leadership represented by the students. Specifically, the provision for female leadership interacted with the range of student cultural backgrounds, which may or may not have been compatible with the concept of female leadership. Interviews with parents and community informants from a variety of backgrounds suggested that among certain cultures, significant tensions would emerge from the idea of female leadership. The remainder of this chapter investigates the outcomes of these crossings.

HEADWOMAN'S BLUES

Headwoman: An Introduction

Weaving Conceptual Connections. The concept of the headwoman in the Iroquois unit was introduced, not as an abstract, isolated concept peculiar to Indian traditions, but as one that embodied qualities with which the students were already familiar. The remainder of this chapter examines small group interactions involving literacy texts and preparatory activities for reading texts during the Iroquois instructional unit. This discussion focuses on the practices of one group consisting of four students: Daniel, a third-grade high-performing boy from the Philippines; Mei, a second-grade Chinese girl from Hong Kong just above the level of limited English proficiency; Mikelle, a second-grade girl from the United States in a lower reading group; and Ravi, a Nepalese second grader in a midlevel morning reading group.

As suggested earlier, not only was there a diversity of culture, reading level, English language proficiency, and grade level, but there also was a diversity of cultural assumptions regarding the concept of "female leadership." Mei, in particular, was shy, rarely speaking above a whisper during classroom activities. Outwardly, she seemed to embody in her behavior traditional Chinese assumptions regarding the role of women and girls. Mikelle, by contrast, had a mother who was a gender activist. In fact, Mikelle missed the first 2 days of school to attend the Women's March on Washington that August. Ravi and Daniel both came from households in which their mothers were responsible for child care while their fathers studied in the university.

Choosing a Headwoman.   In the first activity of the unit, the students were divided into "clans" and instructed to select a "headwoman" for their clan. In keeping with Iroquois tradition, the headwoman would then select the "chief" of the clan. This activity was implemented to impress on the students the fact that in the Iroquois Nation, the chief, a more familiar male model of Indian leadership, was actually selected by a woman.

After selecting the headwoman and the chief, the students were to choose a name for their clan and begin reading an expository text that described the details of Iroquois clan leadership. Figure 3.1 illustrates the cultural crossing of Iroquois gendered leadership assumptions in activity and text with the cultures represented by the children in the reading group.

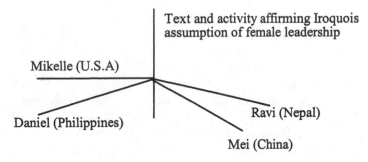

FIG. 3.1.   Crossroads of text and culture.

The crossing of Iroquois cultural assumptions in the text and the prereading activity of leadership selection passed through four cultural domains embodied by the children in the group. This crossing, not only in this group, but also in every group in the class, fostered a disruption of cultural norms, making it difficult for many of the students to select female leaders and engage in a productive reading of the text. This corresponded to the "break" phase of the blues idiom process described earlier. This break and disruption becomes evident in the following student discussion just after groups have been formed and the group is trying to decide who the headwoman is going to be:

Mikelle:	"I want to be the headwoman."
Daniel:	"You can be headwoman, and we can get rid of the headwoman."
Shuaib:	"Can I tape your conversation?"
Daniel:	"Can I say something?"
Shuaib:	"Go ahead, say whatever you want."
Daniel:	"We've got to get rid of the headwoman. We've got to get rid of the headwoman. Okay? That's what it means. Get rid of the headwoman. Get rid of the headwoman? (in a chanting refrain-like rhythm)
Daniel:	"Okay guys, you have to pick; okay you choose the chief. (to Mei) You're the head woman. You have to choose the chief. Between the guys."
Mei:	"No you . . ."
Ravi (to Mei):	"I'm the medium, and he's in the aqua spelling group. He's in the 'Fried Worms.' "
Daniel:	"Okay hurry up. This tape doesn't last that long. Pick the one, pick the uh uh uh uh or whatever, just take one."
Mikelle:	"Me!"
Daniel:	"Noooooo!! You're (Mei) the Headwoman and you have to pick. If you don't pick anything, then nobody's going to be the chief. Then we can't start up [reading] there."

In the passage, Daniel openly resisted the idea of a headwoman. In opposition to the instructions of cooperatively selecting a headwoman, Daniel imposes the role of headwoman on Mei, although Mikelle sought to be named headwoman. It is safe to assume that Mei's shyness, and perhaps Daniel's implicit understanding of her cultural norms, led him to perceive Mei as a more pliable headwoman, in contrast to Mikelle. Thus, the primary decision involved the selection of "chief," the more traditional symbol of Indian leadership. In enacting a criterion for the chief, Ravi suggested Daniel because of his status in the highest reading and spelling groups. Consequently, hierarchies associated with reading became a means of reenacting more traditional gender norms. Because of his reading group status, Daniel, an aggressive, higher-performing third-grade boy, was made "chief" in tandem with Mei, a shy, passive Chinese girl. It is safe to assume that Daniel perceived in Mei's shyness the potential for a more pliable headwoman, in contrast to Mikelle, who aggressively sought the role.

This disruptive and resistant behavior had implications for the proper enactment of reading activities. Not only did Daniel's reading level factor into the decision of his being named chief, but he used his higher reading ability to subvert Mei's authority as a headwoman. Gloria instructed the headwoman to collect and distribute reading materials, designate turn taking with respect to group reading, and monitor the completion of clan literacy work. Clans were instructed to complete assignments cooperatively. The following examples depict the manner in which Daniel subverted this cooperative process as a gesture resistant to female leadership:

Daniel: "Since you are the headwoman, you've got to know everything. And since you are not much of a headwoman, you've got to think and figure it out. And I'm not going to be part of this, 'cause I know what to write already."

In another example 3 days later, Daniel confused Mei by criticizing her written work:

Daniel: "We have to write in complete sentences."

(A look of confusion comes over Mei's face, because she has written complete sentences and does not know what the comment refers to. She eventually begins to erase her previously written answers. Daniel has almost completed his work sheet and is far ahead of the others.)

Resistance to the headwoman was not peculiar to the boys in this group. The pervasive nature of the resistance on the part of the boys in the class influenced Gloria to modify the headwoman identity. Ten days after the clan groups were initiated, Gloria changed the name of the female clan leader from "headwoman" to "clanmother." Clanmother is an implicit domestication of female leadership because it moves the leadership to the more domestic and therefore "normal" domain of "mother."

Mother is a more acceptable designation of leader than woman because of the domestic associations. Gloria also replaced Mikelle with Gina because Mikelle, silenced in her desire to be the headwoman, eventually refused to participate in clan activities.

Mei: Improvising into a Headwoman

As suggested earlier, Mei was selected by Daniel to be the headwoman because of her overt shyness and apparent conformity to more traditional Chinese expectations regarding female behavior. However, interviews with Mei's mother revealed that Mei's background has familiarized her with resistance to the imposition of traditional gender roles and behavior. Mei's mother had to resist traditional norms associated with female roles and behavior to pursue an education. Her parents had sent her to be raised by her grandmother, who discouraged her from pursuing an education. Later, however, as she became older, her mother supported not only her own desire for an education, but that of her children as well:

> Mei's mother: "My Mom is different than my grandmother's opinion. Because she also prefers that me and also my children to study. She has a different opinion. She prefer us to study so she came to live with us to help us so that I can study. So I respect my mom a lot."

The statement of Mei's mother reflects a state of tension and change in Mei's family with respect to gender expectations and education. In addition to a familiarity with cultural tension with respect to gender, Mei also was the product of an extremely rigorous education system in Hong Kong. There, even as a second grader, she had to practice considerable discipline and dedication to education:

> Mei's mother: Yeah, she always crying in Hong, because she has to study until midnight in Hong Kong. And I have to ask an English tutor to help her to study, because she could not keep her grades up in Hong Kong. She was very upset. . . . No social life. So lots of pressure when you go to school in Hong Kong.

Mei, in contrast to more surface appearances, brought considerable discipline to the reading group and to the task of becoming a headwoman. Mei, in her responses to Daniel's aggressive gestures, seemed to draw from these aspects of her background to improvise more assertiveness in her reading group participation. Over time, Mei became far more vocal, moving from silent resistance to vocal defiance of Daniel in the context of reading instruction.

In contrast to her ostensible shyness, at no time did Mei accept the imposition of headwoman role on herself. As the following passage suggests, she resisted until Gloria, not knowing the struggles in the group, told her that she was to be the headwoman:

> (Mei and the other headwomen go up to the front of the room to collect the readings from Gloria, which are to be passed out to the other members of each clan. Mei returns to the table and passes out the papers.)
>
> Daniel: "Okay, I'm going to read the first paragraph."
> Mei: "Stop!!" (looks at Daniel with an angry look, then turns to Mikelle) "Mikelle, would you read the paragraph?"

Mei's resistance to Daniel is constructed as an improvisation because it represents a level of assertiveness that Mei had rarely if ever displayed before in class. This assertiveness enabled Mei to orchestrate a properly conducted reading group session, although she was at a lower reading level than Daniel.

Affirmation and New Understanding

Throughout the clan unit, despite the turmoil surrounding the headwoman concept, Gloria systematically reinforced the authority of the headwoman. Each time the groups assembled, Gloria called on the headwomen to organize and take control of clan activities. Thus, in the midst of cultural and political uncertainty, Gloria continued to affirm the concept of female leadership. This affirmation began with the first clan meeting, when the status of each headwoman was most precarious, and continued throughout the unit. Gloria's affirmation occasioned Mei's acceptance of the role, which she would not take on from the boys. As discussed earlier, Mei's initial resistance involved resisting Daniel's behavior by following through on a threat to tell Gloria about his failure to follow directions. Gloria used the occasion to affirm Mei's improvisation by sanctioning her particular authority over the clan:

> Mei: "He's not cooperating."
> Gloria: "Well then you. He's not cooperating. Alright, so Mei, as headwoman, what are you going to say to him?"
> Mei: "Please cooperate."

Gloria performed such affirmations throughout the unit. On one occasion, when two boys from one of the other clans approached Gloria about a problem in the clan, Gloria returned them to the authority of the headwoman for her to decide. Gloria's affirmations conveyed the message to the entire class that female leadership was an acceptable classroom practice and norm.

In addition to Gloria's affirmations, classroom peers, male and female, began to support the authority of the headwoman. Twelve days after the initial clan meeting, Deron and Murphy, two boys from different clans, acknowledged the hard work and quality leadership of their headwomen. Within Mei's bear clan, affirmation began to emerge slightly more than 2 weeks after the clans began. On a day when Mei was absent, progress on a longhouse construction activity slowed down considerably. At one point, Daniel threw down his scissors and said, "I give up." Gina, Mikelle's replacement, verbalized the impact of Mei's absence, and affirmed her leadership when she said, "We'd be done with this thing if Mei was here." Eventually, Mei took on a legitimate headwoman role, settling disputes, as when Ravi turned to her to settle a disagreement with Daniel, assuming nearly total authority over all clan decisions.

This general affirmation of the new female leadership norm contributed directly to more productive reading group conduct by all the members of the group. Daniel, who eventually adopted a more cooperative disposition during group reading, provided the most profound affirmation. Instead of using his high literacy competency to exert male authority, he became supportive, even helping Mei to decode text. The following passage reflects Daniel's new disposition:

Mei: (reading from the text) "Nuts and berries were also part of the Iroquois meals. (faster than her normal pace). The wild . . ." (tries to decode strawberries)

Daniel: "Where are we? 'The wild strawberries, the earliest . . .' "

Mei: "The earliest fruit of the year was a special favorite. The Iroquois held a feast . . ."

Daniel: "Festival."

Mei: "Festival to celebrate the feast of the rip . . ."

Daniel: "Ripe."

Mei: " 'Ripe berries.' "

Daniel: "Okay, we're done."

Through affirmation, Daniel moved into a helpful, nonhierarchical literacy, which was occasioned by Mei's leadership.

DISCUSSION

Before this Iroquois unit, Daniel was capable of cognitively comprehending the concept of female leadership. However, his cultural and personal biases precluded an acceptance of the term, leading to both cognitive and behavioral resistance. Gloria's weaving of the textual Iroquois leadership theme with classroom practices confronted each student not only with disruptive cultural information, but also with experiences through which they could improvise responses. Mei, usually shy and reticent, dealing with her family's own ambivalent relation to changing female roles, was able not only to read about female leadership, but also to improvise her own leadership practice. Daniel, overtly hostile to the concept of female leadership, also was able to improvise his own acceptance, conveyed not only through verbal recall, but also through his active cooperation with a female peer.

CONCLUSION

This chapter attempts to convey the idea that a reading group, particularly one of culturally diverse students, really is a crossroads of educational and cultural influences and implications. Educators who regard such learning contexts merely in the singular terms of comprehension and coconstructed meaning are missing important variables with respect to the learning experiences that children actually have in these groups. For example, the term "cooperative" in "cooperative learning" is a culturally loaded term. The accounts in this chapter suggest that cooperation is achieved, in some contexts, only as long as certain cultural assumptions are in place. These assumptions place girls at a disadvantage with respect to leading literacy group activities. When these assumptions are disrupted, resistance can result.

As previous studies have demonstrated, cooperative grouping alone does not necessarily lead to cooperative reading practice. Unless certain assumptions are disrupted, culturally diverse reading groups can be a setting in which gender discrimination can be carried out in the name of literacy. Higher-achieving boys can dominate lower-achieving girls, using their literacy competency as an instrument of power.

Culturally diverse contexts and concepts encountered often in literacy instruction confront students with unfamiliar norms that may disrupt cultural and educational assumptions. Disruption in the hands of a skilled teacher, need not be negative, however. Disruption actually can be looked on as a necessary stage through which children grow as they confront diverse norms, improvise accepting responses in a supportive environment, and affirm the validity of these alternatives. At a "postmodern" moment (Jameson, 1984), during a time when the norms in many societies are increasingly uncertain, children need opportunities to read about, experience, and perform new possibilities. Reading groups can be an important place for such performances.

REFERENCES

Baker, H. A. (1984). *Blues, ideology and Afro-American literature: A vernacular theory*. Chicago: University of Chicago Press.

Barnes, D., Barnes, D., & Clarke, S. (1984). *Versions of English*. London: Heinemann.

Berghoff, B., & Egawa, K. (1991). No more "rocks": Grouping to give students control of their learning. *The Reading Teacher, 44*(8), 536–541.

Braddock, J. H., & Dawkins, M. P. (1993). Ability grouping and attainments: Evidence from the national longitudinal study of 1988. *Journal of Negro Education, 62*(3), 324–336.

Cazden, C. (1986). Classroom discourse. In M. Wittrock (Ed.), *Handbook of research on teaching* (3rd ed., pp. 432–463). New York: MacMillan.

Cherland, M. R. (1992). Gendered readings: Cultural restraints upon response to literature. *The New Advocate, 5*(3), 187–198.

Evans, K. S. (1996). A closer look at literature discussion groups: The influence of gender on student response and discourse. *The New Advocate, 9*(3), 183–196.

Garcia, E. E. (1994). Educating Mexican American students. In J. A. Banks & C. A. M. Banks (Eds.), *Handbook on multicultural education* (pp. 372–387). New York: Simon & Schuster.

Gates, H. L. (1988). *The Signifying Monkey: A theory of African-American literacy criticism*. New York: Oxford University Press.

Jameson, F. (1984). Postmodernism, or the cultural logic of late capitalism. *New Left Review*, 53–92.

Keegan, S., & Shrake, K. (1991). Literature study groups: An alternative to ability grouping. *The Reading Teacher, 44*(8), 542–547.

Kreuger, E., & Townsend, N. (1997). Reading clubs boost second-language first graders' reading achievement. *The Reading Teacher, 51*(2), 122–127.

Leal, D. (1993). The power of literary peer-group discussions: How children collaboratively negotiate meaning. *The Reading Teacher, 47*(2), 114.

Lee, C. D., & Slaughter-Defoe, D. T. (1994). Historical and sociocultural influences on African American education. In J. A. Banks & C. A. M. Banks (Eds.), *Handbook on multicultural education* (pp. 348–365). New York: Simon & Schuster.

Lomawaima, K. T. (1994). Educating Native Americans. In J. A. Banks & C. A. M. Banks (Eds.), *Handbook on multicultural education* (pp. 331–342). New York: Simon & Schuster.

Lou, Y., P. C., Spence, J. C., Pulsen, C., Chambers, B., & d'Apollonia, S. (1996). Within-class grouping: A meta-analysis. *Review of Educational Research, 66*(40), 423–458.

MacGillivray, L., & Hawes, S. (1994). I don't know what I'm doing—they all start with: First graders negotiate peer reading interactions. *The Reading Teacher, 48*(3), 210–216.

McMahon, S. I., & Goatley, V. J. (1995). Fifth graders helping peers discuss texts in student-led groups. *The Journal of Educational Research, 89*(1), 23–35.

Meloth, M., & Deering, M. (1992). Effect of two cooperative conditions on peer-group dscussions, reading comprehension, and metacognition. *Contemporary Educational Psychology, 17,* 175–193.

Murray, A. (1970). *The omni-Americans: Some alternatives to the folklore of White supremacy.* New York: Vintage Books.

Rabinow, P. (1984). Introduction. In P. Rabinow (Ed.), *The Foucault reader* (pp. 3–30). New York: Pantheon Books.

Strauss, A. L. (1987). *Qualitative analysis for social scientists.* New York: Cambridge University Press.

Tharp, R. G., & Gallimore, R. G. (1991). *Rousing minds to life: Teaching, learning, and schooling in social context.* New York: Cambridge University Press.

Thompson, R. F. (1984). *Flash of the spirit: African and Afro-American art and philosophy.* New York: Random House.

Tinalli, B., & Drake, L. (1993). Literature groups: A model of the transactional process. *Childhood Education, 5,* 221–224.

Troyna, B. (1992). Ethnicity and the organization of learning groups: A case study. *Educational Research, 34*(1), 45–55.

Vygotsky, L. S. (1986). *Thought and language.* Boston: MIT Press.

West, C. (1982). *Prophesy and deliverance: An Afro-American revolutionary Christianity.* Philadelphia: The Westminster Press.

4

Fostering Collaboration Between Home and School Through Curriculum Development: Perspectives of Three Appalachian Children

Rosary Lalik
Virginia Tech

LaNette Dellinger
James Madison University

Richard Druggish
Concord College

> *Here the living and dead mingle*
> *like sun and shadow under old trees.*
>
> Miller (1975a, p. 348)

Jim Wayne Miller's words capture the spirit of familial continuity and connectedness common in human experience. Appreciation of ancestry, for example, has long been associated with Appalachian culture (Jones, 1996). Miller's image had immediate resonance with our experiences as we spent time with teachers, students, families, and others in an Appalachian community in Southwest Virginia.

Over a 7-year period, we have watched, applauded, consulted, and supported teachers as they developed curriculum that made their mountain culture a central focus of school learning. Through a wide variety of curriculum changes, teachers made local stories and everyday community practices a cornerstone for school participation at Mountain Elementary School, a K–7 school located in an isolated coal mining area of Virginia.

69

An important goal of the teachers was to bring the home and school into collaborative engagement through curriculum. In this chapter, we explore the nature and extent of collaboration between home and school by focusing on the perspectives of three children who attended Mountain Elementary School.

THEORETICAL FRAMEWORK

The work we report relies on a sociocultural perspective of literacies as multiple phenomena that include not only reading and writing, but also a broad array of media and processes used for the construction and reconstruction of meaning (The New London Group, 1995). Through literacy processes, individuals participate as community members to conduct meaningful activities and achieve valued purposes (Heath, 1983). Literacies may be understood as identity kits (Gee, 1990). They inform how we see ourselves and how we are seen by others (Lave & Wenger, 1991). Because literacies emerge and develop as we participate with others, children arrive at school as literate beings with repertories of literate practices and resources (Moll & Greenberg, 1990).

Despite a developing discussion of literacies as sociocultural phenomena, schools typically approach literacy as a narrow set of prescribed knowledge and practices. These practices reflect the two dominant views of literacy (Knoblauch & Brannon, 1993): the functionalist belief (Boyer, 1983) that the goal of literacy is economic or material gain, and the culturalist belief (Hirsch, 1987) that the primary goal of literacy is the transmission of supposedly stable and timeless cultural values inscribed in the canonical literature of Western society. Part of the problem with constricted understandings of literacy is that such understandings often demean those literacy practices that exist outside functionalist or culturalist parameters (Heath & Mangiola, 1991; Shor, 1992). Literacy differences often are transformed into literacy deficits (Taylor, 1991; Taylor & Dorsey-Gaines, 1988), and insufficient attention is given to helping children use their existing cultural knowledge as resources on which to extend existing literacies and build new ones (Moll & Gonzalez, 1994).

This problem is particularly obvious in the education of children from nondominant groups such as African Americans (Delpit, 1995). Teachers of such children often remain unfamiliar with their students' linguistic talents, familial practices, concerns, and aspirations. Rather, teachers typically present a curriculum that celebrates practices and values that may be quite unfamiliar to many children outside the mainstream. Jim Wayne Miller (1975b), an Appalachian poet who has studied and written about Appalachian culture since the early 1960s, when he received his PhD from Vanderbilt University, explained his view of this problem for southern Appalachian children:

> It is difficult for people anywhere to embrace enthusiastically twelve years of formal schooling based on values they don't fully share, reflecting a world they do not live in, a world difficult to connect to their own experience. Too often the schools say to Appalachian children, "If you stick it out and change a few of your peculiar ways, all of this can be useful to you someday." (p. 449)

Purcell-Gates (1995) called for changes in literacy instruction to bridge the gaps between home and school for marginalized children. She argued: "We must arm teachers with knowledge and cultural appreciation and then give them the autonomy, authority and freedom to teach—each and every child" (p. 196). This idea of cultural appreciation also is a central feature of Heath's (1983) work in Piedmont Carolina and of Au's (Au & Kawakami, 1994) work among native Hawaiian children.

METHOD

Research Context

Because we had become interested in teacher-initiated and -led examples of curriculum efforts designed to respect children's home culture, we conducted the study reported in this chapter. Five years earlier, in an effort to examine teacher learning during a graduate degree program in literacy education, we began fieldwork. That is, as Hammersley and Atkinson (1995) suggested, we involved ourselves in the community by "watching what happens, listening to what is said, asking questions—in fact, collecting whatever data are available to throw light on the issues that are the focus of the research" (p. 1). For 3 years, we examined teachers' activities and views as they participated in a graduate degree program in literacy education (Lalik & Boljonis, 1994). For the next 2 years, we examined the classroom and schoolwide curriculum at Mountain Elementary School (Lalik, Dellinger, & Druggish, 1996). We then began the work reported here, an effort that included 2 additional years of fieldwork. To help our readers interpret the students' perspectives reported in this chapter, we use this section of our report to provide a brief summary of what we learned during the first two phases of our research.

At Mountain Elementary School, teachers were cultural insiders who, with only one exception, had been born and raised in the area. (The exception was a fifth-grade teacher born in New York who moved to the region when she married a local man.) As Appalachians, they had developed many of the linguistic and social practices familiar to the children. For example, some teachers collected, recorded, and shared family stories both inside and outside their classrooms. Many of the teachers grew small gardens and preserved their produce in a variety of ways including canning, pickling, and freezing. Others played musical instruments such as guitar and autoharp.

In early interviews, teachers reported that they had gained a heightened appreciation for the importance of Appalachian culture during their participation in the graduate degree program when their professors encouraged them to study Appalachian culture and learn about efforts to record and support its development. They also explained that children at Mountain Elementary School often were ashamed of the values and practices common in the region, and that they, as teachers, could help their students develop greater appreciation for these traditions. They reasoned that as students were given opportunities to study their Appalachian roots through school activities, they would develop greater self-confidence as people and as learners, and in doing so, would become more successful as learners of mainstream curricula. In the slogan they adopted for their school, Nurturing Roots and Inspiring Wings, the teachers summed up their beliefs about how a transformed curriculum might work.

As a culminating project for the degree program, a group of five teachers, who we call curriculum initiators, had planned a variety of curriculum changes to reflect their beliefs. When the graduate program ended, with support from the school principal, the curriculum initiators invited the rest of the faculty, teachers who had not participated in the degree program, to work together to develop further the curriculum they had begun.

Our fieldwork at Mountain Elementary School showed that 16 of the 19 classroom teachers on the faculty as well as the reading teacher, the school librarian, the physical education teacher, and the school principal participated eagerly in the curriculum work. For 2 years they met monthly to generate ideas and plans. On the basis of such plans, teachers began using a variety of local interests and practices as part of classroom and school activities. They developed two storytelling clubs, within which children collected, recorded, and represented family stories through dramatization, song, and other artistic forms. Many of these stories became the bases for classroom lessons designed to achieve more conventional school goals, such as accomplishment of the state-imposed learning standards. Each teacher in the building chose some aspect of Appalachian culture as a 2-year instructional theme. Themes included celebrations, cooking and remedies, tools and toys, and plant life. Teachers incorporated the themes into interdisciplinary activities interspersed across the year to help children learn about Appalachian culture. Several teachers developed extensive inquiry units around community topics such as plants, foods, and genealogy, providing their students with sustained opportunities for community study. In the spring of each year for 2 years, teachers planned and conducted an Appalachian Days Celebration for parents and community members. At each celebration, they displayed many of the classroom artifacts the children had developed as part of their class work, and featured the talents of a number of local artisans, thus bringing the school and the community together in positive engagement.

Methodological Stance

We conducted the study reported in this chapter using an interpretivist lens, inasmuch as we were primarily concerned about the perspectives of our informants: the teachers, children, and families with whom we worked (Erickson, 1986). That is, we believe that one essential aspect for understanding the worlds of teaching and learning is seeing those worlds from the perspectives of the teachers and learners who inhabit them. In doing this research, we followed the advice of Paris (1993), who reminded us that to develop understanding of any event, we must hear from those at its center. In this chapter, we feature the perspectives of three children.

Data Collection and Analysis

To understand relations between school curriculum and home culture, we selected children primarily from classrooms in which we had already been studying the curriculum. That is, with one exception, we selected children from the classrooms in which we had been taking fieldnotes and interviewing teachers for 2 years. For the exception, we selected a youngster whose teacher was one of three in the group of 19 classroom teachers who had not participated actively in the curriculum effort. We thought including such a child as an informant would provide a more balanced picture of the school and curriculum work. To include a broad range of ages, we selected children from one primary-grade classroom, one middle-grade classroom, and two upper elementary-grade classrooms. We continued fieldwork and conducted relevant interviews for two additional years after selecting these informants.

Because we wished to understand the range of perceptions among students, we selected children who differed in a number of significant categories of experience (Andersen & Collins, 1995) including gender (as indicated in school records), social economic status within the community (as indicated by judgment of the school principal), and academic success (as indicated by school grades). Because all of the students attending Mountain Elementary School at the time of this research were identified as Whites, we were not able to include racial differences in this study.

We studied nine children, collecting data on them for a period of 2 years. Our child informants were two girls in a first-grade classroom, two boys and two girls in a combination third- and fourth-grade classroom, one boy and one girl in a seventh-grade classroom, and one boy in a seventh-grade classroom whose teacher had not participated in the curriculum work. We interviewed each child formally twice, and informally five to eight times. We visited them in their classrooms three to four times during the first year of this study. We interviewed their teachers formally twice, and talked with them informally many times about their teaching and students over the data collection period. With the exception of Jeremy, whose grandfather became critically ill during the data collection period, we interviewed parents or other family members twice after selecting the children.

Throughout the 7 years that we studied this community, we used a variety of data collection processes typical of ethnographic work (Hammersley & Atkinson, 1995). During the 4 years that we worked at the school site (1994–1997), we engaged in participant observation in our multifaceted roles as teacher educators, grant facilitators, researchers, presentation collaborators, and participants in community events. We conducted interviews organized around particular teachers' curriculum work across several years and focal children's relational networks within school and family. We collected documents and artifacts (Ely, 1991) including teacher journals, letters, newspaper articles, grant applications, teacher-developed curriculum guides, and student work. We took photographs during classroom sessions, school events, and extracurricular activities. In keeping with Britzman's (1991) argument that there are a multiplicity of realities constructed and reconstructed by individuals and groups within any given culture, our research included multiple conversations with parents, teachers, children, administrators, and school staff.

During the formal and informal interviews that served as a primary basis for this report, we asked children, family members, and teachers about five topics: school tasks children completed, the sources of help used for school projects, curricular changes, home–school relations, and students' aspirations for the future. The particular forms of our questions varied in each interview to minimize the stress on the respondents by maintaining an informal conversational tone, in which the phrasing of questions flowed from the ongoing conversation. We, the authors, conducted all interviews, agreeing that the primary purpose of the formal interviews was to gain respondents' perceptions of how collaborative arrangements between the home and the school were being experienced.

As a first phase of data analysis, we reviewed field notes of our 4-year period of classroom visits and our informal conversations with parents, teachers, and children. We also transcribed formal interviews with students, teachers, and family members, and organized artifacts including class assignments produced by the children, curriculum documents prepared by teachers, newspapers articles, and photographs we had taken during our classroom visits.

We continued our analysis by constructing codes or concepts to label our data and relate them to the concepts important in this study (Coffey & Atkinson, 1996). We generated a variety of codes including school assignments, learning strategies, roles in the classroom, self-assessments, relationships with family, relationships with teachers, assessments of curriculum, and future interests. As we continued our analysis of the students' perspectives, we identified six major themes in the data: avid collecting, consulting elders, spatial experience, temporal experience, heritage, and optimism.

For the purposes of this chapter, we present three cases of the nine we studied, those of Natalie, Jeremy, and Christy. We selected these cases because together they allow us to illustrate the major themes we developed in our analysis of the larger data set within the page constraints of this report. We tell our stories of these three children in third person to reveal our interpretive influence, as Alvermann, O'Brien, and Dillon (1996) suggested. We also acknowledge that a person can never be completely known to us as researchers, nor is the individual able to completely articulate herself, even to herself (Cotterill, 1992).

In constructing cases, we drew liberally on children's actual descriptions and explanations of their lives at school and home. We have done this because the language of the children, like adult language, is constitutive (Luke, 1995). That is, it is a primary human representative form through which reality is defined and constructed, and through which human subjects are positioned (p. 21). Using children's actual words also allows readers to develop their own insights about how these children were experiencing the curriculum (Nespor & Barber, 1995). Following Grumet (1991), we wish to involve readers as part of the community functioning as "multiple interpreters" of the curriculum experience for selected children.

In our work with teachers and children, we meant to be emancipatory. That is, we intended to assist all our informants in gaining strategy and influence so they could more effectively develop and achieve their own life purposes (Dewey, 1938; Lather, 1988). To this end, we shared our cases with the parents and children we studied so they could critique and clarify our perspectives, constructing their own interpretations and considering the forces that have shaped their life stories and our understandings of them. For our informants and other readers, we worked to construct stories of these three children that were attentive to the details of each child's life while portraying the aspects of those lives that encourage readers to reconsider their own taken-for-granted assumptions about learning, schooling, and literacies (Barone, 1995).

INTERPRETATIONS

Natalie

The first time we interviewed Natalie, she was in her classroom. She sat with us at a work table a bit removed from the student desks that had been organized in a horseshoe pattern encircling a large green chalkboard. Natalie was a small, thin fourth-grade child with heather brown hair, cut so that short waves framed her face while long strands fell at her back. She spoke quietly yet confidently with us, and elaborated in a variety of ways on the five topics we explored through the interview.

At Home. When we collected our data, Natalie lived with her mother and father on a parcel of land about 2 miles from the school. Both her parents are natives of the area. They met in junior high and started dating in high school. They broke up before graduation, and only later in life resumed their relationship. When we talked with them, her father owned a small coal mine, and her mother worked part-time in a local bank.

As a infant and young child, Natalie spent most of her waking hours with her maternal grandmother, who had been her primary caretaker during her early years. Natalie's mother, after 16 years of full-time work in the banking industry, an effort she described as "demanding, a lot of effort, and much travel," reduced her office work to part-time. This decision supported Natalie's grandmother, who had become ill and was no longer able to care for Natalie full-time.

In her conversation with the interviewer, Natalie carried on at considerable length without prompting. She also frequently interjected stories about events in her life that she apparently wanted to report, and that gave us glimpses of her life outside school. For example, she told us one story that occurred during one of her frequent visits to her Dad's coal mine. She began her account, "He lets me go up there some time and throw rocks into his pond."

She also told us laughingly about a train ride she took with her uncle, a train engineer, when she was 3 or 4 years of age: "When I came back I fell in the coal pile. . . . She [Natalie's mom] thought that the only coal they had in the train was on top of it. But they have a little pile inside. Me and one of my uncle's friends was playin' around, and I fell in the coal pile."

After school and during summers when her mom worked, Natalie continued to stay next door with her maternal grandmother, a relationship she told us was very important in her life. According to Natalie, stories were a mainstay of her relationship with her grandmother, one that helped her learn a lot about her grandmother's life:

> I've learned most about her childhood by the nights, because she'll tell me like stories when she was little. . . . Sometimes we'll stay up there from 9 o'clock till 11 just talkin'. . . . Most of the time I'll go up there just before she goes to bed and . . . we get caught up in a story.

Natalie connected storytelling to her Appalachian heritage, and she described ways that her grandmother supported her in learning about her heritage. She said she liked sharing stories with her grandmother,

> because it's something about my heritage and stuff that's happened to my ancestors and my grandparents. . . . Right now I've got a picture. It was so old when my granny found it that the picture stuck to the glass. And she fixed it up and cut it and smoothed it, and she put it in a real nice picture frame for me. And I've got it settin' right above my bed so every night I can look at it.

Natalie continued:

> And he [Natalie's great grandfather] was gettin' ready to go into World War I, and he was in his late teens or early twenties when the picture was tookin. It has him all in his uniform and standing beside a white house.

Without any prompting from the interviewer, Natalie reported on various relatives and elaborated on her ancestry, which included enumerating several deaths in her family. Her maternal grandfather died of cancer before she was born:

> So really I've only got a stepgrandpa that's left because all my other grandpas are deceased.

Her aunt, the mother of her two adolescent female cousins, had died of cancer several years earlier when her daughters were children and Natalie was a preschooler. Natalie recalled a special bond between her ailing aunt and her mother.

In describing how Natalie and she spend time together outside school, Mrs. Haskins, Natalie's maternal grandmother, pointed to Natalie's involvement in traditional crafts, church activities, and mainstream sports:

> Well, I've kept Natalie ever since she's been 6 weeks old for her mother to work. And I started teaching her things from a tiny thing up. She catches on real quick, Natalie does. She's nine now and she can embroidery. . . . I just learnt her that a week or two ago, and she's embroidered seven pillow cases. She's done a real good job on them. And naturally I love her. She seems like my own.

Natalie attended church services and activities with her grandmother as often as three evenings a week. Several of the activities were associated with the church service organization in which Mrs. Haskins served as president. According to Mrs. Haskins, the service organization is a mission:

> We help the people in the community. . . . We pick out maybe the poor. They need certain things; we provide them.

Beyond her involvement in traditional activities such as church work and embroidery, Natalie also played golf regularly with her father, and she enjoyed a variety of recreational sports, such as playing point guard on a school basketball team. To assist Natalie, her grandmother sometimes worked with her on basketball at home. In her grandmother's words:

> I help Natalie. . . . [I] get out and play ball with her.

Natalie described herself as very good at sports, and she recounted her experience earning a golf trophy at a parent–child golfing tournament in which she competed with her dad.

At School. Natalie spent most of her school day in a combined third- and fourth-grade classroom. The classroom was housed in one of four temporary buildings located in a small space of land that lay between the main school building and a metal- and stone-framed auditorium–gymnasium.

Natalie's teacher, Mrs. Carmen Tendrill, had been one of the curriculum initiators at Mountain Elementary School, and she had invited us to visit her classroom when we began our fieldwork at the school. She described Natalie as a highly successful student who excelled at school subjects, including reading and writing.

Natalie explained that her teacher, Mrs. Tendrill, had recently read a tale about a journey and journeycake (Sawyer, 1953). The class had made journeycakes themselves, a food that to her tasted surprisingly like the corn bread that was a familiar part of many local families' diets. After Mrs. Tendrill read the story orally to the children, she asked them to write and revise a story of their own about a journey with a favorite family food. Natalie explained that the stories were to be published in a class book that would be put on display for the Appalachian Day Celebration at the end of the school year.

Natalie proudly reported that for her story she had used characters who actually were classmates and friends of hers. Her story followed the efforts of a main character to find a life partner. She named the main character for her cousin, Adam, who was then a fourth grader at Mountain Elementary School.

In her story, Adam brings butter biscuits with him on his journey to Louisiana "to get a girl." On his way, he meets Alma, whom he refers to as "the love of my life." Subsequently, they wed at the "Chapel O' Love" in Louisiana. After a brief marriage followed by a divorce, Adam dreams about his love. In the dream, he successfully fights off a burglar to the admiration of his love.

Natalie explained that the idea was based on an actual dream her cousin Adam had experienced. "His dream was that he was sittin' on the couch one night watching TV and a burglar came in." Natalie explained proudly that she'd changed the dream in her story to, "add more excitement to it."

The story was quite a success at school. Mrs. Tendrill praised Natalie's work, and her classmates rewarded her with their laughter and applause when she shared it with them orally. Natalie also told us how excited her cousin was to be included as a main character.

Natalie also explained that she'd used one of her grandmother's stories to complete a school assignment. First she recounted the story as she remembered it from her grandmother.

> When her[grandmother's] mother was pregnant with them [twins of which her grandmother was one], she went up on a rattlesnake, and when they stick their tongue out like they do. Well, when she [her grandmother] was born, for a little while, she'd turn piety and stick out her tongue just like the snake.

Natalie then elaborated, explaining the term "piety" and its meaning in her grandmother's story:

> Well, piety is like when they get real mad and they kind of get red in the face a little bit. And then she'd get mad and she'd do that and she'd start stickin' out her tongue just like a snake did. (According to a catalog of Appalachian speech [Williams, 1992], "piedy" means "pied," "pieballed," or "spotted.")

Natalie explained that the class assignment was part of the year-long study of recipes and remedies at the third- and fourth-grade levels, and that Mrs. Tendrill had asked the children to bring in a recipe or remedy and the family story that went with it. She had brought in the snake story, as well as a recipe for wild greens, because her great grandmother had been picking greens when she had been confronted by the rattlesnake.

As an aside in her account, Natalie recalled that she, too, had had an experience with a poisonous snake. As a young child, she had been near her front porch when she had jumped over a copperhead. She had not noticed the snake because "it was laying in the power line shadow." Her mother spotted the snake when it "reared up" near her daughter's foot. According to Natalie, her mother responded swiftly to save her from the copperhead, "She threw me on the porch and 'bout broke my arm." Like her grandmother's story, Natalie's story illustrated the dangers of birthing and rearing children and the role of the mother in such situations.

With the development of the Appalachian curriculum, Natalie's grandmother, Mrs. Haskins, had become a frequent visitor at school. For example, one day she arrived at school to assist the third and fourth graders in making fried apple pies, a traditional and locally popular food. Pie making was one of many activities in the year-long focus on Appalachian recipes and remedies that teachers at this grade level used to structure the children's study of Appalachian culture. At a ball game Mrs. Haskins had attended, Mrs. Tendrill, knowing of her expertise at pie making and her willingness to be involved at school, had invited her to help in the activity, which she had planned in part to support the school participation of local families.

Besides helping with activities associated with the Appalachian curriculum initiatives, Mrs. Haskins collaborated with the principal in her role as leader in a church service group that donated school supplies to Mountain Elementary School. She explained the effort:

> In the school here we buy pencils, paper, and all this school needs of supplies. Not all they need, but . . . ever what they use. Once a year, before school starts, the whole church and the WMU (Women's Missionary Union) . . . we buy all that stuff for the school kids.

Mrs. Haskins' description of her role of responding to and initiating connections with the school was consistent with the principal's view that the Appalachian curriculum had successfully involved the families of many children, families who before had avoided school events and activities.

Besides taking an active role in classroom assignments, Natalie participated in school sports and was the point guard for her grade-level basketball team. Mrs. Haskins also supported Natalie and the school in this endeavor by attending "all of Natalie's basketball games since Natalie had begun playing in second grade." As described earlier, Mrs. Haskins also helped Natalie practice basketball as part of activities at home.

Future Interests.   Natalie expressed her hope to play a musical instrument:

> Well, my parents are talking about getting me a saxophone for Christmas, so when band time comes around next year I'll have my own. . . . Ever since I've been a little kid, I've always wanted to play the saxophone. . . . I just think it's a really cool instrument.

Natalie explained that on Sunday nights at her grandmother's house, her Dad often played his guitar for the family.

Natalie had elaborate plans for her future that reflected an interest in following in the path defined by one of two female cousins with whom she had spent time as a young child, and who was a young adult at the time of our interviews. In her plans, Natalie included a contingency in the event of hard times:

> I kina' want to follow one of my cousin's because she's goin' to school right now and she's going into pharmacy and I'm gonna try to follow in her foot-steps and be a pharmacist and get my degree. 'Cause when you take phar-macy, you can take law, and if you take law . . . I mean if the pharmacy doesn't work out, you only have to go back for one or two more years and then you can get your lawyer's degree. . . . And so I'll have something to fall back on.

Without any elicitation from the interviewer, Natalie weighed her plans, comparing them with parental choices and focusing on her inten-tion to remain in the region as an adult:

> I don't really want to follow in my Mom's footsteps or my Dad's. . . . I just never wanted to be like that. I mean like coal mines; it's like country and stuff, but a banker. . . . It seems like it's a city job or something. I think the reason I don't want to be a banker is because I just like the country more than I do the city. . . . Around here you can get like little pharmacies and stuff. It isn't real big, and there's not a lot of people around here. I like workin' in coal mines, but just don't think it'd be right for me.

Jeremy

The first time we asked Jeremy to talk with us in a formal way, he was just finishing a practice session with the storytelling club he had been a member of for two years. Smiling mischievously he told us he would "be honored." He left the gym where the club members had gathered and walked toward the small office where we had set up the tape recorder. Jeremy was simply, yet neatly dressed in black jeans and a pale tee shirt. His shiny black hair was cut into a spiked crew cut that gave him an ap-pearance reminiscent of a British rock star. On entering the office, Jeremy took the time to explain to the school secretary that the broad brown streaks that covered his black jeans were a consequence of bleach rather than dirt.

At Home.   Jeremy did not talk much about his parents, but he did tell us that he remained very close to his grandparents, particularly his grandfather. In describing his relationship with his grandfather, Jeremy explained:

That's pretty good; that's a deep one because I've known him all my life because when I was born, you know, he was the first one to take me home.

Jeremy reported that at that time of his birth, his parents lived in a nearby camper and could not keep him there because they had not "stabled out yet" as a couple.

In talking with us, Jeremy mentioned the name of a place in Kentucky where his mom and dad had lived for awhile, and then as an aside, he exclaimed that his current community is called "Space Holler" because several of the local families have names such as Mooney. He concluded by referring to his activities in the storytelling club:

I thought that was real funny; we ought to do a story on that one. That idea never struck me before.

Daniel, one of the curriculum initiators at Mountain Elementary School and a leader of the storytelling clubs, explained Jeremy's close association with his grandparents as a relationship that grew from Jeremy's infancy when his grandparents cared for him in their home, not far from where Daniel himself lived. According to this account, Jeremy's mom and dad eventually took up residence together, took Jeremy in, and had two more children. During the school year in which we talked with David and Jeremy, both Jeremy's siblings also attended Mountain Elementary School.

Jeremy told us that his parents were doing the best they could, that his father was not allowed to drive and so could not help him get to school activities. He said he relied on his grandparents for transportation to school events and told us that both grandparents enjoyed storytelling. According to Daniel, unlike most parents of children at Mountain Elementary School, Jeremy's mom and dad were unsupportive of Jeremy's keen interest in storytelling, as they were of his other school activities:

They don't really offer Jeremy a lot of support in any of his endeavors actually, and sometimes his father is responsible for him not being able to attend after-school things like the story swaps.

Daniel elaborated his sense of Jeremy's approach to life outside of school:

Jeremy is an amazing little kid; he's resilient; he seems to bear up under the worst of circumstances sometimes and keeps a very good outlook. I don't know if I could do as well.

According to Daniel, Jeremy's grandparents were "very, very supportive and very, very helpful," often bringing Jeremy to school activities
themselves, as well as supporting his story collecting and performing activities in many ways. Daniel told us that Jeremy loved his paternal
grandparents, and that several of the stories he had collected had come
from his grandfather who was a "natural storyteller." He said that he worried about what would become of Jeremy because his grandfather's health
was failing and his grandmother also was ill.

When we asked how he spent time at home, Jeremy reported emphati-
cally that he spent considerable time reading and writing at home.
"That's all I do!" he quipped. He explained that he read the newspaper
and library books, and that he had books at his house. He told us that
Louis L'Amour was one of his favorite authors, explaining that L'Amour
is a Western writer, that L'Amour's book, *The Sacketts* (1980), was a special favorite, and that L'Amour had written about the disappearance of a
group of Indians in a book that combined Western writing with science
fiction. Jeremy added that another of his favorite writers was Isaac
Asimov, asserting, "Asimov, I like Isaac!" He told us that Asimov had
lots of articles in "the older science fiction newspapers," and that he preferred science fiction to true stories.

As for writing, Jeremy explained that he wrote for homework, and that
he also kept up a monthly correspondence with two cousins, Jeannie and
Letha, who lived in a nearby state and visited occasionally. Smiling imp-
ishly, he explained that in a recent letter, he had collapsed more than a
month of his activities into a description of just a few days, making it
seem to his cousins that he lived "an exciting life."

At School.   Jeremy came alive at school during after-school activities
known as story swaps. These were school–community events held about
three times each year, during which students, teachers, parents, and interested community members met after school to eat dinner, share stories, play musical instruments, and perform traditional dances.

We had first met Jeremy during a spring story swap in 1995. Unlike the
other middle-grade participants at story swaps, who divided their attention between listening to stories and interacting with their peers, Jeremy
sat for most of the evening riveted on the storytellers. He was the only
student that evening who offered to participate along with the adult storytellers. For his performance, he told his audience a story about an opossum and a fox. Jeremy seemed in his element here, more adult than child
in these surroundings. Jeremy's eagerness belied his small stature and
gangly thinness, which might have made him otherwise appear fragile.

Jeremy asserted his enjoyment of the story swaps, even as he explained his inconsistent attendance:

> I've only been to three or four because my mom and dad, we don't got no car. Well, we got a car but it don't got no tags on it so we can't go long distances 'cause we'll get caught. But anyway, so we don't ever go anywhere. We wait for mamaw to come and pick us up, and that's mostly my transportation.

Despite his difficulties with transportation, Jeremy continued to attend story swaps for more than 3 years.

For Jeremy, the significant dimension of the Appalachian curriculum during the regular school day was the storytelling club. Daniel, who as one of the club leaders frequently worked with Jeremy on storytelling, described him as, "a very, very intelligent young boy in seventh grade." Daniel pointed out that despite his intelligence, Jeremy was not, "a very good student academically."

For his part, Jeremy talked enthusiastically about his involvement with the storytelling club to which he belonged as a founding member. As a member of the club, he worked twice a week with his peers and teachers to collect, dramatize, and record local stories. Each month, he participated during the school day in workshops conducted by members of Roadside Theater, a group of Appalachian performers who taught workshops on the study of local history and performed representations of that history through song, story, dance, and pantomime.

Jeremy's enthusiasm for storytelling club activities contrasted sharply with his avoidance of our questions about in-class assignments and activities. He told us that not very much was going on in class because his teacher was busy helping students pass the state tests required for graduation. He said that, anyway, he really did not pay much attention in class. Jeremy's appraisal of his classroom was consistent with what we had learned about it. His teacher was one of three who seldom attended faculty meetings, during which curriculum planning was a priority. When we asked the school principal about the three nonparticipating teachers, she declined to discuss the matter.

Noticing Jeremy's reluctance to discuss classroom activities and assignments, we requested instead that he share one of the stories he had developed as part of his participation in the club. Jeremy responded eagerly, "Yeah, I know plenty of stories," offering to tell the one we had heard him tell earlier about an opossum and a fox:

See there was this big land, and there lived a opossum and a fox in it. And there were lots of fruits and stuff in it. And the main fruit that was there was persimmons. (You may have heard of them. It's real big around here.) Well, everybody knows that you can't eat persimmons until it frosts because it will make your mouth real sour. It's almost like a lemon. Well, you see anyway, one morning there came this big frost, and the fox, he thought he'd outwit the opossum. He got up and was gonna go to the persimmon tree. He went over to the persimmon tree, and the opossum was already there. He'd done been there. And he was eatin' persimmons. So the fox called way up to him and said, "Why don't you shake me down some persimmons." And the opossum just goes like this, "KKKKKKK" because that means "no" in opossum language. But anyway the fox just kept trying. You know he said it again, "Why don't you shake me down some persimmons." And the opossum went "KKKKKK" again. Well anyway, he just give up after the third time. He goes home and eats him some Kibbles and Bits®.

Jeremy laughed at the ending, pointing to the collaboration with his grandfather that led to his skill with this story. He explained:

You see, that's not really the real ending of the story, but that's how papaw always told it. . . . You see, he liked the Kibbles and Bits® commercial, so he added that one. . . . I don't know even how it ended. I'm gonna try to find out.

Jeremy went on to critique the story, commenting on its longevity and how it might have changed over the years. He judged it to be "very commercial" and probably quite different from the way his papaw had heard it from his dad years before. He speculated that in earlier times there were no Kibbles and Bits®, and that most people had radios rather than televisions.

Jeremy told us he liked the Appalachian curriculum, which he seemed to connect almost exclusively to the storytelling clubs. He elaborated, explaining his hope for the future of the club, a hope that conveyed his sense of personal responsibility for the club:

I think if we had any extra money, we should make this bigger and try to get lots of people involved. . . . I think more people could get involved if we had more teachers, . . . and some people dropped out because sometimes it gets a little hard to juggle your homework and the Appalachian studies.

Although he avoided talking about classroom tasks and assignments, Jeremy described a high level of personal investment in school activities on his grade level. He described a seventh-grade trip to Knoxville, explaining that the students had raised money for the trip by selling "stuff." He had been quite active in the sale process, using money he got from his mamaw:

Not only am I a producer [of items to sell], but I'm a consumer, too.

He elaborated on his own participation in the fund-raising activities:

I'm doing all I can do, and that's still a pretty good lot. I bring in ice cream and pop and sell stuff.

He explained that the trip to Knoxville was part of a schoolwide effort to study other places, as a complement to studying their own place, by going just to one place. He proposed that other schools should follow their school's lead.

Future Plans. Although we did not ask him to assess his academic future, Jeremy did so as part of his flowing monologue during our first interview. He expressed guarded optimism about his academic future at school, explaining that if he passed seventh grade this year, he would go on to the junior high school. Laughing, he remarked, "There's always possibilities you know," then explained that failing seventh grade was one of those possibilities:

Every kid's gotta worry about that! That's real troublesome.

Jeremy reported that in sixth grade he had failed the state literacy test of reading, writing, and math, by two points on the math. Because he had passed that same test in seventh grade, he explained, with relief, that he would never have to worry about the test again:

The written part was really tough, and the readin' part was easy for me, but the math part it was . . . easier than it was last year. It seemed like I knowd more this year, so I passed it.

In response to our inquiry, Jeremy explained his life plans, letting us know that he had already given the matter some thought:

Well, I been thinkin' on that, and I think a comic book cover artist would be the best thing for me because I draw real good.

He explained that he regularly draws comics at school, and that he had already gotten a whole comic finished. Jeremy reasoned that he could also become a "game doctor" who tests games such as Nintendo and Sega before they are sold because of his "special talent" for such games. He reported that he currently owns a Nintendo®, Game Boy®, and Atari®, and that he was getting a computer so he could get other games.

Christy

Christy was tall "like her Uncle Roger." Her dark hair was kept at shoulder length and drew out her eyes. Freckles highlighted her nose and cheeks. Christy was a seventh grader when we first interviewed her.

At Home.   Christy lived in close proximity to family, and she spent free time gathering stories and learning about family history. Christy combined school assignments and recreational activities in ways that made it difficult for us to distinguish her life at home from her life at school. She talked enthusiastically about her ongoing search for stories, explaining that most of them came from family members:

> Most of them I got off my papaw who lives just right across from me so I can run over there and say, "Papaw, I need a story."

Christy said that once her grandfather "told us a really good one about Black County":

> There was a miner. He was from Mountain. He was from right here when they first opened the mines. And he took off a week and went hunting. He just got tired because he hasn't seen nothing, and he leaned up against the tree to rest. And something—I think he, his heart stopped or he had a heart attack, and he just died. Nobody ever found him. It was 7 years later, and another hunter had came, and he laid back against the tree, and he looked over and he could see the bones and then the rifle. The miner's name was Jay High. And they started calling it that. If you go to Poor Valley in Black County, there's a holler up in there. It's called Jay High Holler.

Without encouragement from us, Christy recounted another story that her grandfather had told her about hearing a galloping horse outside, behind his house:

I've never heard it, but in between my house, there's a little swag place, and when my papaw was younger they heard a horse like going through there, and they could hear it making its sounds and galloping through there. When they looked they could not see a horse.

Christy explained that this story gave rise to the notion that there was a ghost horse in the area. Although Christy had never heard the horse, she told us convincingly that others had heard it over the years.

In addition to the stories she heard from her grandfather, Christy also learned stories from her mom and dad and her two grandmothers. She elaborated:

My grandma she lives up on top of the mountain—up on Pike Mountain— and she's told me some good stories.

Christy talked enthusiastically about the work and interests of various family members. She showed us a picture of her grandmother holding a guitar and explained that she had for years played the guitar and sung at church. Her father worked for the gas company at the time of our conversation. Christy explained that he was worried about the possibility of losing his job, a circumstance that was especially unsettling because it could result in a move for Christy's immediate family away from aunts, uncles, and grandparents who lived nearby. Several members of Christy's family lived within a small distance from each other. In her words, "like a whole lot of my family lives just like in one little clump." She described the family property:

Where our house sits down below, there was a lot where my great grandma and grandpa lived, where their house was, but it's tore down now. And then out behind my house is a log cabin; you know how they fixed it together with the clay and stuff. And then the stone chimney. It's just one room, but inside you can tell it wasn't built recently. It's old because, I don't know, it's kind of like a old-timey smell. And then you can just kind of tell. Plus Papaw's got all of the old tools like when his great-great grandpa and all them had them on the wall. . . . And then there's another cabin—my Papaw's sister's cabin. It's built the same way except it's bigger. It's real nice. I've slept in it a couple times. But it's like the graveyard is right here on the hill and the bedrooms that we always sleep in. The window is right here and I slept up there on a full moon one night, and I was so scared 'cause the moon was just like shined right on the graveyard.

Christy's grandfather had 10 or 11 brothers and sisters. His family celebrated reunions at designated times each year. Christy talked enthusiastically about these family times of celebration:

> I love it. I think it's Labor Day when everybody comes in and they'll start
> one story and they'll say, "Oh you remember that time when we done this.
> Oh yeah, and remember when we done this." You know we could just sit
> there for hours and listen to them talk. I like that real well. And every
> body—wherever you can get a floor, a mat, or a rug, or anything—every
> body just piles in.

Christy told us that kids of all ages play outside together where she lives:

> We all just go ride bicycles in the summer, play basketball or we'll say,
> "We'll go to your house today and play football," and we'll say, "Oh, we'll
> go to your house and play baseball the next day."

In describing her community, Christy explained, "There's not that much crime." She captured her sense of personal space: "It's just like our own little place."

At School.   Christy had been involved in a storytelling club for 2 years. Although she had quit this year to play basketball, storytelling remained an important part of her life:

> Well, even if I'm not in it, I can still be part of it, you know, 'cause I still
> have my folder [of stories] and stuff, and I can still get stories. And I can
> still go to all the story swaps.

Christy was eager to tell us about her genealogy project, a major activity in her sixth-grade English class. To find out about her family, Christy went from house to house in the Brier area where her family lived. Members of each household provided as much information as they could:

> When I'd go to one, I'd say "Can you help me with our genealogy?" Then
> he'd go back—"Well, that's about as far back as I can remember." Then
> you'd go to the next house, and you'd get a couple more.

In completing the project, Christy had been able to trace her family as far back as anyone else in the family had ever done, including one of her cousins who taught at Mountain Elementary School. Christy learned that her great uncle had a book on the Rakes family. She proudly explained that his book did not go back any farther than her own genealogy.

In the course of developing her genealogy, Christy said she discovered much about her family. She shared that her papaw had served in World War II, and that her Uncle Roger had served in the Vietnam War. Christy showed us pictures of her grandfather as she told a story about a Christmas episode that had taken place while he was away at war. Along with the pictures, Christy showed us her grandfather's pocket watch and expressed her personal pleasure at possessing such an extensive collection of family heirlooms.

Besides gathering stories for the storytelling club and developing her genealogy project for English class, Christy had been able to use her knowledge of her family to complete other school assignments. When as part of a class effort to explore the cultural motif of the "trickster" her seventh-grade class wrote stories about relatives who liked to play tricks on them, Christy wrote about her uncle who made her cry as a young child when he told her that her parents, who had been away for the evening, were not coming back for her.

Christy's seventh-grade teacher, Mrs. Jonas, although not a curriculum initiator, was an active member of the curriculum effort. She talked enthusiastically about the curriculum changes she had made as part of the faculty-wide curriculum effort. Changes highlighted by Mrs. Jonas included the trickster story assignment for which Christy had used her memory of experiencing her uncle's "trick."

In describing Christy, Mrs. Jonas explained that a cousin of Christy's had been killed in a car wreck and that this had "really, really made its impact on her." Saying she believed that Christy "has a real sense of family," Mrs. Jonas supported the sense of Christy's commitments evident in her conversations with us. Academically, Mrs. Jonas judged Christy to be a "strong student."

As we continued to converse with Christy, she described how seventh graders were collecting stories, "hunting stories, Christmas stories, winter stories," that then were read aloud to the class. As the teacher read the collected stories aloud, each student was to look for literary elements that might be incorporated into new stories they would write in class. Mrs. Jonas explained that Christy had collected a particular story that she drew on repeatedly in developing new writing. According to her teacher, Christy "took ideas she got in class and developed them. But then she went back and found the story she had brought in that had been told to her and incorporated it into her story." For Mrs. Jonas, this demonstrated Christy's "real strong sense of—this is my story and I want to use it."

In assessing the Appalachian curriculum at her school, Christy concluded that studying the Appalachian culture in school supported her understanding of her culture and her appreciation for it:

> If I'd not got into storytelling when I did, you know, I wouldn't know anything about the past or who my ancestors were or any of the stories or how, like the legends got started and stuff.

Future Plans.   Christy expressed her intention to continue her work on her genealogy as a personal project through which she could explore her mother's side of the family. She also said that she would like to go back and talk more with her grandmother. Another interest she explained was learning how the Brier community where she lives became settled. She proudly reported that the area in which they lived often was called John Rake's Hollow after her great great grandfather.

When asked about her future plans, Christy told us she hoped to get a job in the medical field because it was a job she can do in her home county. She elaborated:

> I kind of want to be a radiologist. I think that would be fun or even a baby doctor. . . . That's really the only thing you can do around here if you want to get a really good paying job.

Christy's parents explained to us that they planned for Christy to attend college. Because finances were uncertain, they wondered whether Christy's skill at basketball might not be a means to a college education. Her teacher disagreed, saying, "Christy, your academic skills are so strong that you have a much better chance of getting an academic scholarship." She did, however, note that Christy was somewhat reluctant as a reader, "Like she'll read R. L. Stine (1996), but that's where she is right now."

As we concluded our last interview with Christy, she reminded us that she wants people outside Appalachia to understand that people in her community "don't go outside barefoot to milk the cow" or gather eggs from the chickens. She explained, "There's more to us than that!"

DISCUSSION

The purpose of the research reported in this chapter was to explore the nature and extent of collaboration between the home and school as experienced by the children whose teachers had designed a curriculum intended to make the school curriculum sensitive to and appreciative of the children's home culture. Six themes emerged in the conversations we had with the children: (a) children as avid collectors of cultural treasures, (b) family members as knowledgeable elders, (c) curriculum as a cross-space experience, (d) curriculum as temporal link to the past, (e) curriculum as a source of ancestral pride, and (f) and the future as an arena for guarded optimism and flexibility. In the following section we discuss each theme.

Children as Avid Collectors of Cultural Treasures

The three children described, like the others we studied, described themselves as avid collectors in their search for cultural treasures in their homes and the homes of their relatives.

Natalie told us how she worked with her grandmother to find treasures that were important to her at home and, with the advent of the Appalachian studies curriculum, also at school. In her third- and fourth-grade classroom, these treasures included stories, recipes, and remedies.

Jeremy eagerly engaged his grandparents, especially his grandfather, as a source for stories and as a model for how to tell stories, and his grandmother as a source of transportation to and shared attendance at story swaps.

Christy interviewed various family members, including her grandparents and aunts and uncles, to locate stories and explore her genealogy. She attended family reunions as a collector of stories and genealogical traces, and as an enthusiastic child member of the group.

Family Members as Knowledgeable Elders

With the advent of the Appalachian curriculum, family members became elders respected for their knowledge and skills. As such, they became important members of the school community who could contribute actively and directly to the children's school knowledge and success.

Natalie had been raised by her grandmother, and each held much affection for the other. Natalie probably would have visited her grandmother in the evening, despite school commitments. What changed with the advent of the Appalachian curriculum was that Natalie's grandmother became a curriculum resource, one acknowledged by teachers and children at school for her skills in local practices, such as pie making.

Jeremy's grandfather was seen at school, not only as a grandfather, but as a skilled storyteller, a performer, recognized for his storytelling abilities. As such, he could help Jeremy establish himself as a talented newcomer, carrying on a family tradition well regarded at school.

Christy's family was no longer simply a large family who kept local customs such as celebrating family reunions. They became a rich network of contributors to the various school assignments that were important to Christy and her teachers. Thus, for example, in her story of her experience being cared for by her uncle, Christy, with the help of her teacher, could represent her uncle, not merely as a helpful family member, but as a recognized cultural archetype, the trickster.

Curriculum as a Cross-Spatial Experience

There was a seamlessness among classroom, school, and community in the curriculum as the children described it.

Natalie's story of the journey was important to her. She had talked with her cousin about his life and adapted it for the purposes of a classroom assignment. The fact that it would be displayed as part of an end-of-the-year school–community event known as Appalachian Days was a source of pride and anticipation for her.

Christy had shared her genealogy project at Appalachian Days the year before she talked with us, and several of her family members had attended and shared her pride in this accomplishment. She looked forward to the upcoming celebration, during which the book of new stories reflecting traditionally used literary devices would be on display.

For Jeremy, there was a sense of participating in the Appalachian curriculum, although his teacher had not been a curriculum developer. This experience was possible because in addition to Appalachian Days, the storytelling clubs were a school-wide activity, one available to children regardless of a particular classroom teacher's involvement.

For these children, the spatial lines between home and school also became a bit blurred. Natalie's grandmother taught her traditional crafts such as embroidery at home, whereas she taught her fried apple pie making at school. Christy did a genealogy project for a sixth-grade assignment, and then as a seventh grader, she committed personal home time to pursuing storytelling and genealogy study. Jeremy told stories at school and made up an embellished account of his life at home for his young cousins with whom he corresponded. Each of the children experienced and enjoyed the presence of family members at school activities such as special classroom activities, story swaps, and Appalachian Celebration Days.

Curriculum as a Temporal Link to the Past

The children experienced the curriculum as a temporal link between past and present. Each engaged relatives in describing people and practices from the past, including events in the lives of their living elders and events in the lives of ancestors who had passed away many years earlier, but whose memories were kept alive through artifacts such as stories, photographs, community names, personal records, and official documents.

In considering our conversations with the children, several of these links between past and present became visible. In Natalie's story about a journey, she chose butter biscuits, a food traditionally eaten at her grandmother's home. She included her cousin Adam's contemporary dream in the story as well as the very modern Chapel O' Love that she described as a one-stop marriage facility.

Jeremy's story of the possum and fox was a traditional story drawn from the past. It actually was a kind of trickster tale common to the folktales of many cultures. Yet it was clear to Jeremy that the story had changed over time. He became interested in its earlier forms and intent on learning more about its origin, even while he was excited about developing it for modern audiences through the performance processes he was exploring in the storytelling club.

Christy's interest in genealogy also focused across time. Indeed, a genealogy is a record that links present to past by documenting those who came before, their life spans, and their significant attributes and accomplishments. By bringing her family's history to school, Christy brought the past with her. By expressing her intention to develop a genealogy of her mother's family, she brought the past through the present into the future.

Curriculum as Generator of Ancestral Pride

The children experienced the school curriculum as a link with their heritage, one that evoked a sense of pride. Both Natalie and Christy spoke openly about the pride they felt in their heritage. We can also infer pride from Christy's commitment to continue her practice of collecting stories and to develop a genealogy for her mother's family. Ancestral pride also was implied in the pleasure she exuded as she shared the family heirlooms she had collected. Jeremy's self-motivated search for developing new stories and learning more about the stories he had already collected as well as the wholehearted performances he gave during story swaps illustrated his sense of delight in his family tradition of storytelling. Finally, we believe that the uninhibited way the children talked with us, moving from one family story to another, suggested unabashed pride in their families, homes, and traditions.

Curriculum as Sustaining an Optimistic, If Guarded, Sense of the Future

Natalie, Christy, and Jeremy had found valuable roles for themselves in the school, roles enhanced by their enthusiasm for and support of the Appalachian curriculum. This optimism also was reflected in their views of future prospects for them. Natalie and Christy both imagined themselves in responsible community positions.

Natalie considered what kinds of jobs would allow her to remain in the area. She discounted coal mining, her father's occupation, believing it would not well suit her, and banking, her mother's career, believing it was too connected to cities to suit her. Having watched her cousins, Natalie selected pharmacy as a likely career for her, and she pointed to the little pharmacies located in her community. She showed awareness of the uncertain economic conditions in the region by developing a contingency plan for going into law if pharmacy lost its economic viability.

Christy expressed interest in the medical field because it would allow her to stay in her home county. She suggested that she might study radiology or obstetrics. Like Natalie, Christy showed concern for economic stability of the region, explaining that the medical profession would provide greater economic stability than most other jobs.

Jeremy had decided that he would be a comic book artist or a "game doctor." Both of these choices related to his understanding of his interests and abilities. Despite his poor academic record at school and his struggle to pass statewide barrier tests, Jeremy had made plans for his future that were hopeful and interesting to him.

CONCLUSION

It is clear that the children with whom we talked at Mountain Elementary School were confident in their sense of themselves and their connections to school, family, and culture. They appreciated the cultural literacies of their home lives. However, each of these children also was influenced by the larger society. We could see those influences in their hobbies and aspirations. Natalie attributed her enjoyment of music to her father's guitar playing, but she wanted to play a different instrument. Jeremy delighted in his grandfather's traditional stories, while enjoying the futuristic writings of Isaac Asimov. Christy loved old stories and family reunions, while being an avid reader of R. L. Stine. Thus the lives of these children may be understood as journeys through a dynamic field of time and space across which they were experiencing the intersections of multiple literacies.

The New London Group (1996) defined literacy in terms of multi-literacies or dynamic, interacting semiotic systems for the construction and reconstruction of meaning. The group has encouraged curriculum based on the notion of learner as designer and transformer of various semiotic systems. With this view of literacy, we can see the three described children as literate individuals who with the help of the school curriculum are creatively interweaving home and school discourses to create a unique fabric that is the evolving story of their literate lives.

In this chapter we explore how the children were experiencing a curriculum effort designed to promote school-based literacy by appreciating and supporting the literacy traditions of the home. The children expressed appreciation for the curriculum and the positive role they and their family members were playing at school. In the classrooms where the Appalachian curriculum was being developed, the children described active engagement in the tasks designed to combine home culture and school-based learning objectives, such as writing new stories using traditional literary devices. Thus this study of children's perspectives supports a sociolinguistic perspective on literacy learning. A strong implication of this study is that teachers can design and implement curriculum changes that allow children to develop new literacies as part of the process of studying and developing existing literacies.

As researchers, we are keenly aware that this particular curriculum effort requires further study before we can confidently assess its success. In the end, we would want to examine children's fluency in two languages: the language of their homes and the language of the public arena. In curriculum research such as this, it may be wise to take a longitudinal view.

Nevertheless, this study supported the sociocultural perspective on literacy learning, which recognizes the intergenerational influence on children's literacies expressed through home culture. Just as Natalie's grandmother put a faded photo of her great grandfather into a new picture frame, literacy is reframed as new generations redesign the past through their own lives. With respect to literacy, we agree with Miller (1975a):

For the dead have come too,
those dark, stern departed who pose
all year in oval picture frames.
They are looking out of the eyes of children. (p. 348)

REFERENCES

Alvermann, D., O'Brien, D., & Dillon, D. (1996). On writing qualitative research. *Reading Research Quarterly, 31*(1), 114–120.

Andersen, M. L., & Collins, P. H. (1995). *Race, class, and gender: An anthology.* New York: Wadsworth.

Au, K. H., & Kawakami, A. J. (1994). Cultural congruence in instruction. In E. R. Hollins, J. E. King, & W. Hayman (Eds.), *Teaching diverse populations: Formulating a knowledge base* (pp. 5–23). Albany: State University of New York Press.

Barone, T. (1995). Persuasive writings, vigilant readings and reconstructed characters: The paradox of trust in educational story sharing. In J. A. Hatch & R. Wisniewski (Eds.), *Life history and narrative* (pp. 63–74). Washington, DC: The Falmer Press.

Boyer, E. (1983). *High school: A report on secondary education in America.* New York: Harper & Row.

Britzman, D. (1991). *Practice makes practice: A critical study of learning to teach.* Albany, NY: SUNY Press.

Coffey, A., & Atkinson, P. (1996). *Making sense of qualitative data: Complementary research strategies.* Thousand Oaks, CA: Sage.

Cotterill, P. (1992). Interviewing women: Issues of friendship, vulnerability, and power. *Women's Studies International Forum, 15*(5/6), 593–606.

Delpit, L. (1988). The silenced dialogue: Power and pedagogy in educating other people's children. *Harvard Educational Review, 3*(58), 280–298.

Delpit, L. (1995). *Other people's children: Cultural conflict in the classroom.* New York: The New Press.

Dewey, J. (1938). *Experience and education.* New York: Collier Books.

Ely, M. (1991). *Doing qualitative research: Circles within circles.* New York: The Falmer Press.

Erickson, J. (1986). Qualitative research on teaching. In M. Withrock (Ed.), *Handbook on research on teaching* (pp. 119–161). New York: Macmillan.

Gee, J. (1990). *Social linguistics and literacies: Ideology in discourses.* New York: The Falmer Press.

Grumet, M. (1991). The politics of personal knowledge. In C. Witherell & N. Noddings (Eds.), *Stories lives tell: Narrative and dialogue in education* (pp. 67–77). New York: Teachers College Press.

Hammersley, M., & Atkinson, P. (1995). *Ethnography: Principles in practice* (2nd ed.). New York: Routledge.

Heath, S. B. (1983). *Ways with words: Language, life, and work in communities and classroom.* Cambridge, MA: Cambridge University Press.

Heath, S. B., & Mangiola, L. (1991). *Children of promise: Literate activity in linguistically and culturally diverse classrooms.* Washington, DC: National Education Association.

Hirsch, E. D. (1987). *Cultural literacy: What every American needs to know.* Boston: Houghton Mifflin.

Jones, L. (1996). Appalachian values. In R. J. Higgs & A. N. Manning (Eds.), *Voices from the hills: Selected readings of southern Appalachia* (pp. 507–517). Dubuque, IA: Kendall/ Hunt.

Knoblauch, C. H., & Brannon, L. (1993). *Critical teaching and the idea of literacy.* Portsmouth, NH: Boynton-Cook.

Lalik, R., & Boljonis, A. (1994, April). *Taking a voice in one's teaching: A study of teachers' perspectives in an Appalachian community.* Paper presented at the Annual Meeting of the American Educational Research Association, New Orleans, LA.

Lalik, R., Dellinger, L., & Druggish, R. (1996). Appalachian literacies at school. In D. J. Leu, C. K. Kinzer, & K. Hinchman (Eds.), *Literacies for the 21st century: Research and practice: Forty-fifth yearbook of the National Reading Conference* (pp. 345–358). Chicago: National Reading Conference.

L'Amour, L. (1980). *The Sacketts.* Garden City, NY: Doubleday.

Lather, P. (1988). *Getting Smart: Feminist research and pedagogy within the postmodern.* New York: Routledge.

Lave, J., & Wenger, E. (1991). *Situated learning: Legitimate peripheral participation.* New York: Cambridge University Press.

Luke, A. (1995). Text and discourse in education: An introduction to critical discourse analysis. In M. W. Apple (Ed.), *Review of research in education* (p. 21). Washington, DC: AERA.

Miller, J. W. (1975a). Family Reunion. In R. J. Higgs & A. N. Manning (Eds.), *Voices from the hills: Selected readings of southern Appalachia* (p. 348). New York: Fredrick Ungate Publishing.

Miller, J. W. (1975b). A mirror for Appalachia. In R. J. Higgs & A. N. Manning (Eds.), *Voices from the hills: Selected readings of southern Appalachia* (pp. 447–459). New York: Fredrick Ungate Publishing.

Moll, L., & Gonzalez, N. (1994). Lessons from research with language-minority children. *Journal of Reading Behavior, 26*(4), 439–455.

Moll, L., & Greenberg, J. (1990). Creating zones of possibilities: Combining social contexts for instruction. In L. C. Moll (Ed.), *Vygotsky and education* (pp. 319–348). Cambridge, England: Cambridge University Press.

Nespor, J. E., & Barber, L. (1995). Audience and the politics of narrative. In J. A. Hatch & R. Wisniewski (Eds.), *Life history and narrative* (pp. 49–62). Washington, DC: The Falmer Press.

Paris, C. (1993). *Teacher agency and curriculum making in classrooms.* New York: Teachers College Press.

Purcell-Gates, V. (1995). *Other people's words: The cycle of low literacy.* Cambridge, MA: Harvard University Press.

Sawyer, R. (1953). *Journey cake, ho!* New York: Viking Press.

Shor, I. (1992). *Empowering education: Critical teaching for change.* Chicago: University of Chicago Press.

Stine, R. L. (1996). *Goosebumps: How to kill a monster.* New York: Scholastic.

Taylor, D. (1991). *Learning denied.* Portsmouth, NH: Heinemann.

Taylor, D., & Dorsey-Gaines, C. (1988). *Growing up literate: Learning from inner-city families.* Portsmouth, NH: Heinemann.

The New London Group. (1996). A pedagogy of multiliteracies: Designing social futures. *Harvard Educational Review, 66*(1), 60–92.

5

Telling the People's Stories: Literacy Practices and Processes in a Navajo Community School

Teresa L. McCarty
University of Arizona

Galena Sells Dick
Rough Rock Community School

> [S]chooling . . . is all about the telling of people's stories, and . . . these
> stories, if they are to include and enable all of the students rather than a
> privileged few, must seek to incorporate the multiple narratives and his-
> tories that constitute difference in a minority language setting.
> Naming Silenced Lives (Daniel McLaughlin, 1993, p. 100).

For more than two centuries, the stories told in school to Native American learners have glorified Western cultural traditions while seeking to
recast Indigenous identities according to Euro-American ideals. Especially since the passage of the 1819 Civilization Fund Act, which empowered the federal government to "civilize" Indigenous children, the goal
has been "to educate Indians to be non-Indians" (Lomawaima, 1995, p.
332).

Since 1988, we have collaborated in one local attempt to reverse the
legacy of colonial schooling. The site of our work is Rough Rock, a community of approximately 1,500 in the heart of the Navajo (Diné)[1] Nation
in northeastern Arizona (Fig. 5.1). Galena Dick, a native of Rough Rock,
taught at the community school for 35 years, and directed the pre-K–6
bilingual–bicultural education program there. Teresa McCarty, a non-
Indian educator and cultural anthropologist, has worked at and with

---

[1]Diné is a collective term used self-referentially, signifying The People (i.e., Navajos).
We use the English translation to frame the title of this chapter.

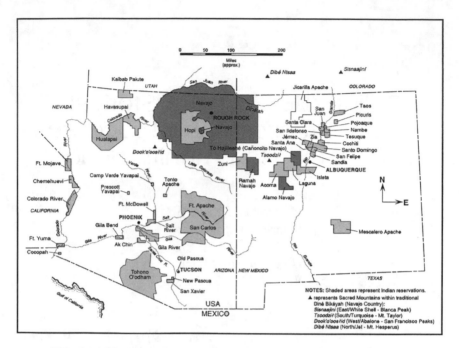

FIG. 5.1.   The Navajo Nation and Rough Rock in the U.S. Southwest.

Rough Rock since 1980 as an ethnographer, curriculum developer, and consultant to the school. Together, we have joined teachers, students, parents, and elders in researching, developing, and implementing a cur-riculum grounded in local texts and lives. This is an account of our long-term collaborative research.

We preface this account with an explanation of our theoretical and ideological orientation to the research and practice reported in this chap-ter. We have been guided by four related bodies of knowledge. First, we have drawn on critical–anthropological theories of minoritized[2] students' school experiences and their "success" and "failure" in school (Gibson, 1997; Jacob & Jordan, 1993; Varenne, McDermott, Goldman, Naddeo, & Rizzo-Tolk, 1999). These theories range from a focus on processes constructed in face-to-face interaction to those embedded in larger rela-tions of power. Freire (1993) points out that, "Curriculum reform is al-

---

[2]We prefer the term "minoritized" to "minority." Navajos living in the Navajo Nation are, in fact, in the numerical majority. "Minoritized" more accurately conveys the power re-lations and processes by which certain groups are marginalized in the larger society. The term also implies human agency and the power to contest and transform existing relations of power (McCarty, 2002, p. xv).

ways a political–pedagogical process" (p. 19). Accordingly, our work has joined attention to face-to-face interaction in classrooms, the school, and the community, with an interrogation of the sociohistorical and institutional forces that both constrain and enable positive change.

Second, we have drawn on research and theory in second language acquisition and bilingual education, in particular, the principle that the acquisition of first and second languages (and) is a reciprocal, interdependent process. Cummins (1989) articulates the principle this way: "To the extent that instruction in L[anguage] x is effective in promoting proficiency in Lx, transfer of this proficiency to Ly will occur provided there is adequate exposure to Ly (either in the school or environment) and adequate motivation to learn Ly" (p. 44). Considerable data on immigrant students in the United States indicate that sustained development of communicative and cognitive–academic abilities in the mother tongue accelerates rather than hinders students' acquisition of English (Crawford, 1997; Grosjean, 1982; Krashen, 1985, 1996; Larsen-Freeman & Long, 1991, Pérez, 1998, Ramírez, 1992; Thomas & Collier, 1997). There also is strong support for Native American mother tongue maintenance for students whose first language is not English (Dick & McCarty, 1996; Holm & Holm, 1990; McCarty, 1993a; Rosier & Farella, 1976; Watahomigie & McCarty, 1996). More recently, Thomas and Collier (1997) have shown that heritage language instruction also is highly effective for children who are "dominant in English [and are] losing their heritage language" (p. 15), a situation that closely parallels that of Native American learners today.

Third, we have been guided by principles of social justice and their realization in participatory action research. This orientation enables us to analyze curriculum transformation as a form of democracy-in-action. As Freire (1993) notes, "[O]ne does not change the 'face' of schools through the central office. . . . One cannot democratize schools authoritarily" (pp. 19–20). Rather, we have worked within a framework of "bottom-up" language and curriculum planning (Hornberger, 1996), situating our inquiry within local contexts and concerns, whereby community stakeholers are positioned as the active agents of research and change. Within such a framework, theory and practice are dialectical, "undichotomizable," and irreducible one to the other. Freire (1993) states that "The very task of unveiling a practice . . . is a theoretical task, a theoretical practice" (p. 102). We have sought to identify and rework the hidden and explicit theories guiding language and literacy teaching at Rough Rock, using an action research cycle of "looking" (gathering data), "thinking" (reflecting, analyzing, and theorizing), and "acting" (planning, reporting, implementing, evaluating, and disseminating) (Stringer, 1996, pp. 16–17; see also Lewin, 1946).

Finally, it should be evident that we have adopted a language-as-resource approach (Ruiz, 1988). We begin with the assumption that the Navajo language is a tremendous intellectual, social, cultural, and scientific resource to its speakers and humankind. Our goal has been to support and capitalize on local linguistic and cultural resources, and to incorporate them into the school curriculum in transformative and liberatory ways.

With this background established, we turn to the sociocultural context in which our theoretical and pedagogical framework has been applied.

MULTICULTURALISM IN A DINÉ CONTEXT

Situated on a red-rock plateau dotted with juniper and sage, Rough Rock rose to international prominence in 1966 as the first school to have a locally elected, all-Indian governing board, and the first school to teach in and through the Native language. Today, the school enrolls approximately 600 students in pre-K through grade 12. Many come from "traditional," often monolingual Navajo households situated off unpaved roads some distance from the school. Their families make their living through a combination of sheep and goat herding, cattle ranching, making and marketing of local arts and crafts, and wage labor associated with construction or mining. A second group of students lives on or near the school campus in modern, tribally or federally financed housing. These are the children of school employees. Although they are exposed to the traditional Navajo way of life through their extended family relations, many of these students speak English as a first language. A final group comes from outside the local area and resides in one of two school dormitories. These students' home backgrounds vary, but in general are similar to the two aforementioned groups. Some are enrolled at Rough Rock specifically because their parents want them to receive a bilingual–bicultural education.

These demographics suggest the situation of language shift under way at Rough Rock, and indeed, in Indigenous communities throughout North America. When we began our work together during the 1980s, it was still the case that the large majority of Rough Rock students spoke Navajo as a primary language. In a single generation, we have witnessed an alarming shift in children's heritage language proficiencies. Currently, about 50% of Rough Rock elementary students are identified by their teachers as "reasonably proficient" in the heritage language. At the same time, however, students tend to speak a Nativized variety of English, and thus to be labeled "limited English proficient." Our work seeks to understand and build on the multiple language and literacy strengths of Rough Rock learners, expanding their proficiencies in the heritage language and English.

In this setting, multiculturalism and its connections to literacy learning carry a distinct significance. At Rough Rock, multiculturalism is not about children studying "people who are different from them" (Rasinski & Padak, 1990, p. 580). Indigenous students have been doing that since the first Indian "praying town" was established in Massachusetts in 1631. Instead, multiculturalism at Rough Rock and, we suspect, in other American Indian communities, is a reenvisioning of curriculum to embrace the lives and stories of children and families from the local community. Rather than a benign pluralism that "celebrates" difference, we understand multicultural education to be an instrument of critical democracy that resists dominant modes of schooling and reshapes them to provide genuine equality of opportunity for all (Aronowitz & Giroux, 1985; Darder, 1991; Freire, 1978; Giroux, 2001; Lomawaima & McCarty, 2002; Sleeter, 1996). The development of multicultural curricula is thus both a critique of colonial education and a proactive, pro-Navajo bridge to English and the wider world.

The Social History of Literacy Learning at Rough Rock

Drawing on notions of dialogism and heteroglossia (Bakhtin, 1981), Cairney (1992) observes that, "Reading occurs against a backdrop of one's prior literary experiences" (p. 502). Over the years, we have held long conversations about the backdrop of literacy experiences among Indigenous peoples, and its meaning for contemporary Native educators and students. For both of us, our school-based English literacy experiences began with the pervasive "Dick and Jane" basal readers. But whereas one of us found some, albeit contrived, connection between those texts and lived experience, the other found confusion and belittlement. Years later, Galena Dick wrote about this in her literacy autobiography:

> Looking at the books in class I wondered where this fantasy was. I used to dream and think, "Will I ever get to see this place some day?" I learned how to read by remembering the formation of individual words and how they looked on a page, the curves and shapes they had. . . . I wasn't aware

that print had a meaning. All I wanted to do was remember all the words to satisfy the teacher (Dick & McCarty, 1996, p. 73).

There is one story from Galena Dick's autobiography that is particularly telling concerning the power of literacy practices such as these to mold children's identities. The story unfolded late one September afternoon, as we were driving from the Rough Rock Elementary School to the district administration building about a mile away. Galena's narrative was interrupted by our bureaucratic mission, but we returned to the story the next day. We present it here as a further "backdrop" to the story of our collaborative work and the larger issues it raises.

Galena said:

> I recall an instance that happened when I came to the public school [in fourth grade]. One day the English teacher assigned us to write a composition paper on "the first time you made a cake." When she finished the instructions about the assignment, I sat there grinning and thinking to myself . . . , "What does this teacher know about me and my home environment?" I wondered if she knew my background and my people and the way we lived. She didn't know I lived in a hooghan [a traditonal earth and log dwelling] with no running water or electricity, modern amenities, or household appliances like a stove. . . . I sat there wondering how I was going to complete my assignment.
>
> I thought about the time my family and relatives were all involved in making my puberty ceremony [kinaaldá] cake. . . . I knew a lot about baking this kind of cake, but this wasn't the cake my teacher had in mind. . . . So after school, [I went to] the supermarket [and] located the shelf where the cake mixes were. I copied the recipe and the directions for mixing and baking a cake. Then I went to [an Anglo] friend's house to make sure I had the recipe the teacher was talking about. Then I ran back to the dormitory. I made up a story about making the cake. I felt nervous and uneasy about writing on a topic which I never experienced with my family. I felt embarrassed about my own culture. I wondered if other students were aware of my error or lack of ability and confidence, and if the teacher was going to point out my mistake. I was humiliated and worried I was going to be accused of making up a story (Dick & McCarty, 1996, p. 74).

In this story, the teacher's literacy practices act as a metaphorical mirror that reflects and helps construct an image of the child and her language and learning potential (McCarty, 1993a). Stories such as these are common at Rough Rock and in other Indigenous communities. They represent one reason why many Native students, to quote a colleague at Rough Rock, have come to view their language and culture as "second best." Our point in presenting these stories is to emphasize that efforts to develop culturally responsive literacy practices and materials must first engage and critique this education history. We argue that only through a process of dialogic and critical reflection can local stakeholders position themselves as the producers of school knowledge, whereby the stories children hear, read, and tell affirm rather than negate who they are (Freire, 1977, 1993, 1998). We turn now to an examination of how such a process was activated at Rough Rock.

REENVISIONING CHILDREN'S LITERACY POTENTIALS

In the fall of 1983, personnel from the Hawa'ii-based Kamehameha Early Education Program (KEEP) came to Rough Rock to test whether the English reading strategies they had developed for Native Hawaiian students would work with children from another culture (L. Vogt, personal communication, August, 1988; Vogt, Jordan, & Tharp, 1993). At the time, Rough Rock had installed a phonics-driven basic skills program in an attempt to stabilize what had become a highly volatile curriculum. (For more on this, see McCarty, 1993b, 2002; Dick, Estell, & McCarty, 1994; also see Auerbach, 1992, for a critique of such programs.) KEEP addressed the very things perceived as lacking at Rough Rock at the time: contextualized reading, cooperative learning, and instruction keyed to the local culture. Third-grade teacher Afton Sells found that KEEP's approach reinforced what she was already doing despite basic skills, and in her words, "I didn't want to give it [KEEP's approach] up."

With Afton Sells' leadership and support from the Anglo elementary principal and director of education, KEEP became the core curriculum in the primary grades, all classrooms staffed with local Navajo teachers. The KEEP strategies did require modification to make them workable with Navajo students. (For a full discussion, see Vogt et al., 1993.) But the most significant changes, and the foundation for our current work, were the ways in which Navajo teachers expanded KEEP's premise of cultural compatibility by tailoring instructional content and participant structures (Philips, 1983) to the local language and culture.

These changes did not happen quickly or in a linear way (Vogt & Au, 1995). They evolved over several years, initially through KEEP's direct and ongoing work in Rough Rock classrooms and, after the formal KEEP–Rough Rock collaboration ended, in sustained professional development activities. As teachers witnessed improvements in children's English language development, they gradually moved from "cloning" KEEP to immersing themselves in research, theory, and practice in American Indian bilingual education (Dick et al., 1994).

In the course of this work, we began to question the limited means available to evaluate what we observed children actually doing in two languages. Neither standardized tests nor a locally developed assessment captured the rich, multilayered quality of the literacy processes we were documenting in Rough Rock classrooms. We therefore turned our attention to understanding those processes better, and to seeking more accurate and meaningful strategies for evaluating the language and literacy abilities students actually displayed.

In the spring of 1992, along with eight bilingual teachers, we formed a study group to investigate alternatives to standardized assessment. Similar to teacher study groups elsewhere (González et al., 1995; Short et al., 1992), our group was voluntary, organized by teachers for their own purposes, and intended to connect a body of scholarly literature to our own classroom research. Over a semester, the group met weekly for a few hours and monthly for a full day, reading and discussing scholarly texts on alternative assessment, keeping ethnographic observations and reflective logs, and monitoring and collecting samples of students' Navajo and English writing. The elementary principal, a strong supporter of the innovations introduced by KEEP, provided release time for teachers and participated in study group discussions himself.

Despite this supportive environment, the residue of colonial education surfaced almost immediately within the group. For example, we began the first group meeting by inviting teachers to brainstorm a web on evaluation. We were startled to hear these veteran teachers claim they knew nothing about the topic, and were "waiting to be told what to do" with the children's writing samples they had gathered. "We tend to accept what somebody else develops" (i.e., standardized tests), one teacher said. "Disempowered," another teacher wrote in her journal. Galena Dick pointed out:

> Teachers often feel they don't know the "answers" or what they know isn't that important. This study group is not just a place where we have to listen to one person and have them give us all the answers. We know our kids better than anybody else. Teachers intuitively know there is more going on than what is represented on standardized tests.

Eventually, teachers began to voice opposition to the institutional constraints on their teaching practice. "Why not use our own teacher-developed tests?" one teacher asked. As we studied students' writing in Navajo and English, it became clear that the prime resources for assessing students' literacy processes were the bilingualism and biculturalism of the teachers themselves.

The study group became the forum not only in which we examined children's literacy(ies)-in-process, but also through which teachers validated their power to effect curricular change. Often, this process recalled painful memories of the teachers' own English literacy experiences in federal boarding schools, where, as Galena Dick's autobiography shows, they had been denied the very opportunities they were now trying to provide for their students.

Over time, this critical inquiry led teachers to develop novel strategies for observing, recording, and assessing students' capabilities in two languages, including holistic writing checklists (Hudelson, 1989) and a portfolio assessment plan modeled after a Navajo ceremonial basket and cornstalk (Fig. 5.2). "What I really gained from this study group," one teacher remarked, "was looking at children's writing and determining how to evaluate what they do know and how to build on that." Another said, "It seems like whenever we all . . . work together, we do get more done, and I'm beginning to understand and answer all the questions I've had." Still another commented, "We found out our students' strengths" (Lipka & McCarty, 1994; McCarty, 1993a).

These reflective statements suggest the power of the study group as a vehicle for positive change. Within this social space, teachers constructed what we have called elsewhere a "zone of safety," an environment in which conventional practices could be questioned and new ones posed and tried (Lipka & McCarty, 1994; also see Begay et al., 1995; McCarty, 2002). Teachers worked as both apprentices and peer mentors (Lave & Wenger, 1991). In Vygotskian terms, they created and worked within a zone of proximal development—an interactional space in which each individual was able to achieve more through collaboration than alone (Cole, John-Steiner, Scribner, & Souberman, 1978). We emphasize that this was not a "comfort zone." There was great personal and shared discomfort as teachers revisited their literacy histories and began to challenge the pedagogical assumptions they had internalized in the course of their own schooling. Yet more than any other single experience since the introduction of KEEP, the study group strengthened teachers' ownership over the process of curriculum change. This became the platform from which we would launch an invigorated new bilingual, bicultural, biliteracy curriculum.

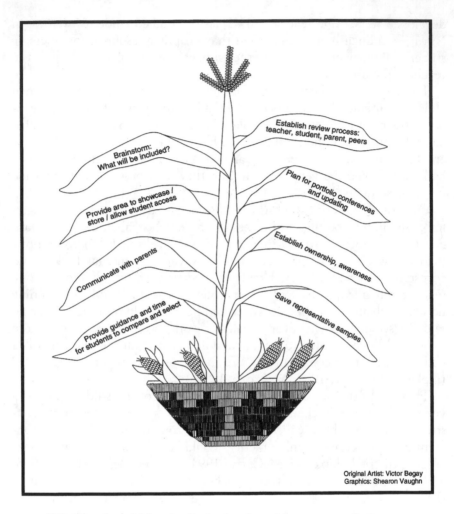

Original Artist: Victor Begay
Graphics: Shearon Vaughn

FIG. 5.2.   A model for a locally developed portfolio assessment (by Lorene
Tohe Van Pelt, second grade teacher, adapted from Tierney, Carter, & Desai,
1991; original art by Victor Begay; graphics by Shearon Vaughn).

CURRICULUM DEVELOPMENT
AS A SOCIAL TRANSACTION

One of the most important innovations introduced by KEEP was the concept of reading and writing as integrated processes rather than products
resulting from the application of decontextualized skills. Initiating these
processes at Rough Rock required letting go of the cultural artifacts
closely associated with schools—basal readers, workbooks, and commer-

cial programs—and relying on teachers and students instead. The "zone of safety" had to be widened. Teachers needed to create the same types of social-mediational structures they found in the study group within their own classrooms and literacy practices.

This was the basis for extending our research and practice to include literacy materials development. Rough Rock has a long history of producing Navajo language materials. The first Native American curriculum development center was established there in 1967. Moreover, unlike many Indigenous groups, Navajos have a relatively long written language tradition dating back to the mid-19th century, a standardized orthography, and a significant corpus of literature. Nevertheless, the quantity and quality of Navajo print materials are limited, especially in comparison with those available in English.

During summer and weekend workshops, teachers and teacher assistants carved out yet another social space for collaborative dialogue and the development of bilingual–bicultural texts. From their own life histories and the stories told by parents and elders, Rough Rock educators began generating a small collection of children's storybooks in Navajo. Macintosh computers, the talents of local artists, and a small printing budget enabled the school to turn these texts into high-quality, beautifully illustrated works (Fig. 5.3). These materials drew upon and validated the local culture, opened new possibilities for teacher–student dialogue, and allowed students to see their teachers as published authors— in Navajo (McCarty, 1993a).

A crucial part of this process was a series of summer literature camps that continue to this day. Organized by the school's bilingual education program, the 2- to 3-week camps are open to all elementary students. They emphasize field-based learning and the co-involvement of children, teachers, parents, and elders. The theme for one summer, hooghan, is illustrative. Aside from its function to provide shelter, the hooghan carries with it a rich oral tradition of stories and songs, as well as a wealth of opportunities for teaching and learning about kinship, Diné values, and the everyday art and science of food preparation and the care and tending of the home. One elder explained the life lessons contained in the hooghan hearth this way:

> The fire stoker and the burning fire, one can talk to. They are useful in that way. They are like our maternal grandfathers and grandmothers. That is how they nourish us. With these we progress and gain strength. These things you must learn, I tell the children. I teach them that way as they watch me prepare food. . . . I still keep my fire burning—that is how it is.

Shicheii Bidóola
(My Grandfather's Bull)

Emma Lewis Hane' Áyiilaa
Gilberto Jumbo Na'azhch'ąą'
AnCita Benally Naaltsoos Ak̓ę́ę́' Niiníníl

Tó Bíká Adeezbąąz

Juanita Estell hane' áyiilaa
Emmett Bia Jr. na'azhch'ąą'
Afton Sells naaltsoos ak̓ę́ę́' niiníníl

FIG. 5.3. Samples of teacher-developed children's storybooks: *Scheicheii Bidóla (My Grandfather's Bull)*, *Tó Biká Adeezbáąz (Getting Water in a Wagon)*, *Łį́į́tsʉoí Ayázhí Nináyiijááh (Yellowhorse Bringing Lambs Home)*, and *Łłoo (A Dog Named Łłoo)*.

During another literature camp, students researched the archaeology and petroglyphs of Dinétah, the Navajo homelands in northwestern New Mexico. This was complemented by a study of local landforms and sacred sites that combined oral history, geography, geology, and mathematics. Engaged in authentic learning experiences such as this, parents, elders, school staff, and students joined in storytelling, song, drama, art, and research and writing projects related to locally relevant themes. The oral tellings emanating from these experiences were recorded on hypercard for classroom use. Many have become the basis for developing new print materials as well.

These examples provide some sense of the ways in which bilingual–bicultural curriculum development at Rough Rock not only has involved the creation of new print materials, but also has entailed a collaborative social transaction between elders, parents, teachers, and youth. In the context of these socially meaningful interactions, children and adults co-construct knowledge from the cultural and linguistic capital (Bourdieu, 1977), or "funds of knowledge" (González et al., 1995) within their community. In this process, they create new opportunities for the development of Indigenous literacies and reaffirm the value of Navajo language and culture in their lives. We remember, for example, one elder's disbelief on being presented with a teacher-produced storybook in Navajo. "I thought only the Anglos wrote books," the elder said. The curriculum development processes and products at Rough Rock have sought to transform these attitudes, and to privilege Navajo knowledge in children's lives.

THE LITERACY CONTINUUM

Out of the processes described in this discussion, locally produced children's literature and other multicultural texts came to anchor theme studies in Rough Rock classrooms. For example, as part of the studies in one-third grade class, students read Ethelou Yazzie's (1971) *Navajo History*, and Marilyn V. Maberry's (1991) *Right After Sundown: Teaching Stories of the Navajos*. They also listened to stories of Navajo origins from elders who joined classroom activities, or whose stories had been previously recorded on audiotape and hypercard.

The third-grade teacher had been looking for ways to connect these literature studies to other content areas. The importance of insects and insect people in Navajo creation stories afforded a natural connecting point to science and entomology. The students became involved in scientific inquiry, literature study, journal writing, creative writing, and publishing, all revolving around a local theme. Oral and written language development and the co-involvement of parents and elders were natural parts of this interdisciplinary enterprise (Begay et al., 1995). The texts in Fig. 5.4, by third graders Morris Denetdeel and Alessandra Teller, illustrate the writing process and what children achieved in this learning–teaching environment.

These classroom practices exemplify what Tohono O'odham linguist Ofelia Zepeda (1995) calls the literacy continuum, a unique form of intertextuality that connects Indigenous oral traditions with written language development in the heritage language and English (Bakhtin, 1981; Hornberger, 1989). Within the literacy continuum, Zepeda (1995) states, each child "reaches deep into a past, a past he or she shares with a community—a past thousands of years old" (p. 11). The literacy continuum affirms that all learners come to the classroom with a storehouse of cultural and linguistic knowledge. In the case of Native students, that knowledge typically includes storytelling traditions, the flow and structure of oral narratives, and the importance of oral traditions within the community (Zepeda, 1995; also see McCarty & Watahomigie, 1998). When teachers and students jointly "reach into" these traditions, they are able to exploit not only culturally embedded forms of intertextuality, but also the essential social and relational qualities of authentic literacy events. Cairney (1992) states it this way: We need to "stir the collective intertextual history of our classrooms" (p. 507).

Through their research and reflection on practice, Rough Rock educators have attempted to do this. As children listen to the unfolding of elders' narratives, as they hear a favorite book or the stories of their peers, students experience, in those moments, an Indigenized form of intertextuality, the joining of oral and written narrative forms. Orality and literacy, Indigenous and Western narrative forms, are united in ways that allow students to use what they know to develop new language abilities, and to inquire about the world from a place within their cultural worlds (McCarty & Watahomigie, 1998). In the process, children experience the power and integration of the spoken and the written word. "This power is different from that which is held by a select few," Zepeda (1995) states. This is "the power ordinary people can have with words" (p. 8).

This is the essence of the literacy continuum. There is no single, uniform literacy, no linear path; nor is the literacy "club" open only to a privileged few (Smith, 1988). Instead, the work at Rough Rock shows the ways in which teachers, students, parents, and elders can co-construct transformative literacy practices that expand children's multiple literacies.

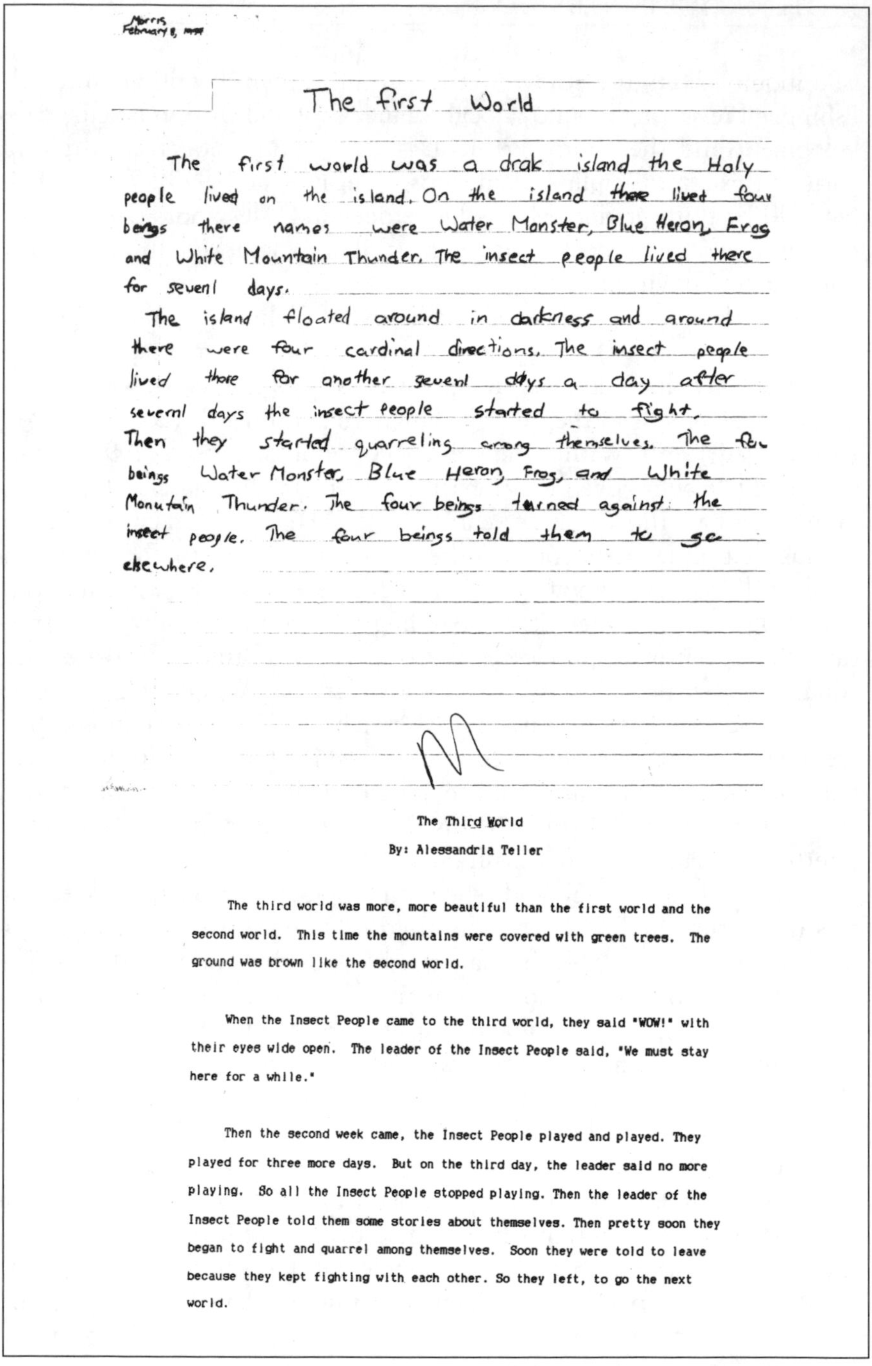

The First World

The first world was a drak island the Holy people lived on the island. On the island there lived four beings there names were Water Monster, Blue Heron, Frog and White Mountain Thunder. The insect people lived there for several days.

The island floated around in darkness and around there were four cardinal directions. The insect people lived there for another several days a day after several days the insect people started to fight. Then they started quarreling among themselves. The four beings Water Monster, Blue Heron, Frog, and White Monutain Thunder. The four beings turned against the insect people. The four beings told them to go elsewhere.

The Third World

By: Alessandria Teller

The third world was more, more beautiful than the first world and the second world. This time the mountains were covered with green trees. The ground was brown like the second world.

When the Insect People came to the third world, they said "WOW!" with their eyes wide open. The leader of the Insect People said, "We must stay here for a while."

Then the second week came, the Insect People played and played. They played for three more days. But on the third day, the leader said no more playing. So all the Insect People stopped playing. Then the leader of the Insect People told them some stories about themselves. Then pretty soon they began to fight and quarrel among themselves. Soon they were told to leave because they kept fighting with each other. So they left, to go the next world.

FIG. 5.4. "The First World" by Morris Denetdeel, and "The Third World" by Alessandra Teller (third grade, 1994), showing the integration of culturally-based content with the writing process—first and final drafts.

116

This work can be seen as a form of resistance to the legacy of colonial schooling. "When we went to school," Galena Dick (1998) writes, "all we learned about was Western culture";

> We were never told the stories that Rough Rock children are now told, and write themselves. We're telling those stories now. In the process, we are reversing the type of schooling we experienced. We see both sides of it, and we're helping children, through schooling, make connections to their own language and lives. (p. 25)

WHAT DIFFERENCE DOES THIS MAKE?

Rudine Sims Bishop (1994) notes that multicultural children's literature can be more than a "demand for inclusion" (p. 6). At its best, she writes, "it is a demand for a complete reenvisioning, reforming, or restructuring of schooling and ultimately of the society itself" (pp. 6 7). If schooling is indeed "all about the telling of people's stories" (McLaughlin, 1993), then such reenvisioning also demands that we ask:

> Whose stories are told?
> By whom?
> For whom and for what purpose?
> What difference does it make to embed curriculum in local stories and lives?

We have so far addressed the first three of these questions. We now consider the last. We would be remiss if we did not comment on the improvements in Rough Rock students' biliteracy, self-efficacy, and academic achievement. Using locally developed assessments and district-required standardized tests, we have conducted longitudinal studies of individual student and grade–cohort achievement. When these data are analyzed for all K–6 students, one overriding pattern emerges: Students who have the benefit of cumulative, uninterrupted initial literacy experiences in Navajo make the greatest gains on both local and national measures of achievement (Begay et al., 1995; McCarty, 1993a, 2002). Many test out of state and federal categories that would label them as "limited English proficient."

But the difference involves much more than the scores on tests. These changes in students' school performances came about as teachers had sustained opportunities to conduct classroom research and thereby better understand the discourse patterns in which local literacies are situated. Through their research, teachers came to view literacy learning as the construction of meaning rather than the mechanical acquisition of skills. These understandings were incorporated into teachers' pedagogy, becoming the basis for community transactions around bilingual–bicultural curriculum development (Auerbach, 1992, p. 77). Herein lies the "difference": As teachers reenvisioned their literacy potentials and those of their students, teachers simultaneously empowered themselves and created the conditions whereby students and their families could do the same.

By sharing and disseminating this work, we seek to make a difference in other Indigenous and minoritized communities. Certainly, the Rough Rock case is unique: The original collaboration with KEEP, the support provided by the former building principal, the level of external funding the school has been able to maintain, and the unique synergy of a group of bilingual teachers are case-specific factors. As Lipka et al. (1998) point out in their analysis of Yup'ik schooling, there is an ephemeral quality to such a case. Its significance lies in the moments of opportunity constructed within a zone of safety, which evolve into productive work (p. 203; also see Cole et al., 1978).

We believe the transferrable lessons in the Rough Rock case lie in the ways wherein such moments of opportunity can be created and effectively used. At Rough Rock, this began with teachers interrogating their own literacy histories and practices, and comparing them with the experiences and privilege of others (Auerbach, 1992; Giroux, 1987). This became the foundation for developing multicultural children's literature "at its best" (Bishop, 1994, p. 6), that is, literature and literacy practices that reimagined, reformed, and restructured the culture of schooling.

Rough Rock's process of curriculum reform is not complete, nor has it been untroubled or without significant setbacks. In particular, recent standardizing mandates threaten to dismantle much of the hard-won changes bilingual teachers were able to effect (Lomawaima & McCarty, 2002; McCarty, 2002). We are nonetheless heartened by the positive changes this process has produced. As testimony to these changes and their significance for children, we conclude with a poem by Melissa Todecheenie, a second grader at Rough Rock during the period of our research. The poem is entitled, simply, "Me." Note especially Melissa's spelling inventions:

I am me.
It is good to be.
I am special to be me,

Just like a bee,
I am a unique person,
I am the only kind son,
Who has a special talent of me,
Above the sailing sea,
It stands the greatful me,
Standing on the hills overlooking me,
I walk to the end of shinning sky,
As I come before I cry,
I will always be me,
No one will take the place of me!

If we are genuinely committed to a critically democratic and eman-cipatory education, then the stories through which children construct their worlds should reflect and validate who they and their communities are. From this perspective, curriculum and pedagogy can enable students to see themselves, in Melissa Todecheenie's words, as truly "greatful"—full of greatness. We hope we have shown in this chapter some possibilities by which this might be achieved.

REFERENCES

Aronowitz, S., & Giroux, H. A. (1985). *Education under siege*. South Hadley, MA: Bergin & Garvey.

Auerbach, E. (1992). Literacy and ideology. *Annual Review of Applied Linguistics, 12*, 71–85.

Bakhtin, M. (1981). *The dialogic imagination* (C. Emerson & M. Holquist, translators). Austin: University of Texas Press.

Begay, S., Dick, G. S., Estell, D. W., Estell, J., McCarty, T. L., & Sells, A. (1995). Change from the inside out: A story of transformation in a Navajo community school. *The Bilingual Research Journal, 19*, 121–139.

Bishop, R. S. (1994). A reply to Shannon the canon. *Journal of Children's Literature, 20*, 6–8.

Cairney, T. H. (1992). Fostering and building students' intertextual histories. *Language Arts, 69*, 502–507.

Cole, M., John-Steiner, V., Scribner, S., & Souberman, E. (1978). *L. S. Vygotsky, Mind in society: The development of higher psychological processes*. Cambridge, MA & London: Harvard University Press.

Crawford, J. (1997). *Best evidence: Research foundations of the Bilingual Education Act*. Washington DC: National Clearinghouse for Bilingual Education.

Cummins, J. (1989). *Empowering minority students*. Sacramento: California Association for Bilingual Education.

Darder, A. (1991). *Culture and power in the classroom: A critical foundation for bicultural education*. New York: Bergin & Garvey.

Dick, G. S. (1998). I maintained a strong belief in my language and culture: A Navajo language autobiography. *International Journal of the Sociology of Language, 132*, 23–25.

Dick, G. S., Estell, D. W., & McCarty, T. L. (1994). Saad naakih bee'enootį́į́lį́ na'alkaa: Restructuring the teaching of language and literacy in a Navajo community school. *Journal of American Indian Education, 33,* 31–46.

Dick, G. S., & McCarty, T. L. (1996). Reclaiming Navajo: Language renewal in an American Indian community school. In N. H. Hornberger (Ed.), *Indigenous literacies in the Americas: Language planning from the bottom up* (pp. 69–94). Berlin & New York: Mouton de Gruyter.

Freire, P. (1977). *Pedagogy of the oppressed.* New York: Continuum.

Freire, P. (1978). *Education for critical consciousness.* New York: Seabury Press.

Freire, P. (1993). *Pedagogy of the city.* (D. Macedo, translator). New York: Continuum.

Freire, P. (1998). *Pedagogy of freedom: Ethics, democracy, and civic courage.* (P. Clarke, translator). Lanham, MD: Rowman & Littlefield Publishers.

Gibson, M. (Ed.). (1997). Ethnicity and school performance: Complicating the immigrant/involuntary minority typology. Special Issue. *Anthropology & Education Quarterly, 28.*

Giroux, H. A. (1987). Critical literacy and student experience: Donald Graves' approach to literacy. *Language Arts, 64,* 175–181.

Giroux, H. A. (2001). English only and the crisis of memory, culture, and democracy. In R. D. González & I. Melis (Eds.), *Language ideologies: Critical perspectives on the official English movement, vol. 2* (pp. ix–xviii). Urbana, IL and Mahwah, NJ: National Council of Teachers of English and Lawrence Erlbaum Associates.

González, N., Moll, L. C., Floyd-Tenery, M., Rivera, A., Rendon, P., González, R., & Amanti, C. (1995). Funds of knowledge for teaching in Latino households. *Urban Education, 29,* 443–470.

Grosjean, F. (1982). *Life with two languages: An introduction to bilingualism.* Cambridge, MA: Harvard University Press.

Holm, A., & Holm, W. (1990). Rock Point, a Navajo way to go to school: A valediction. *Annals, AASSP, 508,* 170–184.

Hornberger, N. H. (1989). Continua of biliteracy. *Review of Educational Research, 59,* 271–296.

Hornberger, N. H. (Ed.). (1996). *Indigenous literacies in the Americas: Language planning from the bottom up.* Berlin & New York: Mouton de Gruyter.

Hudelson, S. (1989). *Write on: Children writing in ESL.* Englewood Cliffs, NJ: Center for Applied Linguistics and Prentice-Hall Regents.

Jacob, E., & Jordan, C. (Eds.). (1993). *Minority education: Anthropological perspectives.* Norwood, NJ: Ablex.

Krashen, S. (1985). *Inquiries and insights: Second language teaching, immersion and bilingual education, literacy.* Hayward, CA: Alemany Press.

Krashen, S. (1996). *Under attack: The case against bilingual education.* Culver City, CA: Language Education Associates.

Larsen-Freeman, D., & Long, M. H. (1991). *An introduction to second language acquisition research.* London & New York: Longman.

Lave, J., & Wenger, E. (1991). *Situated learning: Legitimate peripheral participation.* Cambridge, UK: Cambridge University Press.

Lewin, K. (1946). Action research and minority problems. *Journal of Social Issues, 2,* 34–46.

Lipka, J., & McCarty, T. L. (1994). Changing the culture of schooling: Navajo and Yup'ik cases. *Anthropology & Education Quarterly, 25,* 266–284.

Lipka, J., with Mohatt, G., and the Ciulistet Group (1998). *Transforming the culture of schools.* Mahwah, NJ: Lawrence Erlbaum Associates.

Lomawaima, K. T. (1995). Educating Native Americans. In J. A. Banks & C. A. M. Banks (Eds.), *Handbook of research on multicultural education* (pp. 331–347). New York: Macmillan.

Lomawaima, K. T., & McCarty, T. L. (2002). When tribal sovereignty challenges democracy: American Indian education and the democratic ideal. *American Educational Research Journal, 39,* 279–305.

Maberry, M. V. (1991). *Right after sundown—Teaching stories of the Navajos.* Tsaile, AZ: Navajo Community College Press.

McCarty, T. L. (1993a). Language, literacy, and the image of the child in American Indian classrooms. *Language Arts, 70,* 182–192.

McCarty, T. L. (1993b). Federal language policy and American Indian education. *The Bilingual Research Journal, 17,* 13–34.

McCarty, T. L. (2002). *A place to be Navajo: Rough Rock and the struggle for self-determination in Indigenous schooling.* Mahwah, NJ: Lawrence Erlbaum Associates.

McCarty, T. L., & Watahomigie, L. J. (1998). Language and literacy in American Indian and Alaska Native communities. In B. Pérez et al. (Eds.), *The sociocultural contexts of language and literacy* (pp. 69–98). Mahwah, NJ: Lawrence Erlbaum Associates.

McLaughlin, D. (1993). Personal narratives for school change in Navajo settings. In D. McLaughlin & W. G. Tierney (Eds.), *Naming silenced lives: Personal narratives and the process of educational change* (pp. 95–117). New York & London: Routledge.

Pérez, B. (Ed.), with McCarty, T. L., Watahomigie, L. J., Torres-Guzmán, M. E., Dien, T., Chang, J., Smith, H., & de Silva, A. D. (1998). *The sociocultural contexts of language and literacy.* Mahwah, NJ: Lawrence Erlbaum Associates.

Philips, S. U. (1983). *The invisible culture: Communication in classroom and community on the Warm Springs Indian reservation.* Prospect Heights, IL: Waveland Press.

Ramírez, J. D. (1992). Executive summary. *The Bilingual Research Journal, 16,* 1–62.

Rasinski, T. V., & Padak, N. D. (1990). Multicultural learning through children's literature. *Language Arts, 67,* 576–580.

Rosier, P., & Farella, M. (1976). Bilingual education at Rock Point: Some early results. *TESOL Quarterly, 10,* 379–388.

Ruiz, R. (1988). The empowerment of language-minority students. In C. Sleeter (Ed.), *Empowerment through multicultural education* (pp. 217–227). Albany: State University of New York Press.

Short, K. G., Crawford, K., Kahn, L., Kaser, S., Klassen, C., & Sherman, P. (1992). Teacher study groups: Exploring literacy through collaborative dialogue. In D. J. Leu & C. K. Hunzer (Eds.), *Forty-first yearbook of the National Reading Conference.* Chicago, IL: National Reading Conference.

Sleeter, C. E. (1996). *Multicultural education as social activism.* Albany: State University of New York Press.

Smith, F. (1988). *Joining the literacy club: Further essays into education.* Portsmouth, NH: Heinemann.

Stringer, E. T. (1996). *Action research: A handbook for practitioners.* Thousand Oaks, CA: Sage.

Thomas, W. P., & Collier, V. (1997). *School effectiveness for language minority students.* Washington, DC: National Clearinghouse for Bilingual Education.

Tierney, R. J., Carter, M. A., & Desai, L. E. (1991). *Portfolio assessment in the reading–writing classroom.* Norwood, MA: Christopher-Gordon.

Varenne, H., & McDermott, R., with Goldman, S., Naddeo, M., & Rizzo-Tolk, R. (1999). *Successful failure: The school America builds.* Boulder, CO: Westview Press.

Vogt, L. A., & Au, K. H. P. (1995). The role of teachers' guided reflection in effecting positive program change. *The Bilingual Research Journal, 19,* 101–120.

Vogt, L. A., Jordan, C., & Tharp, R. G. (1993). Explaining school failure, producing success: Two cases. In E. Jacob & C. Jordan (Eds.), *Minority education: Anthropological perspectives.* Norwood, NJ: Ablex.

Watahomigie, L. J., & McCarty, T. L. (1996). Literacy for what? Hualapai literacy and language maintenance. In N. H. Hornberger (Ed.), *Indigenous literacies in the Americas: Language planning from the bottom up* (pp. 95–113). Berlin & New York: Mouton de Gruyter.

Yazzie, E. (1971). *Navajo history.* Chinle, AZ: Navajo Curriculum Center Press.

Zepeda, O. (1995). The continuum of literacy in American Indian communities. *The Bilingual Research Journal, 19,* 5–15.

6

Multicultural Views of Literacy Learning and Teaching

Lee Gunderson
Jim Anderson
University of British Columbia

The purpose of this chapter is to examine how well some current instructional practices fit with the expectations that parents and students from different cultural backgrounds have concerning literacy learning and teaching. We report the results of two studies involving students, teachers, principals, and parents in open-ended and structured interviews. The use of two interviewing techniques allowed us to explore whether the two methods would produce similar responses across groups, in essence replicating findings. The parents were from the same three ethnic groups in the same general geographic area. However, they came from disparate neighborhoods and communities; their children attended different schools; and individuals in particular cultural groups represented different socioeconomic levels.

It is clear that, "five out of six people in the world are non-White," and that the "vast majority of the world's population is non-Christian" (Banks, 1991). Despite this, many North American educators view education from a "mainstream" perspective that reflects a Eurocentric bias, which holds that authentic literature, process writing, reader response, authentic assessment, and emergent literacy are central to literacy learning and teaching. To us, these appear to be views held by many white middle-class North Americans.

An assumption that underlies many of these positions (or views or perspectives) is that literacy learning is "natural." This view is not necessarily shared by all students or parents. Teachers often appear to believe in a theory of learning that is literacy-centered, which views reading and writing as integral activities of thinking human beings. Most teachers seem to be convinced that students should become independent, critical learners.

Belief in the importance of critical, independent reading is not necessarily shared by individuals from all cultures (Early & Gunderson, 1993; Ping, 2000). Delpit (1988, 1991) argued that strategies focusing students' attention on process rather than product and processes that benefit students from the middle class deny minority students access to the "power code." Anderson (1994b) found "that parents from different cultural groups held different perceptions of literacy learning" (p. 13). The parents in his study embraced many views that are antithetical to a holistic perspective. Holistic teaching is a pedagogical phenomenon uniquely imbued with mainstream Euro-centric cultural features.

The schools described in this chapter implemented a curriculum informed by a document entitled *Primary Program Foundation Document* (1988) developed by the Ministry of Education in British Columbia, Canada. It was intended as a set of guidelines, principles, and practices to inform curriculum development and implementation as well as instruction (or pedagogy). Undergirding this document is the philosophy that "the child learns in a holistic way" (p. 127). According to this philosophy, various skills develop as the child interacts in functional and meaningful ways with his or her environment. The child is seen as learning through exploration, questioning, and risk taking. Literacy learning is seen from an "emergent literacy" perspective in that "children begin building their reading and writing behaviors before coming to school" (p. 182). Literacy learning, it is stated, involves the child "taking risks," and reading and writing abilities "develop in a series of successively accurate approximations" (p. 182). Basic to this assumption is the concept that the development of "questioning" children with a plurality of views and openness to a variety of views is valuable. This value is not universally shared (Oster, 1989).

In many countries, books are the absolute source of knowledge, wisdom, and truth (Anderson, Anderson, Lynch, & Shapiro, in press). Many texts read by students in preindustrial countries are sacred. It is not appropriate to question their authority or their contents. Works by Maley (1985), Matalene (1985), Parker et al. (1987), Ping (2000), and others have increased our understanding of intercultural differences in attitudes toward learning in general and toward holistic approaches to teaching in particular. They have shown how and why students from countries such as the People's Republic of China rely on memory and quotation and find our insistence on originality and analysis difficult to embrace.

Those who encourage students to be curious, interested, critical, and communicative; to hold a plurality of points of view; and to desire to question and make sense of it all need to be acutely aware that they are teaching a value system. Moreover, it is a value system potentially in opposition to that held by the families of many students. The following studies explored this mismatch. We begin with a study that involved the quantification of parental beliefs, followed by the results of a more descriptive study.

METHOD

The participants in the first study were 30 parents from three different cultural groups: Chinese Canadians (10 professional-managerial white-collar occupations), Euro-Canadians (10 professional-managerial white-collar occupations), and Indo-Canadians (10 blue-collar occupations) from a large urban area of western Canada. The sample was drawn from three elementary schools (Kindergarten to grade 7) located in areas with fairly large populations of students who spoke English as a second language (ESL). Each parent was interviewed either in the home or in his or her child's school. An open-ended question ("What are the five most important things you are doing to help your child learn to read and to write?") and the Parents' Perceptions of Literacy Learning Interview Schedule (PPLLIS) were used. The parents were interviewed in their first language by a trained research assistant from their same cultural group.

The PPLLIS (Anderson, 1992) is a 33-item interview guide informed by the Deford Theoretical Orientation to Reading Profile (1978). The questions pertain to reading (e.g., Does a child benefit from hearing favorite stories that she has memorized read again and again?), writing (e.g., Should a child learn to print neatly the letters of the alphabet before attempting to print messages, stories, notes, and so forth?) and literacy learning in general (e.g., Do children learn important things about reading and writing before they begin formal reading programs at school?).

The interviews were audiotaped and then transcribed in their entirety. The PPLLIS responses were coded as to their fit with a holistic literacy perspective. Open-ended responses were coded into themes such as "emphasis on neatness," "rote memorization," "providing encouragement," and so forth.

Only one parent could not read or write. Indeed, many of the Chinese and Indo-Canadian parents could read and write English proficiently. The decision to interview the parents in their first language was an attempt to ensure that the nuances of the questions were not lost. Further-more, the interviewers were trained to monitor the interviewing to en-sure that parents were not misperceiving what was being asked. Finally, "member checks" on the data were performed to ensure that the partici-pants' recorded responses were what they intended.

Newtown School is located in a middle- to upper middle-class residen-tial neighborhood. Many of the parents are recently arrived immigrants from Hong Kong and Taiwan. More than half of the 400 students speak a language other than English at home. The school has a French immer-sion stream whose students are drawn from upper middle-class neighbor-hoods surrounding the school. Most of the parents are professionals or entrepreneurs. Four of the Chinese Canadian parents and six of the Euro-pean Canadian parents were from this school.

Newville School is located in a residential–commercial area close to the downtown core. It has approximately 270 students, who come from the immediate neighborhood. The school is ethnically diverse, and English is the second language for more than one third of the students. Many of the parents, who work in the adjacent commercial district, are lower middle class and middle class. Some of the children come from a housing project located in the neighborhood. Six of the Chinese Canadian parents and four of the Euro-Canadian parents came from Newville School.

Parkdale School draws many of its approximately 200 students from the immediate working-class neighborhood. Many of the parents are recent immigrants from India, and Punjabi is spoken in nearly all the homes. The parents tend to work in relatively low-paying service occupations. The 10 Indo-Canadian parents came from this school.

The three schools are generally well equipped, modern buildings with such amenities as school and classroom libraries, computers, and so forth. Some of the students occasionally receive individual or small group instruction in a learning assistance center. Nearly all the students are integrated into regular classrooms for most of the day, although ESL or learning assistance teachers sometimes provide support in the regular classrooms.

Initially, it was intended that 25 parents at each grade level would be interviewed to balance the number of participants according to grade level. However, many parents expressed reservations about participating in the study, even after being reassured about confidentiality through a follow-up telephone conversation. It was believed that the parents who came forward would provide valuable insights, so we decided to proceed with the study with fewer participants than anticipated. The sample thus included: 11 parents of kindergarten children, 10 parents of grade 1 children, and 9 parents of grade 2 children.

RESULTS

The results of PPLLIS (Anderson, 1994a) are reported first, then the responses to an open-ended question "What are the five most important things you are doing to help your child learn to read and write?" This question was asked immediately before the PPLLIS was presented.

Parents' Perceptions of Literacy Learning Interview Schedule

Chinese Canadian Parents.   As shown in Table 6.1, the analysis showed that approximately 54% of the responses from this group were consistent with a holistic perspective. In contrast, Anderson (1994a, 1995) and Fitzgerald, Spiegel, and Cunningham (1991) found that highly literate middle-class parents (as these parents were) supported holistic literacy instruction to a much greater extent.

All the Chinese Canadian parents supported some aspects of the holistic approach, and all of them responded affirmatively to question 24 (Does reading to and with children help them to learn to write?), supporting the symbiotic relation between reading and writing. On the other hand, these parents were divided on some items, with half of them responding affirmatively to question 13 (Should a child learn to print neatly the letters of the alphabet before attempting to print messages, notes, stories and so forth?). One parent, for example, responded: "Yes, she [referring to her daughter] should learn to print neatly first."

The other five parents thought that children could attempt to communicate in writing before they had learned to print neatly. One parent explained: "It doesn't matter because he [her son] is still young. As long as his printing is understandable, it'll be fine. When he is a bit older, we hope he can print more neatly." However, another parent, in responding "no," was less emphatic: "Not necessary, but parents should help their child correct his printing if he made any mistakes in his printing."

All the Chinese parents held traditional views in some areas. All thought that workbooks and basal readers are necessary to help children learn to read (question 3), and responded by saying, "Yes certainly!" and "Yes, I find them quite helpful." One parent also saw workbooks as a way to help her child learn English: "Yes. Since my child is living in a Chi-

TABLE 6.1
Parents' Perceptions of Literacy Learning and Teaching

Question	C-C	E-C	I-C
1. Does a child learn to read by first learning the letters of the alphabet and their sounds, then words, then sentences, and then stories? (N)	2	4	2
2. Is teaching a child to recognize isolated words on sight (flashcards) a suitable technique for teaching her to read? (N)	6	7	2
3. Does a child need workbooks and basal readers to learn how to read? (N)	0	6	0
4. Is this book (e.g., *The Giving Tree*) suitable to read to very young children? (Y)	6	10	6
5. Does a child benefit from hearing favorite stories that she has memorized read again and again? (Y)	9	10	7
6. Should you encourage a child to join in sometimes while you read a book with which he is familiar? (Y)	5	10	8
7. Will you be teaching your child a bad habit if you point to the print as you read? (N)	8	9	10
8. Are you helping a child learn to read by encouraging him to discuss what is being read? (Y)	10	10	10
9. Is it necessary to check a child's understanding by asking him questions at the end of each story? (N)	0	7	1
10. Should you permit your child to "read" familiar books from memory using pictures as cues? (Y)	9	10	10
11. Does real reading begin only when a child begins to say the words as they are printed on the page? (N)	1	9	4
12. Is it necessary for a child to know the letters of the alphabet and the sounds of the letters of the alphabet before she begins to write? (N)	1	5	3
13. Should a child learn to print neatly the letters of the alphabet before attempting to print messages, notes, stories and so forth? (N)	5	8	8
14. Is it necessary for a child to have lots of experience copying words, sentences, and finally stories before she attempts to write on her own? (N)	2	8	7
15. Should a child be encouraged to write only easy words and short sentences when he begins to write? (N)	0	8	0
16. Are a young child's early scribblings (show example) related to later development in writing stories, messages, and the like? (Y)	8	8	10
17. Does a child need workbooks like these to learn how to write? (N)	4	7	4
18. Can a child learn to write before she has learned the correct spelling of words? (N)	7	3	6
19. Should you correct your child if she writes "kt" for the word "cat?" (N)	0	2	0
20. Is a child's confusion of "b" and "d" or "p" and "q" in printing an indication of a major problem? (N)	5	10	6
21. Can a child begin to write (e.g., notes, stories) before she knows how to read? (N)	5	7	5

(Continued)

TABLE 6.1
(Continued)

Question	C-C	E-C	I-C
22. Are learning to read and write similar to learning to talk in that children learn these skills gradually? (Y)	10	8	9
23. Is it only gifted children who learn to read and write before receiving formal instruction in preschool or elementary school? (N)	3	9	10
24. Does reading to and with children help them learn to read? (Y)	10	8	10
25. Do children learn important things about reading and writing before they begin formal reading programs at preschool or elementary school? (Y)	6	9	8
Do the following activities help children learn to read and write?			
a. talking to them? (Y)	9	9	10
b. taking them on outings? (Y)	9	9	9
c. having them pretend to write grocery lists for you? (Y)	9	9	10
d. reading to them? (Y)	10	10	10
27. Should schools be totally responsible for teaching children to read and write? (N)	6	8	0
28. Is it important that children see their parents reading and writing? (Y)	9	10	7
29. Should children have reached a certain age before they can begin to learn to read? (N)	1	9	4
30. Do children need training in eye–hand coordination, recognition of shapes, and so forth before they begin to learn to read and write? (N)	5	5	3

C-C, Chinese Canadian; E-C, Euro-Canadian; I-C, Indo-Canadian ($n = 10$ in each group).
Y and N indicate that the parents would answer "yes" or "no," respectively, if their answer were congruent with a holistic perspective.

nese-speaking environment, we parents couldn't speak English well, and we couldn't also read English. The child can learn English only in school. It's good for him to have workbooks to practice English."

All of these parents ascribed considerable importance to asking children questions on material just read (question 9). A typical response was "Yes it is necessary and helpful." Invented spelling was very problematic for this group, and their disdain for it is exemplified by the parent of a kindergarten child who responded stridently: "Yes, I should [correct a child who writes "kt" for cat] because it's wrong!"

Likewise, nine parents believed that real reading begins only when a child is able to decode print accurately (question 11). A typical response was as follows: "No, I don't think it's real reading. It showed that he just felt interested in the book."

Euro-Canadian Parents.   All these parents supported some aspects
of holistic teaching. As shown in Table 6.1, all these parents supported
shared reading (question 6), which often is seen as the cornerstone of
emergent literacy, and which some educators apparently see as the way
children become literate (Pellegrini, 1991; Anderson, Anderson, Lynch,
& Shapiro, in press). One parent cogently captured the essence of shared
reading when he responded, "[The shared] reading should be interactive," whereas another parent said, "I like it when they interrupt and ask
questions."

No aspect of a holistic teaching and learning approach was rejected by
all the parents in this group. Nevertheless, they tended to have more traditional perceptions of some aspects of literacy learning (e.g., question 1).
One parent thought that "children learn the alphabet first, then some
words and then sentences." Several parents, however, had more holistic
views of learning to read:

> I think a lot of them happen in combination. They will begin to, I think
> initially they will probably begin to recognize the letters when they are very
> young rather than actually to read and spell. Then memorizing books,
> learning stories by heart so they can pick up sentences and recognize words
> as well. They can make a good guess from pictures and so forth. It's a com-
> bination of them.

Another parent suggested the following:

> The most important things is to be reading books, to read the meaning and
> to learn phonics so the child becomes familiar with the functions of words.
> They do a lot of guessing and come through by guessing and learning.
> Sometimes I do [inaudible] guess the words I don't know.

Most of these parents suggested that they would correct a child's invented spelling (question 19). However, unlike some educators who assume either/or positions on issues such as invented spelling (Church &
Neuman, 1990), several parents contextualized their responses, as suggested by one parent: "I do [correct invented spelling] when my child
looks up to me and asks me if it is correct." Another parent stated: "Yes,
if a child is older, but not when a child is young." Interestingly, when
probed as to when such correcting should begin, this parent suggested
that it should be initiated in grade 3. These results are consistent with
those from the Anderson (1994a) study, which found that parents generally had difficulty accepting the concept of invented spelling.

Indo-Canadian Parents.   All of these parents supported some aspects of holistic teaching and learning. All saw value in "reading-like behavior" (question 10). One parent, apparently engaging in "kid watching" (Goodman, 1978) at home, reported, "Yes, my child does that," whereas another suggested that "for young children, it's important." The parents were divided on some items (e.g., question 21), with five of them agreeing that children can begin writing before they learn how to read and the other five maintaining the traditional perspective that children need to learn how to read before they can learn how to write. They had strong opinions on this issue. For example, one parent who did not see reading as a precursor to writing argued, "Yes, a child can write whether he can read or not," while a parent who held the opposite point of view opined with as much conviction, "[Children] have to know how to read first."

All the parents held traditional perspectives regarding some aspects of literacy acquisition (questions 3, 15, and 19). Commenting on workbooks and basal readers, one parent believed that "they help a lot" and another suggested that "they are necessary." This group also vehemently rejected invented spelling (question 19). The following response was typical: "Yes, I would correct the child. If not, child will continue writing in this way."

Whereas there was some support for using flashcards (question 2), among the other groups in this study and among middle-class parents in other studies (Anderson, 1994a), this level of support for this technique has not been evident previously. This finding is consistent with the results of the study by Fitzgerald, Spiegel, and Cunningham (1991), which found that parents with low literacy, such as these Indo-Canadian parents, supported more traditional instructional practices.

Comparisons and Contrasts.   There were only two items (questions 8 and 20) to which all the parents responded in a manner consistent with a holistic perspective (Table 6.1). However, several aspects were supported by the parents in all three groups. For example, eight or more parents (≥80%) in each group thought tracking print was an appropriate strategy (question 7), supported reading-like behavior (question 10), saw a child's scribblings as the genesis of writing (question 16), viewed literacy as developmental (question 22), and supported the social dimensions of literacy learning (questions 26–29).

Fewer than half the parents in each group viewed learning to read as holistic (question 1) and would accept a child's invented spelling (question 19). Given their rejection of invented spelling, it is not surprising that parents tended to reject the notion that children can begin to write (compose) before they know the letters of the alphabet and their sounds (question 12). There also was considerable support for reading readiness (question 33) in all the groups.

Although there were similarities across the groups, there also were differences. For example, eight of the Indo-Canadian parents supported the use of flashcards (question 2), whereas the other parents tended not to favor the practice. The Euro-Canadian parents ascribed less importance to basal readers and workbooks (question 3), showed less inclination toward checking a child's understanding after reading a text (question 9), and tended to support a developmental view of learning to read (question 11). The Chinese Canadian parents tended to value the importance of paired reading less (question 6), ascribe more importance to form in printing (question 13), and, support the role of copying from texts in learning to write (question 14).

Open-Ended Question

Prior to the administration of the PPLLIS, each parent was asked, "What are the five most important things that you are doing to help your child learn to read and to write?" The answers are shown in Table 6.2.

Chinese Canadian Parents.   One theme that emerged from the responses of these parents was the concern with form, "teaching children to print properly." These parents also perceived accuracy and precision, not "risk taking" and "invention," to be important in literacy learning. They believed that one of their roles was to monitor the child's performance. Similarly, they tended to perceive their role as that of transmitting knowledge or information to the child. Only two of the parents identified reading to children as a factor in helping children learn to read.

Euro-Canadian Parents.   As previous research has shown (Anderson, 1994a), reading to a child is the factor identified by "mainstream" parents (Pellegrini, 1991) as contributing to children's literacy development. The parents in the current study also perceived modeling and demonstrating literacy and providing materials as important. Although some of the parents identified the teaching of specific skills such as phonics and spelling, very little emphasis was placed on such instruction. Instead, they emphasized activities and events that would socialize children into literacy.

Indo-Canadian Parents.   Reading to children was the factor identified most frequently as contributing to early literacy development. The teaching of spelling and numbers was next in frequency. It is interesting

TABLE 6.2

Parents' Perceptions of Their Roles in Literacy Learning

Chinese Canadian parents (*n* = 10)	
Teach child to print neatly	8
Check understanding when child is reading	4
Teach child to spell	3
Read to child	2
Recite story	2
Teach child to concentrate	2
Teach child how to write	2
Teach child to pronounce clearly	1
Have child sit at desk properly	1
Help child understand the use of learning	1
Have child read fast and correctly	1
Have child complete homework	1
Correct grammar	1
Teach child how to listen	1
Teach child to speak mother tongue well	1
Euro-Canadian parents (*n* = 10)	
Read to child	10
Have child see significant others read	6
Provide books regularly	3
Encourage child with homework	3
Go to books to pull out information	2
Make reading a pleasure for the child	2
Point to pictures	1
Provide paper, pens, and pencils	1
Let child use computer	1
Spell words for the child	1
Start child in early literacy (phonics) program	1
Have child read to parents	1
Encourage child to write stories	1
Have child practice pronunciation, phonics	1
Child taught himself	1
Restrict TV	1
Teach alphabet	1
Show that reading has practical application	1
Indo-Canadian parents	
Read to child	7
Teach spelling	3
Teach numbers	3
Answer child's questions	2
Encourage child to watch television	2
Bring books from store	1
Take child for outings	1
Correct pronunciation of difficult words	1
Explain meaning of vocabulary words to child	1
Look at flyers from stores with child	1
Encourage child to play	1
Buy a computer game	1
Help child write letters to friends and relatives in India	1
Tell stories	1
Provide lines for child to print on	1

that the teaching of numbers and playing cards, which also could involve numbers, was mentioned in response to a question about literacy learning. Two parents mentioned watching television as a special contributing factor in their children's literacy development. One Euro-Canadian parent indicated that she was helping her child's literacy development by restricting television. Whereas this group identified several factors consistent with the literacy socialization perspective of the Euro-Canadian parents, they also identified other factors that more closely matched the transmission-skills orientation of the Chinese Canadian parents.

The second study focused on attitudes and beliefs in a more descriptive fashion.

METHOD

The second study involved three schools located in three school districts. The first author had worked as a researcher in each of the schools for a number of years before the study. Semistructured interviews were conducted with parents, students, teachers, cultural liaison workers, and administrators over a period of 1½ years. Interpreters who also were members of the same cultural and linguistic communities conducted the parental interviews in parents' first languages. Systematic classroom observations were made to confirm or disconfirm that teachers were consistently applying the features of instruction they had identified as important. The researcher's conclusions and observations were shared with the participants to ensure that they were accurate. The study involved 22 teachers, 3 principals, 1 vice principal, 3 cultural workers, 51 parents, and 63 students. Details of this study are reported in Gunderson (2001).

Upton Elementary School

Upton is a school of approximately 500 students in an upper middle-class neighborhood in a large West Coast metropolitan area in Canada. Students are enrolled in grades kindergarten through 7. Kindergarten to grade 3 is organized into ungraded family units. The population of the school changed during the period of 1989 to 1993, with immigrants from Taiwan and Hong Kong making up the majority of new students. In 1989, the school was approximately 10 percent ESL, and by 1993, the proportion of ESL students had risen to 52% with 96% from either Hong Kong or Taiwan (Mandarin and Cantonese speakers). Of the students at Upton, 90% had attended Christian preschools in their home countries.

Such preschools are viewed as good preparation for school in general, and the Christian schools in Hong Kong and Taiwan are viewed positively because instruction is in English (Gunderson & Clarke, 1998).

The Upton teachers abandoned basal readers and workbooks. They initiated and maintained literature-based literacy programs. Report cards were anecdotal without traditional letter grades. Classroom newsletters were a feature in most of the classes. Parent meetings were held to explain the programs.

Parental dissatisfaction with the literacy program increased as the school population changed. Discontent at Upton was fueled by a general dissatisfaction with the literacy program, which prompted the Premier of the province to reconsider the holistic literacy program and to bring back letter grades and a focus on basic skills. The teachers at Upton capitulated and brought back workbooks, basal readers, and rote memorization. The situation at Upton was extremely difficult for teachers, administrators, students, and parents because there were deep-seated value systems in conflict. The parents, mostly Asians, were convinced that teaching and learning should focus on memorization and facts, whereas the teachers mainly believed they should focus on process and exploration.

Oakville School

Oakville is in an affluent suburb of a large West Coast city in Canada. The school has approximately 500 students in grades kindergarten to 7, comprised primarily of students from upper-middle socioeconomic status families. About 45 of the students, varying in ages and grade levels, were Farsi- and Persian-speaking immigrants from Iran. About 50% were English-speaking bilinguals. All but two of the families were Muslim. A cultural-liaison worker reported that these individuals were devout Muslims, but not fundamentalists. She noted that many had left their home country from fears of persecution.

The teachers at Oakville were divided in their views or philosophies of teaching and learning. The primary teachers were the most enthusiastic about holistic teaching and learning, whereas the intermediate teachers were skeptical and unreceptive. Indeed, the teachers were divided into two camps: a strong holistic teaching group (kindergarten to grade 3) and a skills-based group in the intermediate grades (grades 4 to 7). Some intermediate teachers did use trade books and reading centers in their instructional programs. However, they also used traditional spelling and basal reading instruction, although the use of basal readers was not prescribed. One primary teacher argued that the skills group had become involved with literature programs because the province had authorized the expenditure of funds for children's trade books. Workbooks continued to be used for both reading and spelling, often paid for by teachers' personal funds.

The primary teachers encouraged their students to write as soon as they entered school, even the kindergarten students. They involved their students in the language-rich, meaning-centered activities that have become associated with holistic teaching and learning (Gunderson, 2001; Gunderson & Shapiro, 1988).

As the students moved from the primary to the intermediate grades, they crossed a boundary, one that separated the two philosophic camps. In the intermediate classrooms, they were asked to do workbook activities and memorize spelling words. The intermediate teachers complained about their students' writing habits, their apparent dislike for workbooks, and their inability to sit still for long periods filling in workbooks. There was much teacher room talk about poor work habits, sloppy learning attitudes, and students who apparently had been taught nothing. The primary teachers strongly defended their programs and their students' achievements. As criticism across the province escalated in the media, the cleavage between the primary and intermediate teachers widened, a gap that intensified the conflict developing between the immigrant parents' expectations for their children and the implicit and explicit expectations of the literacy program their children were experiencing.

Meetings at Oakville, informational sessions organized by the teachers, were not well attended. In general, most of the immigrant parents did not attend them. Formal, individual parent–teacher meetings were scheduled during November and May. These sessions were led by students as part of a program designed to include them in discussions about their learning. The student-led conferences were extremely successful for all except the immigrants. The immigrant students were unable to lead conferences. The parents were unable to accept what the children said about their own progress. The student-led conferences appeared to generate distrust. Individual parent–teacher contacts were made mostly as students were being picked up after school by their parents, almost always their mothers. The mothers were reluctant to speak with the teachers about their children's progress, but when they did, they were mostly concerned about their primary students' progress and the apparent lack of traditional school methods and approaches.

Parent–teacher contacts were difficult for the primary teachers, and very difficult for the parents. A cultural-liaison worker informed the teachers that the parents were reticent about interacting with authority, and that they, the teachers, were viewed as authorities. Parker and the Educational Services Staff at AFME (1986) noted that, "hostility and suspicion may well be characteristics of the Middle Eastern student when he first arrives in the United States" (p. 96). It should be noted that hostility and suspicion often are displayed by students who experience culture shock in culturally unfamiliar contexts (Furnham & Bochner, 1986; Storti, 1989, 1994). However, it is not correct to describe the behaviors of these parents as hostile or suspicious. They displayed reticence in interacting with teachers, a tendency the cultural-liaison worker suggested was a result of their experiences with authorities in their home country. As time passed, the number of primary-age immigrants decreased dramatically as their parents enrolled them in a nearby private school that featured traditional skills-based instruction.

Bottomland School

Bottomland School is located in a suburb of a West Coast metropolitan center in Canada. The community is located on an island formed at the mouth of a major river. Its rich earth had been used primarily as farmlands until the 1970s, when the expanding population of the nearby metropolitan center began to encroach. The late 1980s and early 1990s saw the immigrant population expand and the number of ESL students increase from approximately 1% of the school population to about 35% in 1994 (Gunderson & Carrigan, 1993), mostly Chinese from Hong Kong and Taiwan.

Bottomland School is located in an area still used almost exclusively for farming. It is a small school of approximately 175 students in kindergarten to grade 8. Some grades are combinations (e.g., third–fourth grade). Approximately 80% of the students are Punjabi-speaking East Asians from farming families who own or work on the surrounding farms. All the parents had been educated in India. None had attended university or sat for university examinations.

Bottomland's primary teachers had already begun to implement their holistic programs when the holistic teaching program was adopted. The intermediate teachers adopted many features of the suggested curriculum. Because the school was small, there were only eight teachers and a positive sense of togetherness.

Punjabi-speaking Indian Muslim farmers have a strong sense of commitment to the land. Their families are patriarchal. Sons are highly valued, and it is generally acknowledged that they are overindulged. Indeed, a great deal of antipathy has been generated by the news that an American medical doctor travels to British Columbia to provide the services allowing East Asian women to know the gender of their unborn babies so that female fetuses can be aborted (Staff Writer, 1994). Most East Asian marriages in the Bottomland service area are arranged, with potential wives brought to Canada from India. Bottomland farming families are extended families, with grandparents, cousins, aunts, uncles, brothers, and sisters often living together. Everyone except the young boys is expected to work on the farm, especially during the harvest season. It is not uncommon for visiting relatives to come from India during harvest season to work, often bringing a suitcase full of farming tools.

As Bottomland's program became more student-centered and individualized, parental dissatisfaction grew. This dissatisfaction was communicated to teachers and the principal through increased personal afterschool contacts with the fathers. The program was rapidly becoming viewed as suspect. Students were not given regular homework assignments. They did not have regularly scheduled spelling tests, and they were not involved in formal reading groups. Their written work was not corrected, and they did not "sit" for formal tests. They also did not receive traditional grades. What bothered most of the fathers was that their children were asked to select their own books. This was incomprehensible to the parents. In addition, as Muslims, these parents indicated to both the teachers and the cultural-liaison worker that they were offended that their children were encouraged to read and guess about what they were reading. It was incomprehensible that they were asked to read and make predictions. Most of the East Asian boys at Bottomland attended classes at a mosque, where they learned to read the Koran. The parental view of reading had been formed by the parents' experiences as Muslims.

The parents at Bottomland believed treating reading as an activity that should be enjoyed, and one that should include an often imperfect "oral interpretation" of what is written was offensive. According to these parents, teachers are supposed to teach students to read the words perfectly aloud, not to guess or predict, nor to interpret. This does not suggest that thinking critically was not a feature of their culture. It was a view that seemed to result from a complex interaction between parents' religious beliefs and their own expectations for school and schooling that they had learned in India as elementary students.

The program at Bottomland School was designed on a set of beliefs about teaching and learning that focused on the central view that language is inquiry. The parental view of teaching and learning differed. The teacher was viewed as the center, the one who had knowledge to be communicated to students. That the primary teachers were female caused considerable difficulty for many Bottomland parents because it violated their own notions of power and authority. The parental view of reading was that books contain knowledge that students could come to know through perfect oral reading. The parental view also included the notion that learning was like any task, which consisted of steps learned in order. A learner's task was to acquire the knowledge represented by each step, and to be awarded a grade that showed how well she or he had succeeded. Communication difficulties continue to be a feature of the program at Bottomland School. Cultural aides who are knowledgeable have attempted to bridge the gap that exists between the cultural notions parents and students have for school and schooling and the explicit and implicit beliefs that informed the school's program. Accommodation on the part of teachers, parents, and students has ameliorated the difficulties somewhat, but Bottomland continues to be a school in which holistic beliefs and practices meet Eastern beliefs and notions.

CONCLUSION

The research reported in this chapter involves an analysis of groups identified by culture. The ethnographic descriptions in the second study corroborate the more quantitative data in the first study. It is apparent, however, that the groups were not monolithic. Each was unique in that it represented different mosaics of beliefs.

Generalizations suggested in this discussion relate specifically to the groups discussed and represent only general trends. It cannot be said that they are representative in any systematic way of larger populations, only that they do to some degree represent the beliefs of these particular groups at a particular time. Variation should not be surprising. For instance, the debate among North American educators about whole language and phonics is eloquent testimony to the variation that exists among teachers.

The way individuals view teaching and learning, including the role of literacy, varies across cultural groups, especially views regarding holistic teaching and learning. However, this is not a particularly surprising finding considering that the views, even among middle-class mainstream families, are mixed. Indeed, those who report that they favor holistic instruction also report that skills such as phonics should be explicitly taught (Anderson, 1994b).

Any effort to search out literacy universals or universal processes of literacy may itself be a thoroughly Western-oriented undertaking. There is an essential conundrum. Holistic approaches seek to empower individual students, to give them voice, yet individual voice is antithetic to some cultural views. Holistic teaching seeks to show students that meaning is not in text, and that reading is creative prediction. Yet in some cultures text represents truth.

The schools described in the second study represent three different situations and three different outcomes: confrontation, avoidance, and uncomfortable coexistence. Three solutions took place within an overall context of antiholistic sentiment.

Many of the pedagogical practices to which the parents in these studies objected were supported and encouraged in the *Primary Program Foundation Document* (1988). Ironically, this program purports to value the role of parents:

> The Program values teachers and parents as partners in the child's education. Teachers and parents consult and collaborate to create for the child a climate of respect, success, and joy necessary for lifelong learning. (p. 15)

Many parents in this study did not see themselves as partners in their children's education, and indeed, many of them felt isolated from the school.

If we are to help students from other cultures become academically successful, we have a responsibility to help them engage in the kind of seeing and thinking that this system demands, to help them understand "mainstream" literacy attitudes and strategies, and to empower them by assisting them in learning the discourse of the dominant culture (Delpit, 1988). We also must keep in mind, however, as Harman and Edelsky (1989) noted: "Literacy is not necessarily liberating." Students and parents are empowered by learning that their voices are heard and valued in the school community.

Early and Gunderson (1993) suggested that teachers should "conceive of the classroom itself as a community, one with its own practices, principles, and values" (p. 104). They also suggested that linking home and school practices requires teachers "to design classroom instructional practices which reach out to the broader community" (p. 106). They added that the classroom should foster a classroom community, and that some ways of doing so include the use of student-run postal systems, dialogue journals, the writing and publishing of class newspapers, cross-age and peer tutoring programs, and schoolwide topical projects. They concluded that linking home and school literacy can be achieved by designing "classroom instructional practices which reach out to the broader community" (p. 106), which can include, "studying the local community, interviewing residents, writing histories, drawing maps, searching local archives, collecting photographs and the like, taking field trips to local places of interest, and involving community members, including parents, in classroom activities as guest speakers, helpers or guests at special events" (p. 106). Parents who are monolingual speakers of languages other than English can be involved positively in school activities such as reading aloud in their first languages (Walters & Gunderson, 1985). Such activities bring students' first cultures into the classroom and do not interfere with their overall language learning.

We must always be aware, however, that we are teaching students views that may be antithetical or heretical, notions viewed with disgust by members of the cultures from which they come. We must also be aware that there may be some cases in which a student's or a parent's view, one that is culturally based, may be abhorrent. Views that are violent, racist, or sexist should be confronted in thoughtful ways. It is not acceptable, for instance, to abort fetuses because they are female.

Education is the instrument by which governments, both national and local, inculcate in their citizens the beliefs deemed correct and appropriate, beliefs that include the dominant social values that may reproduce an oppressive stratified society (Barrs, 2000; Giroux, 1983). Holistic teachers believe in the value of process, critical independent thinking, and inquiry. This set of beliefs appears to be distinctly North American, generally considered appropriate for students and held by teachers to be essential. In some cases, immigrant parents and students must accommodate to new views. In other cases, the teacher must recognize difference, accept it, and try to integrate it into his or her teaching. What seems true across cultures and political affiliations is that parents, teachers, and other interested adults seek "the best" for students.

The upper middle-class Chinese parents viewed the best as being a product, the accumulation of knowledge to enable their children to pass a test that will allow them to enter a university and subsequently to graduate and become a member of a profession. Some interpret this as a politically conservative approach to the values of schooling that aims to maintain an oppressive, stratified society that had worked for the parents themselves. The Asian parents believed that a holistic teaching and learning approach violated their children's right to learn the knowledge they needed to succeed. Traditional schooling works for some individuals within the established system. That is, it empowers some to acquire the knowledge they need to be successful in school and subsequently in a class-stratified society. The understanding that the holistic approaches represent a view differing from the view held by many parents and students is an important step.

POSTSCRIPT

A group of Chinese Canadian parents in the Greater Vancouver area of British Columbia, "unhappy with the work their children are doing in . . . public schools," has embarked on creating a traditional school (Sullivan, 1998, p. 15). The guiding principles behind the proposed school will include "teacher-led instruction, a homework policy, [and] . . . regular study and conduct reports" (Sullivan, 1998, p. 15). To date, officials have not acceded to this initiative, although pressure from parents to establish such a school continues. We believe that the more affluent parents from the various cultural groups in our study will be able to avail themselves of this alternative. Some will be unable to afford such an option. Some parents and children will be privileged on the basis of class, and "the solution" raises new issues.

REFERENCES

Anderson, J. (1992). *Emergent literacy: The beliefs and practices of parents of preschoolers*. Paper presented at the annual conference of the Canadian Society for the Study of Education. Charlottetown, Prince Edward Island.

Anderson, J. (1994a). Parents' perceptions of emergent literacy. *Reading Psychology, 15*(3), 165–187.

Anderson, J. (1994b). *Parents' perspectives of literacy acquisition: A cross-cultural perspective*. Paper presented at the annual Conference of the College Reading Association, New Orleans, Louisiana.

Anderson, J. (1995). How parents perceive literacy acquisition: A cross-cultural study. In E. G. Sturtevant & W. Linek (Eds.), *Generations of literacy* (pp. 262–277). Commerce, TX: The College Reading Association.

Anderson, J., Anderson, A., Lynch, J., & Shapiro, J. (In press). Storybook reading in a multicultural society: Critical perspectives. In A. van Kleeck, S. A. Stahl, & E. B. Bauer (Eds.), *On reading to children: Parents and Teachers* (pp. xx–xx). Mahwah, NJ: Lawrence Erlbaum Associates.

Balcom, S. (1993). Parents are unhappy about schools. *The Vancouver Sun*, p. A1.

Banks, J. A. (1991). *Teaching strategies for ethnic studies* (4th ed.). Needham Heights, MA: Allyn & Bacon.

Barrs, M. (2000). Gendered literacy. *Language Arts, 77*, 287–293.

Church, S., & Neuman, J. (1990). Myths of whole language. *The Reading Teacher, 44*(1), 20–26.

Deford, D. (1978). *A validation study of an instrument to determine a teacher's orientation to reading instruction*. Unpublished doctoral dissertation, Indiana University, Bloomingham, IN.

Delpit, L. D. (1988). The silenced dialogue: Power and pedagogy in educating other people's children. *Harvard Educational Review, 58*(3), 280–298.

Delpit, L. D.(1991). A conversation with Lisa Delpit. *Language Arts, 68*, 541–547.

Early, M., & Gunderson, L. (1993). Linking home, school and community literacy events. *TESL Canada Journal, 11*(1), 99–111.

Fitzgerald, J., Spiegel, D. L., & Cunningham, J. (1991). The relationship between parental literacy level and perceptions of emergent literacy. *Journal of Reading Behavior, 23*(2), 191–213.

Furnham, A., & Bochner, S. (1986). *Culture shock: Psychological reactions to unfamiliar environments.* London: Methuen.

Giroux, H. (1983). *Theory and resistance in education: A pedagogy for the opposition.* South Hadley, MA: Bergin & Garvey.

Goodman, Y. (1978). Kidwatching: An alternative to testing. *National Elementary Principal, 57*(4), 41–45.

Gunderson, L. (1997). Whole language approaches to reading and writing. In S. Stahl & D. Hayes (Eds.), *Models of literacy learning and teaching* (pp. 221–247). Mahwah, NJ: Lawrence Erlbaum Associates.

Gunderson, L. (2001). Different cultural views of whole language. In S. Boran & B. Comber (Eds.), *Critiquing whole language and classroom inquiry* (pp. 242–271). Urbana, IL: National Council of Teachers of English.

Gunderson, L., & Carrigan, T. (1993). *A three-year study of the achievement of immigrant students.* Paper presented at the National Reading Conference, Charleston, South Carolina.

Gunderson, L., & Clarke, D. K. (1998). An exploration of the relationship between ESL students' backgrounds and their English and academic achievement. In T. Shanahan & F. V. Rodrigues-Brown (Eds.), *National Reading Conference Yearbook 47* (pp. 264–273). Chicago: National Reading Conference.

Gunderson, L., & Shapiro, J. (1988). Whole language instruction: Writing in 1st grade. *Reading Teacher, 41*(4), 430–437.

Harman, S., & Edelsky, C. (1989). The risks of whole language. *Elementary School Journal, 66*(4), 392–406.

Maley, A. (1985). On chalk and cheese, babies and bathwater and squared circles: Can traditional and communicative approaches be reconciled? In P. Larson, E. L. Judd, & D. S. Messerschmitt (Eds.), *On TESOL '84.* Washington, DC: TESOL.

Maley, A. (1987). XANADU: A miracle of rare device: The teaching of English in China. In J. M. Valdes (Ed.), *Culture bound: Bridging the culture gap in language teaching* (pp. 102–111). Cambridge, UK: Cambridge University Press.

Matalene, C. (1985). Contrastive rhetoric: An American writing teacher in China. *College English, 47,* 789–808.

Oster, J. (1989). Seeing with different eyes: Another view of literature in the ESL class. *TESOL Quarterly, 23*(1), 85–103.

Parker, O. D., & Educational Services Staff of AFME. (1986). Cultural clues to the Middle Eastern student. In J. M. Valdes (Ed.), *Culture bound: Bridging the culture gap in language teaching* (pp. 77–84). Cambridge, UK: Cambridge University Press.

Pellegrini, A. (1991). A critique of the concept of at risk as applied to the concept of emergent literacy. *Language Arts, 68,* 380–385.

Ping, H. (2000). *Teaching Chinese ESL Students in a Writing Workshop: A Cross-Cultural Perspective.* Unpublished doctoral dissertation, Simon Fraser University, Burnaby, British Columbia, Canada.

Primary Program Foundation Document. (1988). Victoria, BC: The Queen's Printers.

Scarcella, R. (1990). *Teaching language minority students in the multicultural classroom.* Englewood Cliffs, NJ: Prentice-Hall Regents.

Staff Writer. (1994). American doctor criticized for providing gender revealing services in British Columbia. *The Vancouver Sun*, p. B3.

Storti, C. (1989). *The art of crossing cultures.* Yarmouth, ME: Intercultural Press.

Storti, C. (1994). *Cross-cultural dialogues: 74 brief encounters with cultural difference.* Yarmouth, ME: Intercultural Press.

Sullivan, A. (1998). Chinese lead traditional school drive. *The Vancouver Courier, 89*(20), p. 16.

Walters, K., & Gunderson, L. (1985). Effects of parent volunteers reading first language (L1) books to ESL students. *The Reading Teacher, 39*(1), 66–69.

7

Spanish in Latino Picture Storybooks in English: Its Use and Textual Effects

Rosalinda B. Barrera
Ruth E. Quiroa
Rebeca Valdivia
University of Illinois at Urbana–Champaign

Latino children's literature in English reflects varying degrees of Spanish usage. In some books, the only semblance of Spanish is in the form of personal or place names. In other books, the use of Spanish language elements is more extensive, ranging from different single words to assorted phrases and sentences, each occurring once or multiple times within and across pages. The common denominator among these books is that English is clearly the primary, or base, language of the text, and Spanish is the secondary language. During the past decade or so of expanded publishing of multicultural–multiethnic children's literature in the United States, the use of Spanish in the texts of Latino children's literature in English appears to have grown (Barrera & de Cortés, 1997; Barrera, Quiroa, & West-Williams, 1999; Barrera, Thompson, & Dressman, 1997). Languages other than Spanish also appear in contemporary English-language children's books, among them Japanese, Navajo, Ojibwa, Thai, and Yiddish.

To critics of multicultural and bilingual education, such as Stotsky (1999), the inclusion of secondary, or "foreign," language elements in English-language textbooks is particularly troublesome, viewed as a threat to U.S. children's academic achievement. According to Stotsky, only some languages, namely, French and Latin, are seen as fit for inclusion in English-language textbooks and trade books. In contrast, from a multicultural–multiethnic literature perspective, there is recognition that secondary language and dialect can be used for significant literary effect, especially for adding realism to story aspects such as characterization, setting, and theme, thus enhancing the cultural authenticity of English-based narratives. However, there also is awareness that secondary language and dialect might be used ineffectively or inappropriately to the disservice of the literary work, its subject, and the reader or listener.

Latino children's literature in English that incorporates Spanish is of interest to us from both literary and readership standpoints. As we see it, these books have potential for attracting a wider domestic audience than might be drawn to monolingual Spanish editions, or even bilingual editions offering parallel Spanish and English texts in the same book. Monolingual English-speaking teachers and librarians, who make up the majority of the nation's teacher and librarian work force, might be more inclined to avoid those types of books than an English-based book. This is not to say that mainstream resistance to the content of multicultural–multiethnic literature in general, in addition to its text language, is not a continuing problem. But it is saying that when produced with skill and care, Latino books in English with some Spanish should hold literary and linguistic appeal not only for monolingual English readers, young and old alike, but also for bilingual Spanish–English individuals, making for a larger potential audience. Ultimately, in the mind of the reader or listener of either language background, the use of Spanish in an English-language text should not get in the way of the story being told.

In this chapter, we analyze three contemporary Latino picture storybooks in English, with a focus on the use and textual effects of the Spanish-language elements on their pages.[1] We examine the usage of these elements by means of criteria adapted from recent research in Latino adult literature. Concomitantly, we identify patterns of usage and consider the impact or effects that such patterns might have on the literary works. Although linguistic aspects of text figure into the analysis, our textual investigation is primarily a literary analysis. In the sections that follow, we articulate the theoretical constructs that guided our exploration, explain our analytical procedures, present selected findings, and

---

[1]Mary Mehlman Burns in Anita Silvey's *Children's Books and Their Creators* (Houghton Mifflin, 1995) organizes picture books into "at least five categories." One category is "the picture storybook and the picture information book: In these books the illustrations are as integral to the content as the text" (p. 522). Her other categories are "the 'pure' or 'true' picture book with little or no text" (e.g., ABC, counting, and other concept books); the wordless book with no text; toy and movable books (e.g., pop-up, lift-the-flap, and pull-tabs); and the illustrated book, which "may have more text than pictures" (p. 522).

point out implications of our observations for future development and publication of Latino children's literature.

THEORETICAL FRAMEWORK

Attention to the use of Spanish in Latino children's literature in English has centered mostly on orthographic or grammatical aspects, not literary considerations. This has not been the case, however, with Latino literature in English for adult readers. Here there has been attention to the use of Spanish in English text from linguistic as well as literary perspectives, particularly in the area of Chicano literature (Burciaga, 1996; Keller, 1984; Keller & Keller, 1993; Penfield & Ornstein-Galicia, 1985; Rocard, 1989; Rudin, 1996). It is from this line of studies, particularly the recent work by Rudin (1996) on the Chicano novel in English, that we drew key concepts and constructs for informing our investigation, theoretical as well as methodological. In this section we briefly discuss two theoretical notions that we found relevant to our inquiry into Latino children's literature: (a) literary bilingualism and (b) the author as cultural translator.

The Nature of Literary Bilingualism

English storybook text with Spanish-language elements has sometimes been referred to as "bilingual" or even "semibilingual" (Agosto, 1997). According to distinctions drawn by Rudin (1996), however, neither of these terms is appropriate:

> The great majority of works that at first sight may present themselves and are sometimes marketed as bi- or even multilingual literature are cases of "bilingualism in literature" rather than "bilingual literature.". . . While bilingual literature proper is hard to find, literary bilingualism—the use of secondary language elements in monolingual literature—occurs frequently and has many different forms. (p. 10)

As such, the use of literary bilingual techniques, devices, or strategies constitutes "literary bilingualism" rather than bilingual literature per se in which both languages are "of equal weight, format, or scope" (Rudin, 1996, p. 10). It should be noted that in Chicano adult literature, the existence of bona fide bilingual works (also described in the professional literature by modifiers such as "fully," "true," and "authentically") appears to be mostly in poetry rather than prose (Keller, 1984; Penfield & Ornstein-Galicia, 1985; Rudin, 1996).

Scrutiny of literary bilingualism in Chicano adult literature apparently has been conducted more frequently through linguistic and sociolinguistic lenses than through literary lenses. Not surprisingly, its relation to societal or community bilingualism has received a fair share of the attention. As a result, the incorporation of Spanish words into English text has been juxtaposed with community code switching, the alternation of Spanish and English in bilinguals' speech, a salient characteristic of bilingualism in some contexts. However, literary critics such as Keller (1984) (focused on code switching in bilingual Chicano poetry) and Rudin (1996) (focused on Spanish in the Chicano novel in English) point to the independence of literary bilingual techniques. They have noted that such phenomena do not necessarily have to mirror their societal or community counterparts because in literature, an aesthetic canon is obeyed, not a social, communicative one (Keller, 1984; Rudin, 1996).

Whether their major function is realistic (i.e., mimetic) or artificial (i.e., experimental), literary bilingual techniques, like the use of a secondary dialect in English-language literature (Holton, 1984), need only suggest social reality, not reproduce it exactly. Illustrative of this point, Keller (1984) noted that code switching, even in bilingual poetic text, does not have "to reflect the community's bilinguality nor even be semantically or syntactically acceptable in the ordinary sense" (p. 284). In essence, the author can have secondary language elements serve a number of different functions under the two broad categories of realistic and artificial uses, generating a variety of textual effects for maximum literary impact.

According to Rudin (1996), in the "contact zone of literature and bilingualism" (p. 11), various social and individual factors as well as genre influences are operative, aspects that reflect on the relation of the languages involved and the relation of the author with these languages. Another relation, that of the author with the reader, will be reflected in part through various facets of the secondary language elements used, such as their form, type, semantic aspects, and method of incorporation. In the next section, we elaborate on the task and role of the author of Latino children's literature in English.

The Author As Cultural Translator

Authors of primarily English texts in Latino children's literature may be "insiders" or "outsiders" in relation to the culture(s) depicted, and proficient in Spanish to varying degrees. The potential readers of their works may be just as culturally and linguistically diverse, with knowledge of the culture and the Spanish language ranging from extensive to minimal or non-existent. Therefore, the author who chooses to incorporate Spanish elements into English-language text for young readers must do so, at the least, in a manner that enhances the literary merit of the story and makes it comprehensible and appealing to both monolingual–monocultural English readers and Spanish-English bilingual readers.

In his analysis of 19 Chicano prose narratives in English (17 novels and 2 autobiographies published between 1967 and 1985), all of them written by Chicanos, Rudin (1996) applied to Chicano literature the views of German philosopher Friedrich Schleiermacher on different methods of translation. Rudin asserted that "Chicano authors, as well as the authors of other 'New Literatures in English' and of 'minority' literatures in general, are comparable to translators" (p. 60), although they are involved in translating cultural texts, not literary works. He analogized that in the process of cultural translation, as in literary translation, the distance between author and reader is bridged in general either by the reader moving toward the author's text language and cultural meaning, or by the author moving toward the reader.

Keller (1984) also spoke to the process of cultural translation from the point of view of intended readership. He noted that when Spanish and code switching are used to represent the cultural world of Latinos, the author or poet might adopt either a cross-cultural or a bicultural orientation. The former approach is carried out in "anthropological fashion," with the author "taking his reader by the hand through the esoteric or unknown world of Chicanos," introducing a Spanish concept or term and then explaining it for the English monocultural reader. In contrast, in a bicultural approach, the author or poet "switches between the two languages with a bilingual's natural ease" and may use a number of "identity markers" (p. 174) to establish rapport in Spanish with his or her Chicano readers.

In his study, Rudin (1996) came to an overarching conclusion about the distance between author and reader: In order to traverse cultural and linguistic differences, it was generally the author of the Chicano novel in English who moved and not the monolingual reader. The author provided ample translation and textual cushioning, often guiding the monolingual reader with extreme carefulness through the text. In effect, Spanish was used with the monolingual reader in mind and not the bilingual one. Additionally, Rudin (1996) concluded that for the bilingual reader, the same Spanish elements in these texts would most likely amount to needless redundancy and excessive repetition. Keller (1984) would refer to these same texts as "cross-cultural" in orientation.

Some other specific findings from Rudin's (1996) study follow: Most Spanish entries could be considered easily understandable for monolingual readers because they are loan-words, clichés, or cognates. A high degree of literal translation of Spanish entries was evident, with limited use of contextual translation. Spanish was used mainly for mimetic purposes, "as a token of the Spanish-speaking community portrayed" (p. 228). Overall, Rudin (1996) concluded that the use of bilingual techniques in these works "doesn't break much fresh ground" (p. 230). Experimental use of bilingual techniques was minimal, not to mention subversive use of these elements, too.

METHOD

Rudin's (1996) research provided us not only with theoretical insights, but also with methodological procedures for exploring the use of Spanish in Latino children's literature in English. We regarded his analytical procedures as a starting point, to be modified as necessary in light of the two different book forms involved: the pictureless novel for adult readers studied by him and the picture storybook for child readers that was our focus. In the following discussion, we describe how we applied these procedures, then give synopses of the books examined.

Analytical Procedures

The analytical criteria applied by Rudin (1996) to Spanish words and word sequences to be coded, or Spanish-language entries, consisted of length, method, placement, and function (applied to all entries), word class, semantic field, and type (applied only to single-word entries), and structure (applied only to multiword entries). We added an additional criterion, namely, illustration, to examine possible relations between the Spanish entries and the respective artwork of the focal books. The criteria were operationalized by means of the following questions:

- Length: How many words does the entry encompass?
- Grammatical aspects: What word class is the Spanish element? (for single-word entries) or Is the entry a complete or incomplete sentence? (for multiword entries)
- Semantic field: What domain of meaning does the entry represent?

- Type: What degree of familiarity does the entry have to monolingual English readers?
- Method: How is the entry translated in the text?
- Placement: In what part of the text does the entry occur?
- Function: What literary purposes does the entry serve?
- Illustration: Is the entry elucidated by the artwork?

Possible categories for responses to these questions, drawn largely from Rudin's (1996) study, are identified and discussed in the Results section, as well as adjustments that needed to be made for the purposes of our study. It should be noted that one criterion (i.e., function) did not lend itself to quantitative treatment for reasons explained later.

Coding the Data

We jointly determined that Spanish elements would be counted as entries according to guidelines we developed. Only initial occurrences of identified Spanish words and word sequences were counted and coded for computer analysis. Repetitions of any words or word sequences were noted but not counted. The following additional guidelines emerged during the coding of the data:

- Related noun forms differing only in terms of number (*remedios/ remedio*) were counted and coded in the singular form.
- Nouns marked possessive according to English grammar (e.g., *Abuelita's, mamá's*) were counted and coded in the base form (*Abuelita/ mamá*).
- However, related multiword entries differing by a word (e.g., *corazoncito mío/corazoncito*) were counted and coded separately.
- Personal names (e.g., Fernando, Isabel, Elena) were not counted.
- Nicknames with connotative meaning but left unexplained by the author (e.g., Chato and Novio) also were counted and coded, as were animal names with denotative meaning (e.g., Urraca, Cristál).

The resultant categorical data for each focal book were recorded on a multipage coding form developed for this study. For each book, we also recorded numerical data from counts of text words (Spanish, English, and total), text pages (total and those with Spanish entries), and Spanish-language entries (total and repeated).

Focal Books

The three picture storybooks chosen for this analysis were *Abuelita's Heart* by Amy Córdova (1997), *Isla* by Arthur Dorros (1995), and *Chato's Kitchen* by Gary Soto (1995). For the sake of brevity, the two multiword titles are referred to as *Abuelita* and *Chato*. All belong to a corpus of recently published Latino picture storybooks the first two authors presently are examining in a larger investigation of Spanish use in picture storybook text in English. These particular books were chosen because they were at the high end of the corpus in terms of number of Spanish words and reflected some interesting similarities and contrasts.

Isla is a first-person narrative told by a young girl about an imaginary trip she and her grandmother take to an island, apparently in the Caribbean, where the family had its roots and relatives still reside. The two fly fantastically like birds to a city highly evocative of San Juan, Puerto Rico, visit with their family members, and tour the contemporary island environment—forest, seaport, and countryside—with the grandmother as avid guide before returning at the end to New York City where they presently live. It seems that similar imaginary flights occur whenever the grandmother shares stories with her granddaughter. The story ends with promise of another such experience.

Abuelita is another first-person narrative told by a young girl about a walking journey she and her grandmother take one evening in the desert environs near the woman's home in the southwestern United States before the return of the girl and her parents to their distant city home. With its modern-day setting in what appears to be New Mexico, the story mixes various elements ostensibly of Latino and Native American culture. For example, the grandmother wears a *rebozo* (shawl) and sings "*Cielito Lindo*" (Beautiful Sky), but also makes beaded moccasins for her granddaughter and sprinkles blue cornmeal on the ground in gratitude to Mother Earth. Many abstract references to light, love, and the heart, especially at the end of the story, give it a New Age flavor.

Chato is a contemporary animal fantasy narrated in the third person and set in the barrio of East Los Angeles. Chato, a "low-riding" striped cat who stalks sparrows and cooks tortillas, connives to make a family of five mice, who have just moved to the neighborhood, his next meal. He and his best friend, Novio Boy, work hard for hours preparing assorted dishes for a fiesta in which, unbeknown to the mice, they will be the cats' main course. But the two wily felines ultimately are surprised and thwarted by a friend of the mice, Chorizo, another "low-riding" animal who serves as the rodents' limousine and protector.

Of the three books, two have glossaries (*Isla* and *Chato*). Unlike the glossary for *Chato*, the one in *Isla* includes a phonetic key to aid readers in pronouncing Spanish entries. These two books rely consistently on italics to highlight Spanish words on the page. In *Abuelita*, there is no visual distinction of the Spanish words.

FINDINGS

Before presenting results of the criteria-based analysis, we provide counts of text words, text pages, and Spanish entries from the focal books (Table 7.1). We found that the proportion of individual Spanish words (not entries) was higher for *Isla* (15%) than for *Abuelita* (9%) and *Chato* (9%). However, Spanish words appeared on about the same proportion of text pages in the three books: *Isla* (76%), *Abuelita* (79%), and *Chato* (79%). The number of Spanish language entries per text was nearly the same across the three focal books, ranging from 33 to 39 entries, as was the number of repeated entries per text.

Length

All the entries were coded for length according to the three categories shown in Table 7.2. *Isla*, the book with the most Spanish words numerically and proportionally, also was found to have the highest number and proportion of multiword entries, both short and long. Single Spanish words accounted for only 39% of its total entries. The short entries included a fair amount of three- and four-word sequences. In contrast, the proportions of single-word entries were 64% for *Abuelita* and 71% for

TABLE 7.1
Counts of Words, Pages, and Spanish Entries

Feature	Abuelita	Chato	Isla
Total no. of text words	1,049	1,103	951
No. of English words	954	1,005	807
No. of Spanish words	95	98	144
Total no. of story pages (text + picture pages)	28	29	36
No. of pages with text	14	19	25
No. of pages with Span. entries	11	15	19
Total no. of Spanish entries	33	35	39
No. of repeated entries	8	8	9

TABLE 7.2
Length of Entries

	Abuelita (n = 33)	Chato (n = 35)	Isla (n = 39)
Single word	21	25	15
Short (2–4 words)	10	10	22
Long (5+ words)	2	0	2

TABLE 7.3
Single-Word Entries by Grammatical Class

	Abuelita (n = 21)	Chato (n = 25)	Isla (n = 15)
Noun	14	19	9
Adjective	2	1	0
Adverb	2	0	0
Interjection	1	4	2
Imperative	2	1	4

Chato. *Chato*'s lengthiest entry was a short sequence of three words (*de veras, hombres*). All of its other short entries were only two words each.[2]

Grammatical Aspects

In this part of the analysis, single-word entries were classified according to grammatical class as shown in Table 7.3, which includes only those word classes actually encountered. Multiword entries, both short and long, were classified according to grammatical structure: complete or incomplete sentence.

Class. The most frequent word class represented was the noun. Most of the single-word entries across all three books were in this class. In *Chato*, more than three fourths of the single-word entries were nouns, in *Abuelita* two thirds, and in *Isla* slightly more than half. In alphabetical order, nouns across the trio of books ranged from *abuela/o, abuelita/o, algodones,* and *arroyo* to *tamarindo, tía/o,* and *tortillas.* Common nouns occurring more than once were *chamiso, corazón,* and *remedio*(s) in *Abuelita;* *barrio* and *tortillas* in *Chato,* and *mangos* in *Isla.* Common nouns with Spanish determiners, such as *la isla* that appears several times in *Isla,* were

---

[2]Our analysis did not require the use of Rudin's (1996) fourth category for length (i.e., songs).

coded as short entries. Among the imperative forms, *mira* appeared in all three books, *ven* in two books. The interjection *bienvenida/ bienvenidos* appeared in two of the books.

Structure. Across the three focal texts, most of the multiword entries were found to be incomplete sentences: 58% (14 of 24) for *Isla*, 67% (8 of 12) for *Abuelita*, and 70% (7 of 10) for *Chato*. In *Chato*, examples of incomplete sentence entries included *chiles rellenos, chorizo con, las tortillas*, and *muy simpático*. Among those in *Abuelita* were *La Cueva del Corazón, mi favorita*, and *sopa de frijoles con salsa verde*. In *Isla*, incomplete sentences included *como la noche, mi esmeralda*, and *y una sombrilla*. Full sentences in *Isla* included *Hay mucho más que ver, Nos cantan*, and *Vamos a la selva*. The only full sentences in *Abuelita* were *Como estás hoy dia?* and *La tierra está encantada aqui*; and in *Chato, No [es] problema* and *¿Qué no [es]?*

Semantic Field

From a semantic standpoint, a sizable proportion of the single-word entries in all three books were terms of address, as shown in Table 7.4, particularly in *Isla*, in which they comprised almost three fourths (73%) of all entries, including the kinship terms *Abuela, Abuelo, tío*, and *tía*. This semantic category accounted for 43% and 44% of the total entries respectively in *Abuelita* and *Chato*, including the kinship terms and terms of endearment *Abuelita* and *corazoncito* in *Abuelita* and *Mami* and *Papi* in *Chato*. Entries of a culinary nature (e.g., *arroz, enchiladas, frijoles, guacamole*, and *salsa*) were equally high in *Chato*, and were the only other semantic field for *Isla*. Words dealing with the environment (e.g., *arroyo, chamiso*, and *coyote*) were second in *Abuelita*. If some short entries are considered, then the environment-related field would increase for

TABLE 7.4
Single-Word Entries by Semantic Field

	Abuelita (n = 21)	Chato (n = 25)	Isla (n = 15)
Terms of address	9	11	11
Environment	6	2	0
Values	4	0	0
Social life	0	1	0
Material tokens	2	0	0
Culinary terms	0	11	4

TABLE 7.5
Single-Word Entries by Type

	Abuelita (n = 21)	Chato (n = 25)	Isla (n = 15)
Loan-word	3	12	3
Cliché	0	2	2
Etymological pair	2	3	1
Hermetic Spanish	16	8	9

Abuelita, with entries such as *un conejo, adobe casita*, and *yerba buena*, and the food-related field for *Chato* would be higher, with entries such as *las tortillas, carne asada, chiles rellenos*, and *chorizo con*).[3]

Type

This criterion addressed the degree of familiarity of the Spanish entry to monolingual English readers. Hermetic entries, Spanish words whose meaning is considered unfamiliar to the monolingual English reader, accounted for more than three fourths of the single-word entries in *Abuelita* (76%) and more than half such entries in *Isla* (60%), as shown in Table 7.5. In *Chato*, fewer than one third of the single words were hermetic entries, and nearly half (48%) were loan-words, Spanish words that have become part of the mainstream English lexicon and are likely to be known to the monolingual English reader. In *Abuelita* and *Isla*, loan-words were only 14% and 20%, respectively, of the single-word entries. Some of the loan-words found included the following: *barrio, salsa*, and *fiesta* in *Chato; mangos, papayas*, and *cocos* in *Isla*; and *arroyo, coyote*, and *rebozo* in *Abuelita*.[4] Apart from the hermetic and loan-word categories, Spanish words in the focal books also included etymological pairs and clichés. Two etymological counterparts for the English word "mama" were *mamá* in *Abuelita* and *mami* in *Chato. Sí* and *pronto* were coded as clichés in *Isla*, as were *Híjole* and *hola* in *Chato*.[5]

---

[3]Rudin (1996) used five semantic categories. We used two of these in our analysis (i.e., terms of address and culinary terms) and subdivided his "ethnographic" category into the other four categories shown in Table 7.4.

[4]In accord with Rudin's (1996) procedures (p. 81), a Spanish-language entry was classified as a loan-word if it was listed in *Webster's Third New International Dictionary* and had preserved its spelling.

[5]We concur with Rudin's (1996) observation about two criteria: type and method. He stated that neither criterion "implies clear-cut boundaries between its subgroups, and many Spanish entries can be ascribed to more than one type and one method" (p. 115).

TABLE 7.6
Translation of Spanish Entries

	Abuelita (n = 33)	Chato (n = 35)	Isla (n = 39)
Literal	28	8	28
Contextual	1	12	7
None	4	15	4

Method

Regardless of the degree of familiarity of the Spanish entries to monolingual English readers, there was a marked tendency for them to be translated literally in two of the focal books, Abuelita and Isla.[6] As shown in Table 7.6, approximately 85% of the entries in Abuelita and 72% in Isla were handled in this manner. In contrast, only 23% of the entries in Chato were translated literally.

Two modes of literal translation, often involving direct speech, prevailed in Abuelita:

1. A Spanish entry was followed directly by its English translation separated by a period or comma (e.g., "Corazoncito mío, my dear heart," she sings.)
2. A Spanish entry was preceded directly by its English counterpart separated by a period or comma (e.g., Abuelita says, "The earth is enchanted here. La tierra está encantada aquí.").

Disjoined literal translation, in which a Spanish entry and its English counterpart are separated by a number of words (e.g., "Bendito sea," hums Abuelita. "Blessed be."), occurred less frequently in this book.

In Isla, direct and disjoined literal translations also were evident. More obvious in this book, however, were literal translations in which the first-person narrator assumed the role of translator for her grandmother (e.g., "¡Qué pescado!" Abuela says, telling me what a fish it was). In a variant of this mode, the grandmother speaks in sentence fragments that then are translated into complete English sentences by the child narrator (e.g., "De todo el mundo," Abuela tells me. They come from all over the world).

Chato also made use of literal translations, direct and disjoined, but they did not dominate the text. What predominated was the book's siz-

---

[6]See note 4.

able presence of both contextually translated and untranslated entries, resulting no doubt from the very nature of the Spanish words in the text (i.e., mostly loan-words and clichés) and the inclusion of a glossary. Several examples of untranslated Spanish entries in *Chato's Kitchen* involve Chato's direct speech, a dialect of the barrio. Two nearly contiguous examples from the same page follow: "*Órale*, neighbors," Chato purred. "Don't be scared of me . . ." and "No, *de veras, hombres*, I'm ok," Chato reassured. Plenty of contextual cues to aid the reader are provided with the assorted food items that figure thematically into the story.[7]

Placement

All entries were classified by placement into direct speech or narrative segments. In two of the focal texts, the entries were distributed fairly evenly between direct speech and narrative, 55% and 45%, respectively, for *Abuelita* and 46% and 54%, respectively, for *Chato*. The distribution in *Isla*, however, was markedly skewed, with about 82% of the entries in characters' talk and only 18% in the narrative. Of the 32 entries in direct speech in *Isla*, 27 (84%) were by the grandmother, who speaks only Spanish and converses frequently throughout the story with her companion, her bilingual granddaughter who serves as the first-person narrator. Other Spanish-speaking characters with minor speech segments are Tío Fernando, Cousin Elena, and the people at an open-air market. The young girl speaks directly to her grandmother in Spanish only twice toward the end of the story, to say *es mágica* and *la isla*. Only a few different Spanish entries appear in her narration, among them, several terms of address (*tío, tía, Abuela, Abuelo, mamá*), *la isla*, and *las estrellas*.

In *Abuelita*, both the grandmother and granddaughter appear to be bilingual, congruent with the story's U.S. setting. Of the 18 Spanish entries in direct speech, 15 (83%) are by the grandmother. The granddaughter speaks in Spanish only in the opening pages of the story. However, both also speak English throughout the story. Some of their speech segments begin in Spanish and others in English, with both intrasentential (i.e., within the sentence) and intersentential (i.e., across sentences) code switching as a part of their speech. But, perhaps partly because there is no glossary, the two characters continually produce speech segments composed of identical Spanish and English words and phrases, in essence, generating concurrent translations. (This aspect of their talk is discussed

---

[7]We did not record any examples of nonliteral translations of Spanish entries, a category positioned by Rudin (1996) between literal and contextual translation.

further in the next section.) The granddaughter sprinkles Spanish throughout her first-person narration, much of it in the form of culturally specific terms such as *chamiso*, *rebozo*, and *Cielito Lindo*, producing more intrasentential alternations.

In *Chato*, Spanish words can be found in direct speech segments produced by several of the major and minor characters. Of the 16 Spanish entries in direct speech, 6 are by Chato, 4 by Chorizo, 3 by Papi mouse, 2 by Novio Boy, and 1 by Mami mouse. Intrasentential code switches in the characters' speech are more numerous than intersentential ones. Most of the Spanish entries used by the third-person narrator, who speaks mostly in English, are food items and the repeated word *barrio* in reference to the story's setting.

Function

Of the two major functions described by Rudin (1996), realistic/mimetic (i.e., to add authenticity to story elements) or artificial/experimental (i.e., to innovate with language), the former seemed to drive the use of Spanish in the three focal books. The latter function was not observed at all. In the realistic or mimetic mode, the incorporation of Spanish served a number of other functions identified not only by Rudin, but also by children's literature specialists such as Lukens (1999), Nodelman (1996), and May (1995). The functions of secondary language relate directly to the elements of literature, namely, character, plot, theme, setting, tone, style, and perspective. That is, Spanish-language elements can be used to enhance or advance any or all of these elements in a particular text. For example, the function of a Spanish entry might be to convey a character's language background, or to represent the Hispanophone nature of a particular setting, inject a humorous tone through word play, or contribute to development of the theme, among others.

Given the interrelated nature of the aforementioned literary elements, it follows that an entry can serve more than one function at a time, making it difficult to quantify such data. We found this to be case repeatedly in our analysis, as did Rudin (1996) in his study. He noted that the "[function] categories are by no means mutually exclusive; most secondary language entries correspond to two or more of them" (p. 15). Consequently, we provide a narrative account of the findings for this criterion without a numerical treatment of the data.

The use of Spanish to enhance characterization was evident in all three books. For example, in *Chato*, some Spanish words serve to mark the story ethnolinguistically. In fact, both speech and dress mark the characters as Latino urban gang members (e.g., Chato's utterances of *No problema, Órale,* and *de veras, hombres.* Novio Boy's English speech is marked similarly by "Yo! Cool Cat of East Los, Homes!" and "Whatcha doin'?"). In *Isla,* consistent Spanish usage by the grandmother serves to identify her as a monolingual Spanish speaker, who although now living in the United States, does not speak English, like a number of this nation's first-generation immigrants. Spanish usage identifies the granddaughter-narrator as a bilingual Spanish–English speaker who can communicate with her grandmother (i.e., *Abuela*) in Spanish but with others also in English (e.g., the book's English-speaking readership), comparable with many of this nation's second- and third-generation immigrants.

In *Abuelita,* the use of Spanish marks the characters as bilingual, bicultural individuals, apparently for whom code switching is a salient feature of their speech. Interestingly, the grandmother's first utterance begins in English: "The earth is enchanted here. La tierra está encantada aqui." Subsequent directives to her granddaughter open with either English or Spanish, such as "Mira, look, Corazoncito" and "Come. Ven, Corazoncito." And in some utterances, Spanish and English are juxtaposed as opening words: "Bienvenida, welcome, Corazoncito mío, to the Cave of the Heart. La Cueva del Corazón!" and "Here, aqui. Adentro, inside." Utterances by the granddaughter-narrator, on the other hand, tend to open with Spanish, as in the following: (a) "Hola perrita, mi amigita. Hello little dog, my dear friend. Como estás hoy dia? How are you today?" (b) "Abuelita, my grandma." (c) "Mi favorita, my favorite!" In her narration, the young girl alternately uses Spanish and English first: (a) Encantadas . . . enchanted. (b) A rabbit, un conejo, bounces out from behind the bush.

The use of Spanish elements to help define the story's setting is fairly obvious in the text of *Isla* and *Abuelita.* For example, the granddaughter's use of Spanish in *Isla*'s narration serves to advance the Spanish nature of the story's setting, which is Puerto Rico, the grandmother's home country. The place name, *la isla,* is used several times in reference to it. The language of the setting also is reflected in the book's illustrations which show written forms of Spanish on several pages, particularly as environmental print in the city and marketplace. Finally, consistent Spanish usage by the minor characters visited in Puerto Rico further defines the setting.

Adding local color representing Spanish-language facets of the American Southwest appears to be a major function of the Spanish words in the first-person narration in *Abuelita,* an aspect reflected in the book's ethnographic theme. In her narrative, the granddaughter refers to sundry flora, fauna, and food by their Spanish names, as does her grandmother when she speaks. Although some of the terms rendered by her in Spanish might be considered specific to the desert Southwest (e.g., *chamiso* and *Maravilla* bush), others like *cocina* and *conejo* are not so unique, but seemingly are included to further evoke this region and its Hispanophone nature. The use of the word *encantada* also is an explicit referent to New Mexico's assignation as the Land of Enchantment.

In contrast, the bicultural, bilingual nature of the setting in *Chato* is reflected in both the text and its award-winning artwork that depicts both written Spanish and English environmental print. Some items are labeled in Spanish (e.g., *arroz, La Piña, mayo*), whereas others are labeled in English (U.S. Mail, Rosebud matches). On two different pages, a letter of invitation by Chato and one of acceptance by Papi mouse show several English words in full and part of one Spanish word.

Finally, it should be noted that the narrator's playful tone in *Chato* also reflects the use of Spanish (as well as English) for humorous effect, a function observed only in this book. Two examples of this are the following word plays: (a) What did they make? *Quesadillas*, of course, featuring their favorite ingredient—cheese! (b) "We can have *chorizo con* mice." Novio Boy grinned.

Illustration

Because the focal texts were picture storybooks, cues to identifying some of the Spanish entries also could be found in a book's illustrations, not just in its text. More than one third of the entries in *Isla* (38%; 15 of 39) and *Abuelita* (36%; 12 of 33), and one fifth (20%; 7 of 35) of those in *Chato* were depicted in the artwork. We examined two categories, illustration and method of translation, for any discernible patterns between illustrated and nonillustrated entries. In *Isla*, slightly more than half of the illustrated entries (e.g., *las estrellas* and *los niños*) also were translated literally in the text, whereas the rest of the illustrated entries (e.g., *plátanos, mangos*, and *papayas*) were not. However, as might be expected, in the glossary-less *Abuelita*, most of the illustrated entries (e.g., *rebozo* and *un conejo*) also were translated literally in the text, just as were all their nonillustrated counterparts. Predictably in *Chato*, most of the illustrated elements were translated contextually or not at all (e.g., *quesadillas* and *tortillas*), just as were all the nonillustrated entries.

DISCUSSION

In each book, Spanish was used primarily to add authenticity to characterization and setting. Spanish was not used for artificial or experimental purposes apart from its realistic or mimetic functions. But major differences surfaced in the effects that each book's use of Spanish had on the text.

Undesirable Effects

The text analysis of *Abuelita* and *Isla* showed that Spanish words translated literally, for the most part, tend to have a deleterious effect on the literary integrity of the text, particularly from the perspective of the Spanish-language reader, disrupting the text's flow and creating needless redundancy. In the case of *Abuelita*, literal translation of the Spanish entries tended to create characters with "unreal" rather than authentic language patterns, which produced repeated talk that made them appear silly from a linguistic standpoint. This technique produced some rather jarring text segments (e.g., Abuelita's speech that follows: "*Mira*, look, Corazoncito. We call these that grow near the *arroyo*, the stream, *yerba buena*, the good herb"). *Abuelita*'s text also displayed overtranslation, a by-product of a cross-cultural approach. For example, on one page, the granddaughter-narrator states: "Abuelita tells stories of the healing plants, her *remedios*, that grow everywhere around us." Five pages later, Abuelita reiterates this definition: "I have shown you my *remedios*, the healing plants that grow outside, but here, on the inside, is the greatest healer on Earth," whispers Abuelita.

In *Isla*, literal translation of Spanish made for a plodding, didactic text within which the narrator seemed to function largely as a translator for her grandmother's speech, or as a "spokesperson," by interpreting sentence fragments spoken by the elderly woman. Furthermore, in this book overreliance on literal translation to explain the meaning of Spanish entries made the glossary wholly unnecessary. In essence, repeated literal translation created an embedded glossary/dictionary in the text. The overall effect is an anthropological text in which the first-person narrator is the guide to an exotic Spanish-language environment. *Abuelita*'s overuse of literal translation might be more easily excused because it lacks a glossary, but *Isla*'s inefficient use of this method is difficult to justify in light of its extensive glossary.

In sum, *Abuelita* and *Isla* reflected a cross-cultural approach and all it implies from a literary perspective (Keller, 1993). In each book, it clearly is the author who moved toward the monolingual English reader by providing ample literal translations of Spanish entries, instead of the reader who moved toward the author. As a result, the interests of the bilingual reader are not served as well by these books.

Strategic Effects

The text analysis of *Chato* shows that Spanish entries of minimal length (i.e., one and two words long) can have substantial literary impact by suggesting and evoking various aspects of characters and setting. Simply stated, the strategic use of single Spanish words can go a long way in recreating characters' speech and social background, although sometimes stereotypically. Accordingly, if the humor and jest in this book's story is missed, then Chato's speech can be interpreted as exacerbating what might be considered content and illustrations stereotypical of urban Latino youth culture. From a literary perspective, *Chato* makes more effective and efficient use of Spanish entries than the other two books, weaving in Spanish words without needlessly interrupting the flow of the story and creating opportunities to use contextual translation or avoid translation altogether by relying on its glossary. These nonliteral methods, in concert with a glossary, can contribute to a more seamless text.

It also should be noted that strategic word choices in *Chato* reflect attention to both monolingual English and bilingual Spanish–English readers and listeners, a strong sign of this text's bicultural orientation. Thus, the author's use of loan-words and clichés and relatively short entries ensures that monolingual English readers will not be overly taxed by secondary language elements. At the same time, the author's more generous use of contextual translation, or no translation at all, rather than literal translation ensures that bilingual readers will not be insulted or bored by redundant English equivalents. The book's glossary is there to assist monolingual readers in these instances. Interestingly, the author does not translate the names of two of the story's main characters, Chato and Novio Boy. He apparently leaves both names to "insiders" to decipher on their own.

CONCLUSIONS

First, our study demonstrates that textual analysis procedures and findings from the world of multicultural–multiethnic literature for adults can be useful for the study of texts in multicultural–multiethnic children's literature. We think the research by Rudin (1996) and Keller (1984) on the use of Spanish in English-language and bilingual Spanish–English prose and poetry provides an important base to inform the exploration of Spanish use in Latino children's literature in English. Certainly, we anticipated that Rudin's (1996) text criteria and classifications might need to be modified to some degree to suit our study, and these modifications almost defined themselves. However, his overall analytical scheme served us well. All in all, we found a high degree of congruence between his findings and ours across the various criteria for analysis.

Second, our analysis underscores the folly of conservative critics' attempts to curtail the use of "foreign" language elements, including Spanish, in English-language texts. The dynamic and ever-changing nature of language, including English, was repeatedly made obvious to us, particularly as we engaged in verifying the status of loan-words contained in the focal texts. We were surprised at the number of Spanish words that have entered the English mainstream in recent years and now appear in the dictionary. Even words that could not be counted and coded as loan-words because they have had their spellings changed (e.g., yucca, cactus, chilies) emphasized the fact that language change is continual and pervasive.

Finally, this study has borne out our belief that the use of Spanish in Latino children's literature in English should not compromise the literary quality of any text from the standpoint of either monolingual or bilingual readers. Secondary language elements can have a significant literary effect, but they must be strategically chosen and skillfully incorporated by writers and editors. Otherwise, Spanish elements will not be integral to a text, but merely token or superficial. Such elements can and should serve a variety of functions, not only adding realism to prose and poetry, but also stretching the linguistic bounds of these texts. On the basis of the data presented here, it seems that we have barely begun to tap the functional possibilities of Spanish in Latino children's literature in English.

REFERENCES

Agosto, D. (1997). Bilingual picture books: Libros para todos. *School Library Journal, 43*(8), 38–39.

Barrera, R. B., & de Cortés, O. G. (1997). In V. J. Harris (Ed.), *Using multiethnic literature in the K-8 classroom* (pp. 129–154). Norwood, MA: Christopher-Gordon Publishers.

Barrera, R. B., Quiroa, R. E., & West-Williams, C. (1999). *Poco a poco*: The continuing development of Mexican American children's literature in the 1990s. *The New Advocate, 12*(4), 315–330.

Barrera, R. B., Thompson, V. D., & Dressman, M. (Eds.). (1997). *Kaleidoscope: A multicultural booklist for grades K–8* (2nd ed.). Urbana, IL: National Council of Teachers of English.

Burciaga, J. A. (1996). Spanish words in Anglo-American literature: A Chicano perspective. In F. R. González (Ed.), *Spanish loanwords in the English language: A tendency towards hegemony reversal* (pp. 213–230). Berlin, Germany: Mouton de Gruyter.

Burns, M. M. (1995). In A. Silvey (Ed.), *Children's books and their creators* (pp. 522–525). Boston: Houghton Mifflin.

Gove, P. B. (Ed.). (1993). *Webster's third new international dictionary of the English language.* Springfield, MA: Merriam-Webster.

Holton, S. W. (1984). *Down home and uptown: The representation of Black speech in American fiction.* Rutherford, NJ: Fairleigh Dickinson University Press.

Keller, G. D. (1984). How Chicano authors use bilingual techniques for literary effect. In E. E. Garcia, F. A. Lomelí, & I. D. Ortiz (Eds.), *Chicano studies: A multidisciplinary approach* (pp. 171–190). New York: Teachers College Press.

Keller, G. D., & Keller, R. G. (1993). The literary language of United States Hispanics. *Handbook of Hispanic cultures in the United States: Vol. 1: Literature and art* (pp. 163–191). Houston: Arte Público Press/Madrid, Spain: Instituto de Cooperacíon Ibero-americana.

Lukens, R. J. (1999). *A critical handbook of children's literature* (6th ed.). New York: Longman.

May, J. P. (1995). *Children's literature and critical theory: Reading and writing for understanding.* New York: Oxford University Press.

Nodelman, P. (1996). *The pleasures of children's literature* (2nd ed.). White Plains, NY: Longman.

Penfield, J., & Ornstein-Galicia, J. L. (1985). *Chicano English: An ethnic contact dialect.* Amsterdam: John Benjamins.

Rocard, M. (1989). *The children of the sun.* Tucson: University of Arizona Press.

Rudin, E. (1996). *Tender accents of sound: Spanish in the Chicano novel in English.* Tempe, AZ: Bilingual Review Press/Editorial Bilingue.

Stotsky, S. (1999). *Losing our language: How multicultural classroom instruction is undermining our children's ability to read, write, and reason.* New York: The Free Press.

BIBLIOGRAPHY

Cordova, Amy (1997). *Abuelita's heart.* New York: Simon & Schuster.

Dorros, Arthur (1995). *Isla.* New York: Dutton.

Soto, Gary (1995). *Chato's kitchen.* New York: G. P. Putnam's Sons.

8

From the Mountain to the Mesa: Scaffolding Preservice Teachers' Knowledge About the Cultural Contexts of Literacy

Sally M. Oran
Northern Arizona University

THE MOUNTAIN CAMPUS
AND SALLY ORAN'S CLASSROOM

Northern Arizona University's (NAU) main campus, nicknamed the Mountain Campus, is located in Flagstaff, Arizona, a growing town of about 52,000 at an altitude of 7,000 feet and just 80 miles from the Grand Canyon. Tourists, residents, and students enjoy Flagstaff's mild climate, beautiful environment, recreation opportunities, and cultural attractions on the nearby Navajo and Hopi Reservations. My students begin their courses in teacher education at the Mountain Campus with the classes I teach: theories and methods for teaching reading and language arts in nine semester hours of instruction. These undergraduate students come with notions of literacy education that typically reflect their experiences as elementary students, most often in small, predominantly White schools in Arizona.

My primary goal is to provide theory, knowledge, and experiences for preservice teachers that support equitable literacy education in a variety of cultural contexts. My instruction raises new questions in students' minds. How do I manage instruction that builds on the prior knowledge of diverse learners? Why should multicultural children's literature be used as the basis for a literacy program? Why does this type of literature "feel" so different? Because most of my students are Anglo women, the predominant population in teacher education programs throughout this country, learning how literacy education may disable rather than enable literacy achievement for children of diverse cultures is new ground.

Eager and willing to become good teachers, students are surprised when some course content confronts their cultural values, beliefs, and comforts. I often enlist the help of others to cross these boundaries. During this study, I gained the assistance of sixth graders and their teacher at the Yá'át'ééh Mesa Boarding School on the Navajo Nation. My students exchanged letters with the sixth graders and gained real data about the lives and literacy achievement of students in a culture very different than theirs. It was a volunteer project. All of my students during the 1996–1997 academic year agreed to become pen pals with students at the Yá'át'ééh Mesa Boarding School. We were researchers together in literacy education.

This chapter is the story of our research, a collaborative effort of 19 Navajo sixth graders, 29 preservice teachers, and their teachers, Tom Tomas and Sally Oran. I begin with a brief review of the literature that guided this study. Next, I provide information about the participants, their cultural contexts, and the preparation of the two teachers. I explain the research methods and give an example of a typical correspondence. After a presentation of the themes that emerged from our data, I close with a discussion of the study and its implications for teacher education.

LITERATURE REVIEW

Scholars examine the social contexts in which young learners acquire language and literacy skill. An understanding of "the zone of proximal development," that critical place Vygotsky (1986) described, in which learner and expert meet to construct dialogues and experiences that support learning, is central to developmentally appropriate literacy instruction. Cazden (1988) and Graves and Graves (1994) described such dialogues and experiences as scaffolds for successful language and literacy development. Heath (1983), McCabe (1996), and Rosenblatt (1978) focused on rich descriptions of how culture has an impact on language, early narratives, and the written texts children create, whereas Calkins (1994) and Genishi and Dyson (1994) offered strategies for negotiating cultural boundaries with young learners. The message from all these researchers is this: Teachers who understand that children's emerging literacy skill is a product of culture will construct environments to support those skills, and will know they can expect healthy progress from every learner.

Other researchers have focused on school settings and instruction. Goodman and Wilde (1992) explored the rich context of authentic learning. Pearson (1996) named authentic literacy events, using language and literacy to communicate in real ways, as among the most important outcomes of the whole language movement in schools. Turner and Paris (1995) characterized engaging literacy lessons as those that include collaborative tasks over which learners have choice and control. The idea of authentic literacy leads to a critical examination of the artificial content and construction of traditional classroom lessons. Edelsky (1991), Bennett (1991), deMarrais and LeCompte (1998), and Shannon (1989) uncovered traditional classroom practices that camouflage poor literacy instruction, particularly for students outside the dominant culture. Trueba (1989) warned of our tendency, and often our obsession, to focus on the academic failures of certain student populations and ignore educational practices central to those failures.

Literacy education for preservice teachers requires learning about the real contexts of children's language and lives. The New London Group (1996) suggested that we "[negotiate] a multiplicity of discourses" and "extend literacy pedagogy to account for the context of our culturally and linguistically diverse and increasingly globalized societies" (p. 61). Gutierrez, Baquedano-Lopez, and Turner (1997) challenged educators to offer authentic literacy instruction in multiple discourses to "ensure that students participate fully in public, community, and economic life. Literacy [for experts and for learners] includes developing both linguistic and sociocultural knowledge about language and its uses" (p. 369).

Such multiple discourses shape unique learning environments. Gutierrez et al. (1997) proposed a "third space" that

> is not a compromising liberal and comfortable middle or "balanced" curriculum, but rather a new theoretical and pedagogical space in which learning takes precedence over teaching; instruction is consciously local, contingent, situated, and strategic; and our current knowledge about language learning and language users informs the literacy curriculum. (p. 372)

Learners with their language and their whole identities become the center of learning. Teachers create climates in which all participants "become linguistic and cultural brokers" (Gutierrez et al., 1997, p. 376). Such spaces encourage us to examine language communities in relation to dominant language repertoires. This study, a year-long correspondence between my teacher education students and Navajo sixth grad-ers, was an opportunity to study the social and cultural contexts of liter-acy education.

YÁ'ÁT'ÉÉH MESA
AND TOM TOMAS' STUDENTS

The Navajo Nation, occupying a land area about the size of West Vir-ginia, stretches over the high desert and mountain forest regions of northeastern Arizona, northwestern New Mexico, and southeastern Utah. Yá'át'ééh Mesa (a pseudonym) is in the middle of the reservation in northeastern Arizona, far from interstate highways that intrude on Na-vajo traditions in many border towns. Yá'át'ééh Mesa Boarding School is nestled below high mountains, buttes, and mesas criss-crossed by net-works of dirt roads typical on the reservation. Once a boarding school op-erated by the Bureau of Indian Affairs, the school is now a contract school administered by the local community through a contract agree-ment with the Bureau. Most of the children ride the school bus daily, al-though some stay in dormitories during the school week if the distance home is too great for a daily commute.

Tom Tomas has spent weeks in the summer readying the classroom for his sixth graders. The walls await the students' work. Desks are arranged for small teams. Tomas has secured funding for new books, most with Na-tive American themes, that fill the book shelves. His Navajo students speak Navajo fluently and name it as their first language. Tomas already knows them because he has been their art teacher for 5 years. This is his first year as a regular classroom teacher, and his students easily greet him at the beginning of the school year.

There are 6 girls and 13 boys, who range in age from 11 to 13 years, in Tomas' sixth-grade class. Two students are of Navajo and Hispanic heri-tage, and one student is Navajo and Hopi. Only five of the students live at the boarding school during the school week. Fifteen of Tomas' stu-dents speak fluent Navajo. Bilingual instruction, now provided in grades K–2 at Yá'át'ééh Mesa Boarding School, was not available for Tomas' students when they were in those grades.

Navajo community life at Yá'át'ééh Mesa includes activities children have anywhere. Tomas' students do chores around the house or with the livestock, help grandparents with the same kinds of duties, play with friends, watch television, and participate in community events. Navajo culture provides the contexts for these experiences. Chores around the house for Navajo children might include carding wool for Mother's weaving, talking to a baby sister in her cradle board, or spending all Saturday herding sheep. Community events include rodeo competitions, traditional dance contests, and listening to the cultural stories told by elders during long winter evenings. Most of Tomas' students know how to make fry bread and slaughter a sheep for a community meal, and they know what to do during traditional healing ceremonies in ancient hogans.

NORTHERN ARIZONA UNIVERSITY'S TEACHER EDUCATION AND SALLY ORAN'S STUDENTS

The fall and spring cohorts at NAU consisted of 24 female and 5 male students. Most of them were Arizona natives and Anglo. None of them were of Navajo descent. They ranged in age from 20 to 26 years, except for one 51-year-old female during the spring semester.

Only the few students who had chosen elective courses in English as a second language (ESL) instruction or bilingual multicultural education had learned much about cultural issues or language diversity in schools before enrolling in my course. I provided strategies for welcoming every child's language into the classroom, used children's literature from a broad variety of cultural traditions, and taught emergent literacy and narrative styles across cultural contexts. I also supervised my students as they taught literacy lessons each week in a Flagstaff elementary school that serves urban Native American and Hispanic students. Learning how children's culture influences teaching was new to most of my students.

My students' interests included skiing, snowboarding, hiking, social activities typical on college campuses, and managing part-time jobs with full-time university schedules. Most had cars and traveled home frequently. For many of them, this meant trips to the warmer climate of the Phoenix area, referred to as "the valley," or small towns in the Southwest desert regions. None of the NAU students lived in rural settings isolated from mainstream suburban or urban areas.

ORAN AND TOMAS' PRIOR KNOWLEDGE OF CULTURAL CONTEXTS

Tomas, who is Anglo, enrolled in the Cultural Immersion Project at Indiana University while working toward a degree in Art Education at another institution. The project included gaining knowledge about various cultures, models of cross-cultural communication, skills to live and work in another culture, and lengthy reflective assignments during his student teaching at a Navajo school in New Mexico. On completion of his degree, he accepted a position as art teacher at Yá'át'ééh Mesa Boarding School in Arizona. He lived in a traditional Navajo hogan during the first 2 years there and was adopted into his host family's clan. Tomas was invited to Navajo ceremonies, learned more about relationships between Navajo clans, and discovered his new clan relationship to many of his students. He lived in an apartment on the school compound during the year this research was conducted and continued to participate actively in community experiences that enabled him to understand the cultural knowledge his students brought to his classroom.

My preparation for this study was quite different. As an Anglo woman, I had taught in public elementary schools in rural Appalachian and urban African American settings in the southeastern United States. During my graduate program at a large, Southeastern university, I completed ethnographic studies that focused on the interface of diverse cultures in schools. I also helped to direct a teacher education program that prepared students to teach in multicultural, poor, urban communities. On completion of my graduate program, I accepted a teaching position at NAU's Center for Excellence in Education. At the beginning of this study I was still new to the Southwest and knew little about Navajo culture. I did, however, know ethnographic skills for studying diverse contexts. As an ethnographer, I examined the lives of participants from their perspectives, honored their stories, and learned to use that knowledge to become a welcome, knowledgeable participant in cultural contexts very different from my own. My ethnographic skills and knowledge of culturally relevant literacy instruction became major themes in the teacher education courses I taught.

RESEARCH METHODS

My initial question was, "What happens when university students and sixth graders at a Navajo school engage in a year-long letter exchange?" Because I teach the value of authentic literacy events, I reasoned that both my university students and Tomas' sixth graders would benefit from this letter exchange. We decided on a regular correspondence schedule. Tomas and I e-mailed our reflections throughout the study, and I copied all of the correspondence for documentation. My students used the letters they received from Tomas' students as primary data to study children's writing development (Fig. 8.1).

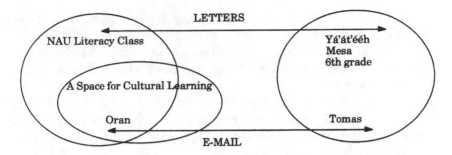

FIG. 8.1.   A model of the research design for From the Mountain to the Mesa: Scaffolding Preservice Teachers' Knowledge About the Cultural Contexts of Literacy.

Tomas used the letter exchanges as opportunities for his students to gain writing skill, so his students responded to letters from their university pen pals during class time. Tomas taught writing workshop skills, so his students learned to peer edit their letters. They sent cinquains, descriptive paragraphs, jokes and riddles, reader responses to *Dogsong* by Gary Paulsen, and their letters to my university students.

My students wrote most of their letters outside of class. They shared them with friends and, because I was concerned about the models they provided for clear writing, they received editing advice from peers and me at the beginning of the study. I soon realized that this intervention might prevent some important lessons, so I simply copied the letters and sent them to Yá'át'ééh Mesa Boarding School in one large envelope. I distributed letters from the Navajo students during class time and encouraged my students to talk about their letters. My students also sent a newsletter, an alphabet book, a "how to" book, and a movie/video rating guide to Tomas' class. There were three letter exchanges during the fall semester and eight exchanges during the spring semester.

Tomas and I e-mailed one another regularly throughout the fall and spring semesters. Our e-mail conversations began as a way to monitor the letter exchanges, but quickly developed into professional conversations about teaching, ideas about instructional strategies, and information my students requested about the boarding school and Tomas' students.

JUANA AND MICKEY'S PEN PAL EXCHANGE

Juana, an NAU student of Mexican heritage, and Mickey, a Navajo boy, exchanged three letters during the fall semester. I offer excerpts from their correspondence to characterize the letter exchanges between students on the Mountain Campus and sixth graders at Yá'át'ééh Mesa.

Juana began the letter exchange, telling Mickey about Tucson, her home town, and Flagstaff, where she was pursuing a teaching degree. She invited Mickey to write back and "tell me about yourself," so Mickey began his first letter with part of a traditional Navajo introduction: "Hi, my name is Mickey Benally. My clan is Tó'áhani. It means 'near the water.' " He told her about his family, his favorite football and basketball teams, and his birthday. Mickey wrote about a visit to a Flagstaff dentist once when he lost two teeth in a bike wreck. His first letter closed with information about Yá'át'ééh Mesa.

Juana's second letter mentioned the sports teams she liked, including Mickey's favorite, the Chicago Bulls. She told about the snow in Flagstaff and asked Mickey about his favorite subjects in school. Juana closed her second letter with these words: "Please write back soon. I can't wait to hear from you again!"

In Mickey's response, he wrote about a recent snow at Yá'át'ééh Mesa, his favorite subject in school (science), and the treehouse he was building. He asked questions about Juana's favorite school subject and whether she had a treehouse. He also wrote, "I want to be a cartoon drawer because I like to draw."

Juana's response included a description of a treehouse she and her siblings had once built. She asked Mickey for a description of his treehouse. She wrote that her favorite subject was English, although she liked science too. She responded to his comment about drawing this way: "So, are you good at drawing? I think it would be neat if you could send me a picture."

Mickey's response indicated that snow had delayed the construction of his treehouse. He included a picture he had drawn for her and this explanation: "I am going to draw an eagle for you. I am going to draw the head. If you want a body in one say yes or no. Because I can make the body on it. So do you want the body or not." Mickey concluded his letter with a paragraph about his favorite movies.

THEMATIC DATA PRESENTATION

Various themes emerged from an inductive, qualitative analysis of the data, which included the letters, the e-mail messages between Tomas and me, and the instructional discourse in my university classroom. These themes were evidenced in our data: characteristics of writing development, evidences of engagement, the impact of modeling, and the cultural contexts of schools.

Tomas' Students: Writing Development

Tomas' students' letters showed progress in length, sentence construction, and punctuation skill over the course of the year. Some students
lengthened their letters or used compound constructions before they had
acquired skill with punctuation to accommodate these constructions.
Here are examples of Mark's letters from the fall and spring that display
this development:

September, 1996

Dear Stephan,

Hi, how are you? Me I'm doing fine. and I have some friends and there
name is Mike, Larry, Earl, Mickey, robert. and how many friends do you
have. and yá'át'ééh Mesa it is good place and there is many Animal and
there is grass everywhere and I like thes plase alot. (Mark)

February, 1997

Mary,

Hi its me again. Hou are you doing? I am just fine. and will the weather is
coming dack fine it is sunshine. There are students from San Miguel that are
coming into our community. We are going to invite them into our homes.
They are going to stay in our community for 3 days. We are going to take
them hiking and take them fishing and we are going to take them to [the
canyon] to show them the ruins. We are going to there community to and
we are going to stay with them for 3 days. There family are going to invite us
into their homes. And sleep over at their houses. We are going to do all
kind of thing the way we did to them [when they visited]. Yá'át'ééh Mesa is
a good place to live. during the summer we are going down to Phoxeix. My
family are going to visit my older sister and her two kides and her dady son
to. We are going to stay with her over there for one week. (Mark)

The students used inventive spelling in their letters. Students whose
reading levels were in the second- to third-grade range used more inventive spellings than those who had developed more competence in reading
and writing. All the spellings indicated a logical selection of symbols for
sounds. Here are examples from a letter written by Rachael to her NAU
pen pal:

Dear Rob,

Hi, I'm doing find. Oh do you want to no about the Monster bird. Will
the Monster bird book was told in 1991. In this abventure, huge bird are

plaging the people of the Anasazi Villages. The tiwns, twleve year old sons of the changina Woman and Sunbearer, use their garndmother Spider Woman to defeat the Monster bird and turn their fledlings into an owl and an eagle, whose claws and feathers are used by the people for healing. (Rachael)

Conversational expressions were especially difficult for Tomas' students. One such expression they had likely not seen in print. Here are examples of ways this casual expression was written in three Navajo students' letters:

How are you doing? Me just fine. (Kristy)
Hi. How are you? Me I'm doing fine. (Mark)
Hello, How are you doing, me fine. (Harry)

In conversation, voice pitch carries meaning. A correct written version might be, "Me? Just fine!" At any rate, this example caused my students to consider reasonable explanations for grammatically incorrect sentences. It also raised the question of speech registers in friendly correspondence and the differences in writing and speaking. Would it have been more appropriate only to teach, "How am I? I'm just fine!" as an acceptable opening in a letter? This was a good question for my students to consider.

All of Tomas' students increased sentence length and complexity in their letter writing during the year. They also increased their reading levels by one to three grade levels, as measured on the same Brigance word test Tomas administered at the beginning of the study. The letters indicated their reading and writing progress.

Oran's Students: Writing Development

My university students were immediately confronted with their own incorrect sentence constructions and spellings. Most of my students said they had spent time proofreading their handwritten letters. Some of them with learning disabilities knew to seek out help to be sure their letters were error free. Other students casually drafted their letters with little thought of their spelling and punctuation, fully expecting friendly words to override any spelling or usage errors. Several preservice teachers who wrote well were bombarded with questions from their peers about writing conventions students normally learn in elementary school. In short, their writing development displayed a wide range of achievement for college students. I did not have writing samples from my students before the beginning of this project, although I asked them to draft their first letters in class to get a sense of their proficiency. Here are some examples of the errors my students made:

> I enjoy being outside. Yesterday I went sleeding with four kids I babysitt. Sometimes it's hard to babysitt because the three brothers sometimes fight. How is you're brother and sister's doing. (Kelly)

> Home for me is Napa, near San Francisco . Have you heard of San Francisco and do you know wear it is? (Cody)

> I grew up in southern California buy the ocean. I saw on the map where you live. Have you seen Ship Rock and all the beutifull areas you're around? (Jeanie)

How is it that errors we view as developmental are still displayed in the writing samples of university juniors? What do such errors in adult writing indicate? Class discussion around these errors was filled with remarks such as "I never did understand that," and "I don't ever remember being taught that," or "I can't remember whether to use 'me' or 'I' in the predicate of a sentence." My students began to question their own education, particularly in English grammar and usage. Because all but one claimed English as a first language, they had to consider how English is taught in public schools and what the implications were for their own teaching. They were forced to consider writing development as something that continues over time in every population, regardless of one's native language. These issues shaped a meaningful interpretation of writing development.

Tomas' Students: Engagement

Tomas noticed his students' increased willingness to write for longer periods of time and to spend additional effort on their letters. Many sent drawings, incorporating jokes and riddles, and several wrote their letters using the class computer. By the middle of the spring semester, Tomas realized that his students spent a substantial amount of class time writing, editing, and revising their letters. Here is an e-mail excerpt Tomas sent to me in the spring:

> Sally,

> The students' letters [arrived at] the noon hour. When I returned to the classroom, my students were reading their D.E.A.R. (Drop Everything and Read) books. Immediately, the students asked if I had retrieved their let-

ters. When I asked them if they wanted to read the letters now or wait until after D.E.A.R. time, they unanimously wanted to read their letters. After a few of the students had read the letters, they asked if they could begin writing their responses.

Tomas noticed his students' willingness to share personal information. A model for communication he recalled from the Cultural Immersion Project at Indiana University was helpful. Much like an iceberg, conversational exchanges include safe, visible information such as the weather, one's family configuration, or mutual friends. As people establish trust, other topics surface, such as information about cultural traditions and family problems or concerns, information typically less visible. Here is an example of cultural and personal information Tomas' students shared that indicates increased engagement:

> When the San Miguel students came to the school, it was a good visit because we butchered a sheep. They ate some sheep meat. Some kids went to the wash when the sheep was still cooking. I stayed and helped my mom cook and clean. After we finished eating, we went to the home of a man named John Bitsoe and he showed us how they make cradleboards and how they cut the wood. There were small, small cradleboards that he made. It was a very good visit with the San Miguel students. (Jarrick to Cathy)

Oran's Students: Engagement

It was difficult for my students to compose interesting letters. They knew their pen pals should want to write back, not just have to write back, and this made them consider the content of their letters in thoughtful ways. An e-mail message I sent early in the study reflects this issue:

> During class on Tuesday we hashed around the dilemma of how you make a letter interesting after all the introductions are completed. Susanne said, "Well, I've answered her questions and she's answered mine—now what?"

Many of my students carefully constructed sentences to catch the interest of their pen pals. Here is an example from Felicia, an NAU student, to Robert:

> Hello! Thank you so much for that drawing. It is *so* cool! Hope you like the picture I colored for you.
> PS I was wondering if you have any pets? I have a dog at home in California. Here is a joke for you.

Question: How do you keep a fish from smelling?
Answer: Cut off his nose! Ha! Ha!

Tomas' Students: Modeling

Certain words or phrases my students used in their letters seemed to prompt changes in their pen pals' letters. Cody, an NAU student, used the casual word "buddy" in all his letters. Here is an example of Cody's casual style in his first letter to Matt:

Hey, Matt,

Matt, what a great name. Matthew is my middle name, Cody Matthew Mallone.

Cody ended this first letter with: "Talk to you soon, buddy," and his second letter with "Take care, buddy."

Matt's letters, although friendly were more formal. His third letter, however, copied Cody's casual tone:

Dear Cody Mallone,

Hey buddy how are you doing? [Body of letter]
Good-by buddy have a nice Christmas. And have a happy New Year.

Your friend,
Matt Thompson

There was a particularly delightful example of an attempt by one of the Navajo students to mimic the casual language my students used. One of my students wrote about "Flag," a local term for Flagstaff. The pen pal wrote back and shortened the name of her Navajo community using only the first syllable!

Oran's Students: Modeling

My students saw their errors repeated by their pen pals. Calbert, a Navajo student, closed his December letter to Jenny with these words, "Your pen pal, Calbert." In January, Kellie, Calbert's new university pen pal ended her letter with, "Your pen pall." In the next two letters, Calbert closed with, "Your pen pall, Calbert." My students' inconsistent or incorrect punctuation, particularly in the greeting or closing of the letters, seemed to confuse the sixth graders, perhaps delaying mastery of these skills.

Their own negative models convinced my students of the power their models had for children, perhaps in a way positive models could not.

Oran's Students: Learning About the Cultural Contexts of Schools

As I began to analyze the data for this study and reflect on my teaching for the 1996–1997 academic year, I began to see that the pen pal letters created a new space for learning in my university classroom. This new space appeared early in the study. I was at home responding to dialogue journals my students submitted weekly. On this particular week, they had described their pen pals at Yá'át'ééh Mesa Boarding School, a portrait I had asked them to write using the first two letters they had received from their pen pals. My eyes froze on a line Joanie had written: "Marlene [her Navajo pen pal] seems to come from a wealthy family. She attends boarding school and summer camp in Oklahoma." I suddenly was confronted with my assumptions about my students. I had assumed, because most of them were Arizona residents, they knew about the history of American Indian education and the socioeconomic conditions of many Navajos on the reservation.

I began a file of new instructional strategies for the literacy education class. The first strategy was to illustrate graphically their knowledge of boarding schools. I will not forget the next class period. I asked each student to draw a semantic web including everything they knew about boarding schools. When everyone finished, we combined individual webs into one representation of collective knowledge. The final graphic display indicated that my students knew only about boarding schools wealthy children attend, those often depicted in films and the media. They knew nothing of boarding schools on the Indian reservations in their own state.

Boarding schools and other experiences puzzled my students. Here are my e-mail messages to Tomas in which I inquire about cultural knowledge:

> My students opened their letters in class yesterday. I was pleased that they asked lots of questions, pointing out that they just don't know much at all about Navajo culture, even though most of them are native Arizonans. They all want to know about how Navajos greet new people by telling their clan. Can you give us some more information about this? Any info you can send me on Navajo traditions around introductions and gift giving would be greatly appreciated.

Tomas responded as follows:

Here is the clanship system. A student's first clan is his mother's clan. The second clan is his father's first clan (the father's mother's clan). The third clan is the mother's father's first clan (maternal grandfather's first clan). The fourth clan is the father's father's clan (paternal grandfather's first clan). Next, regarding gift giving, Navajos give gifts to people departing from their community. It could be a son or daughter going off to school. The gifts are usually handmade by the gift giver or purchased from another craftsman.

I e-mailed this reflection about cultural learning in the spring:

My students are really learning a lot, Tom. One of the things that really stumps my students is the fact that your kids ride horses—and some of them herd sheep while doing it! Another thing is the business about butchering a sheep when the kids from San Miguel come. Not quite the same as taking guests to the Hard Rock Cafe in Phoenix!

My students began to see the limitations that urban culture and dominant culture experiences make on their general knowledge.

Given their own errors in written language, my students questioned their ability to provide literacy lessons for diverse populations, particularly ESL students. We considered two important issues: Why do schools confer privilege to some students without language proficiency (themselves) and demand language proficiency from other students (ESL students)? How does our membership in the dominant culture have an impact on our literacy instruction?

CONCLUSIONS

This study encircled the lives of 19 Navajo sixth graders, 29 university students, and their teachers and created a new space for learning about literacy education. My students learned about the writing development of Navajo sixth graders and preservice teachers. They learned how their own writing influenced, engaged, or disengaged their pen pals. They began to see their pen pals' writing as evidence of developing competence instead of deficiency. They struggled to connect with students whose lives were very different from theirs, and they considered how limited or inaccurate knowledge of children's cultural experiences restricts teaching.

Literacy pedagogy, texts, and goals now had to be examined in light of the pen pal experience. The usual curricula, language, and materials for preservice teachers and elementary students, materials likely to reflect dominant culture norms, were not enough. The pen pal letters led us far away from the micro-arguments of phonics versus whole language or basal texts versus literature-based curricula to multiple literacies that included life experiences, languages, cultural traditions, and privilege.

These multiple literacies shaped our "third space," where we studied the cultural contexts of literacy skills. Our concerns were real. Our questions were central to making meaning of our experience. Our learning was authentic. We confronted biases about ESL learners because we could no longer dismiss writing errors as indicative of limited English proficiency. In light of struggles to write engaging letters to Navajo students, we questioned how such populations were so easily labeled "at risk." Instruction shifted from literacy education theories and instructional strategies for a limited, often anonymous community to those that enlarged and identified the communities, multiplied the texts, expanded our responsibilities as educators, and emphasized the lessons Navajo children taught us.

We never completely finished our "third space," although we did manage to find time and ways to reflect about our study. This unfinished space caused me to examine the course I deliver and its purposes more closely. I wanted my students to understand how instruction that ignores cultural contexts privileges children from the dominant culture and disenfranchises others. I wanted them to attain pedagogical competence in providing culturally relevant literacy instruction to any child. I wanted them to be convinced that emergent literacy is based in cultural contexts, and that literacy development depends on instruction that includes those contexts.

I learned from this study that it is unrealistic to expect my students to gain a thorough understanding of the cultural contexts of literacy in one semester. My course, at the beginning of the professional program, may give impetus to that understanding, but cannot complete it. Preservice teachers, particularly those from the dominant culture, need effective learning scaffolds throughout their professional programs. These scaffolds should include authentic experiences in diverse contexts over time, guided reflection with people who understand these contexts, continued use of multiple literacies, and participation in learning communities that cross traditional university boundaries. Teacher educators who honor the learning development of preservice teachers and understand the cultural contexts of literacy will design professional programs that invite students to construct unique "third spaces" where learning for everyone takes precedence over and directs teaching.

ACKNOWLEDGMENT

Sally M. Oran wishes to thank Tom Tomas, now a teacher at Little Singer School, Little Singer, Arizona. Tom continues to provide superior literacy instruction and culturally responsive, effective education by examining his own practice, the materials and pedagogies he uses, and the cultural contexts of his school and students. In doing so, he honors the traditions of his Navajo students and the best purposes of education.

REFERENCES

Bennett, K. (1991). Doing school in an urban Appalachian first grade. In C. C. Sleeter (Ed.), *Empowerment through multicultural education* (pp. 27–48). Albany, NY: SUNY Press.

Calkins, L. (1994). *The art of teaching writing*. Portsmouth, NH: Heinemann.

Cazden, O. (1900). *Classroom discourse: The language of teaching and learning*. Portsmouth, NH: Heinemann.

deMarrais, K. B., & LeCompte, M. D. (1999). *The way schools work: A sociological analysis of education* (3rd ed.). New York: Longman.

Edelsky, C. (1991). *With literacy and justice for all: Rethinking the social in language and education*. London: Falmer Press.

Genishi, C., & Dyson, A. H. (1994). Conclusion: Fulfilling the need for story. In A. H. Dyson & C. Genishi (Eds.), *The need for story: Cultural diversity in classroom and community* (pp. 237–244). Urbana, IL: National Council of Teachers of English.

Goodman, Y. M., & Wilde, S. (1992). *Literacy events in a community of young writers*. New York: Teachers College, Columbia University.

Graves, M. F., & Graves, B. B. (1994). *Scaffolding reading experiences*. Norwood, MA: Christopher-Gordon.

Gutiérrez, K., Baquedano-López, P., & Turner, M. G. (1997). Putting language back into language arts: When the radical middle meets the third space. *Language Arts, 74,* 368–378.

Heath, S. B. (1983). *Ways with words: Language, life, and work in communities and classrooms*. Cambridge, UK: Cambridge University Press.

McCabe, A. (1996). *Chameleon readers: Teaching children to appreciate all kinds of good stories*. New York: McGraw-Hill.

Pearson, P. D. (1996). Reclaiming the center: The search for common ground in teaching reading. In M. F. Graves, P. van den Broek, & B. M. Taylor (Eds.), *The first r: Every child's right to read* (pp. 259–274). New York: Teachers College Press.

Rosenblatt, L. M. (1978). *The reader, the text, and the poem*. Carbondale, IL: Southern Illinois University Press.

Shannon, P. (1989). *Broken promises*. Branby, MA: Bergin & Gravey.

The New London Group. (1996). A pedagogy of multiliteracies: Designing social features. *Harvard Educational Review, 66,* 60–92.

Trueba, H. (1989). *Raising silent voices: Educating the linguistic minorities for the 21st century*. Boston, MA: Heinle and Heinle.

Turner, J., & Paris, S. G. (1995). How literacy tasks influence children's motivation for literacy. *The Reading Teacher, 48*, 662–673.

Vygotsky, L. (1986). *Thought and language*. Cambridge, MA: Massachusetts Institute of Technology Press.

9

English as a Second Language, Literacy Development in Mainstream Classrooms: Application of a Model for Effective Practice

Diane M. Truscott
Buffalo State College

Susan Watts-Taffe
University of Minnesota

Meeting the needs of English-language learners is a major challenge facing teachers today. With an increasing number of students learning English as a second language (ESL) in U.S. schools, it is a challenge that cannot be ignored. Moreover, as evidenced by the 1998 decision of the California legislature to abolish bilingual education, it is a highly politicized challenge. Theoretically, several programmatic options are available for ESL learners, but, realistically, only a few are usable. Most second-language learners spend most of their school day in a mainstream classroom setting with a teacher who has no special preparation for working with them. How can such teachers contribute to the literacy development of these students?

In this chapter, we provide a response to this question, presenting a research-based model for effective ESL literacy instruction in mainstream classrooms. We use this model to examine actual classroom teaching, synthesizing our classroom observations into recommendations for teacher development and practice. This model challenges the traditional focus on oral reading proficiency as a prerequisite for literacy instruction and instead emphasizes reading comprehension and purposeful language tasks. In addition, it is based on what researchers know about effective practice and is grounded in studies specific to the literacy instruction of

ESL students. To set the stage for a different way of thinking about literacy instruction for second-language learners, we begin by discussing the current experience of many ESL learners in American schools.

LINGUISTIC DIVERSITY IN TODAY'S CLASSROOMS

Walk down any hall in any public city school, in any state, and you will notice that the voices have changed. Recently, the United States has seen the arrival of the largest immigrant group in its history (Lewis, 1991). According to the 1990 U.S. Census data, 14% of the total school-age population live in homes wherein a language other than English is spoken (National Association for Bilingual Education, 1993, as cited in Perez, 1998). Gains in the number of nonnative English speakers have been reported for 39 states in the nation (U.S. Department of Education, 1995), with certain states having particularly large proportions of second-language learners. For example, in 1997, one in every four students in K–12 schools in California was a second-language learner. Currently, in kindergarten and first grade, 40% of the students are nonnative English speakers (Gandara, 1997). Furthermore, it has been predicted that by the year 2030, the number of second-language learners in California will rise to 70% (Garcia, 1992).

The American school experience for many ESL students is a difficult one (Igoa, 1995; Nieto, 1996; Valdés, 1998). In addition to the cultural differences they experience, most ESL students do not receive instruction in their native language. The U.S. Department of Education (1995) reports that only 15% of ESL students nationwide are educated in programs designed specifically for second-language learners. In California, 70% of ESL students receive instruction in English-only classrooms, with little or no outside support for English language learning (Gandara, 1997).

One reason for this is that many schools lack adequate funding to provide special programs for second-language learners, especially when the numbers of children from one language group are few (Garcia, Montes, Janisch, Bouchereau, & Consalvi, 1993). Even in schools offering ESL support, it often is the pullout variety that sometimes leads to diminished instructional time for students (Clair, 1995). A second reason is the social, political, and historical emphasis on English-only instruction, especially in relation to recent immigrants from South America, Southern and Eastern Europe, and China (Perez, 1998).

A third reason is the lack of research showing one particular type of school program to be clearly more effective than others for increasing Eng-

lish language reading achievement (Fitzgerald, 1995). Two studies conducted by the National Research Council concluded that comparative investigations of programs emphasizing instruction in the native language
versus English-only instruction have limited value (August & Hakuta,
1997). According to Tedick (1998), such studies are complex because of
the teacher's pivotal role in determining the success or failure of any particular approach. Despite a lack of data supporting one program over another, many schools are shifting from bilingual programs to full integration
(Schirmer, Casbon, & Twiss, 1996), thus placing the responsibility for literacy instruction in the hands of the regular classroom teacher.

Without professional support or training for mainstream classroom
teachers in general, "sink or swim" approaches to mainstreaming often
lead to student frustration and academic failure (Bos & Reyes, 1996).
Despite the fact that general education teachers are responsible for much
of the literacy instruction for students with linguistically diverse needs,
most of them are underprepared and hold uninformed views and beliefs
concerning ESL students' literacy learning (Flatley & Rutland, 1986;
Penfield, 1987). Only 6% of regular classroom teachers have had any formal coursework addressing ESL issues (Fitzgerald, 1995; National Center
for Educational Statistics, 1997).

Furthermore, neither reading journals nor basal teaching manuals provide much help to teachers (Garcia et al., 1993; Schumm, Vaughn,
Klinger, & Haager, 1992). Garcia et al. (1993) found that only 6% of the
referred articles published in *The Reading Teacher* and 3% of the referred
articles published in *Language Arts* from 1979 to 1990 dealt with ESL issues. Of these, more than half were written specifically for bilingual or
ESL teachers rather than mainstream teachers. An analysis of five basal
reading series for grades 1, 4, and 6 yielded similar results. Most information provided by the basals focused solely on oral language development
rather than overall literacy development. In a more recent content analysis of a leading literacy journal (*Journal of Literacy Research*, formerly *Journal of Reading Behavior*), Garcia, Willis, and Harris (1998) found that only
8% of the articles published from 1992 to 1996 dealt with linguistic diversity. As noted in Fitzgerald's (1995) comprehensive literature review, research on literacy instruction for second-language learners is scarce.

With so little information available to teachers (Faltis & Hudelson,
1994), it is clear that teachers need guidance and support in responding
to the needs of linguistically diverse learners in the classroom (Constantino, 1994). The model that follows provides teachers with some direction for thinking about their classroom practices relative to ESL students. An important aspect of the model is that it does not require

teachers to change their current pedagogy completely. Instead, the framework helps educators recognize those literacy elements that are pedagogically sound and found to be particularly effective for ESL students. Teachers are encouraged to emphasize these components as they rethink and modify other instructional elements needing attention.

A MODEL FOR EFFECTIVE ESL LITERACY TEACHING

The model for effective ESL instruction (Fig. 9.1) is grounded in several sources of information: (a) existing research reviews of ESL learning and teaching in the elementary and upper grade levels (Fitzgerald, 1995; Garcia & Padilla, 1985; Weber, 1991; Wong-Fillmore & Valadez, 1986); (b) descriptions of exemplary ESL programs identified by the National Diffusion Network and other large, federally funded studies (e.g., Tikunoff, 1985); and (c) content from 60 additional current articles and studies on ESL literacy instruction. The model reflects seven effective practices for the literacy instruction of ESL learners: activation/use of prior knowledge, purposeful language tasks, scaffolded use of English vocabulary, focus on comprehension, incorporation of various media, variation of discourse styles, and explicit communication. This series of effective practices was converted into an observational checklist for examining actual classroom practice. Data were collected by means of the checklist in two fourth-grade and two fifth-grade mainstream classrooms during social studies lessons by the regular classroom teacher. Each teacher was ob-

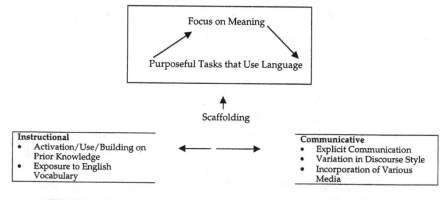

FIG. 9.1.   A model of effective instruction for second-language learners in the mainstream classroom.

served for two approximately half-hour periods. (For a more complete description of this study, refer to Truscott & Watts-Taffe, 1998.)

Meaning and Language Use

The goal of literacy instruction for ESL students should be on the construction of meaning through the purposeful use of reading, writing, listening, speaking, and thinking. Whereas an emphasis on active construction of meaning during literacy events is widely recommended, a focus on meaning or comprehension, as opposed to accurate word pronunciation, represents a theoretical shift from traditional thoughts on ESL instruction (Fitzgerald, 1995). Few reading problems experienced by second-language learners result from deficiencies in oral language skills (Reves, 1993), and programs that emphasize oral word accuracy over comprehension appear to be unproductive (Elley & Mangubhai, 1983; Fitzgerald, 1995; Schirmer et al., 1996). For construction of meaning, teachers are encouraged to use reading materials at levels higher than ESL students' oral proficiency (Raphael & Brock, 1993), thus providing students with opportunities for vocabulary expansion, background knowledge development, and participation as real members of the classroom. This emphasis also requires instruction in comprehension strategies for connected text (Au, 1998; Jiménez, 1997). Many of the comprehension strategies found to be helpful for native English speakers are also helpful for second-language learners (Au, 1995; Flatley & Rutland, 1986; Reyes & Molner, 1991), including the teaching of text structures and metacognitive strategies (Droop & Verhoeven, 1998; Roberts, 1994).

The model highlights the reciprocal relation between the construction of meaning and tasks that engage students in the purposeful use of language. It acknowledges that meaningful language is ultimately more useful, and thus better learned than decontextualized language (Bos & Reyes, 1996; Henry, 1998; Krashen, 1981; Moll & Diaz, 1987; Roberts, 1994; Wilkinson, Courtney, Robertson, & Kushner, 1992). In addition, authentic use of language supports the "legitimate and extensive uses of reading and writing" (Faltis & Hudelson, 1994, p. 459) and serves as a motivational tool because learners need to use the language to share constructed meanings (Elley & Mangubhai, 1983). Because literacy develops within specific social and cultural settings (Au, 1998; Perez, 1998), purposeful tasks can serve as "opportunities [for students] to read, write, and speak themselves into the curriculum" (Henry, 1998, p. 234). There are numerous ways of using language in real ways during literacy events including book clubs, in which students come together to discuss and con-

struct their understanding of readings (Raphael & Brock, 1993), and cooperative grouping, in which students use language to achieve a common
goal (Athanases, 1998; Au, 1998; Bos & Reyes, 1996). When assessing
whether an instructional activity uses language purposefully, a teacher
should simply ask, "Do students have to use English in real ways to complete the assignment?"

Use of Scaffolding

Scaffolds represent variations in the amount and type of instructional
support available. We found that many activities recommended in the literature provide varying degrees of support for students as they engage in
literacy learning (Peregoy, 1991). We see these practices as scaffolds because they acknowledge and adapt for unique learner characteristics, assume some type of social interaction, and serve as temporary frameworks
(Wood, Bruner, & Ross, 1976). Two types of scaffolds are presented in
our model: *instructional scaffolds* (the instructional methods used to facilitate and support student learning) and *communicative scaffolds* (the ways
that teachers can support ESL students through the communication patterns they maintain in their classrooms). Needless to say, these two types
of scaffolds influence one another and work in concert.

• Many practices that can be instructional scaffolds for second-
language learners are the same ones used to support the learning of English-speaking students. Having students activate and use existing background knowledge is critical to the meaning-making process for all students. For second-language learners, it is particularly important because of
cultural differences that may affect concept knowledge. In many cases,
new background knowledge must be developed (Droop & Verhoeven,
1998; Flatly & Rutland, 1986). However, caution should be exercised not
to equate second-language learning with a void experiential base (Flores,
Cousin, & Diaz, 1991). Many second-language learners come to school
with rich experiences that can serve as valuable instructional resources for
teachers who acknowledge and welcome cultural and linguistic diversity in
their classrooms (Cummins, 1994; Moll & Gonzalez, 1994; Reves, 1993;
Schirmer et al., 1996).

• Instructional activities that expose students to English vocabulary
and scaffold the use of new words orally and in writing are essential for the
literacy development of second-language learners (Au & Carroll, 1997;
Tikunoff, 1985). It is important to consider the role played by practice, authentic application, and motivation in vocabulary development. Second-

language learners acquire and extend vocabulary when they are engaged in tasks that require thinking and practice using new words in supported ways (Garcia, 1992). Vocabulary use should not be confined to reading instruction. Studies indicate that many second-language learners can begin to write in English long before they become fluent speakers (Hudelson, 1984; Rigg, 1989; Urzua, 1987). Writing activities should be strongly encouraged because they support both reading skills and oral language development. Vocabulary development also can be fostered through the use of cooperative and collaborative learning, reciprocal teaching, and shared reading (Garcia, 1999; Hough, Nurss, & Enright, 1986; Means & Knapp, 1991; Raphael & Brock, 1993).

Communication is key to learning in a classroom with many voices. Oftentimes, teachers' messages to students and expectations for student behaviors are confusing to second-language learners, partly because of competing cultural norms (Delpit, 1995; Heath, 1983; Roberts, 1994; Tikunoff, 1985).

• The use of communicative scaffolds means, among other things, being explicit about classroom rules, patterns, and routines. It should be clear to students how they are expected to participate in the classroom community and what is expected of them to achieve success in this community (Delpit, 1995; Little & Sanders, 1989). Related to this is the importance of exuding an attitude that all students are academically able (Schirmer et al., 1996) and that all students are reaching for the common goal of academic success within a classroom community setting.

• Another way teachers can support communication in their classroom is to vary their discourse styles (Au, 1995; Fitzgerald, 1995; Flatley & Rutland, 1986). Among the several ways to modify language during instruction are speaking clearly and slowly, avoiding idioms, defining key words in context, and encouraging cooperative or joint responses (Schirmer et al., 1996; Tikunoff, 1985). Teachers also can use a variety of verbal and nonverbal cues during instruction to help students identify and focus on the essential lesson components. For example, teachers can pause to indicate a change in events, change their pitch and volume to stress character voice, and use exaggerated intonation for key words (Elley & Mangubhai, 1983; Hough et al., 1986). Nonverbal cues include using facial expressions, pointing to illustrations, and using gestures to accompany story actions (Hough et al., 1986).

• A final way teachers can incorporate communicative scaffolds is to use various types of media including technology. This is particularly impor-

tant for less proficient speakers of English because it enables them to participate in learning. Visual approaches include using graphics, demonstrations, and hands-on models and activities (Fitzgerald, 1995; Flatley &
Rutland, 1986; Reves, 1993).

A LOOK AT PRODUCTIVE PRACTICES

In our observations of mainstream classroom teachers at the fourth- and
fifth-grade levels, we saw teachers implement a number of the instructional and communicative scaffolds recommended in the literature. For
example, one element of effective literacy instruction for ESL learners observed as commonplace in elementary classrooms was the activation, use,
and/or building of prior knowledge. In most of the lessons we observed,
teachers activated students' topic schemata, and in half of the observed
lessons, teachers demonstrated sensitivity to assumed prerequisite concepts. An excellent example of activating and building background
knowledge comes from Stephen, a fourth-grade teacher, as he sets the
stage for a new social studies unit:

Teacher: "Transportation. Raise your hand if you've heard the word before."
(Hands are raised.) "Good. We're in good shape. In groups I want
you to come up with forms of transportation. Let's come up with
some examples." (Teacher and class generate examples.) "Okay. I'm
going to give you another example to show the range. A skateboard.
A skateboard is a form of transportation." (Students work as groups
while the teacher monitors. Both ESL students seem actively involved.)

Teacher: "What's important is that everyone in your group had a chance to
participate, not that we have a ton of these." (Teacher then pulls
student names randomly from a stack of cards and lists responses on
the overhead projector.)

Teacher: "Look at this list on the overhead. You can set your list aside. Now,
here's a question for you, and I'm gonna need you to think about
this a little. Which one is best? And I'm gonna need you to tell me
why."

Student: "Bus, city bus, 'cause you can get on at different points. Semi-
trucks—sometimes they crash."

Student: "Airplane—gets you there faster."

Student: "Spaceship—you can go farther."

Student: "I have one that isn't up there and it's your feet. They're easier and
doesn't cost you anything."

Student: "Paddleboat because you can use your feet, and you don't have to pay for it."

Teacher: "Did you notice we all came up with different ones. I also noticed that we all had different reasons. The question 'What's the best?' isn't a good question. The better question would be . . . depends on what you're transporting, how fast you need to get there, and how much money or energy you're willing to spend." (Teacher then relates the story to being stranded without a car at a cabin and considers various forms of transportation. Students proceed to read aloud from the social studies textbook the selection "Moving People and Goods.")

Explicit communication is an element of good teaching in any classroom. Communicative scaffolds such as explicit classroom rules and expectations for success are especially important for ESL students as ways to help them anticipate transitions and participate as classroom members. We observed all the teachers emphasizing clear communication through posted classroom rules. Classrooms often were portrayed as structured learning communities, with desks organized into quads and clear daily routines and patterns. Most teachers gave clear directions and demonstrated, in some observable way, an attitude that the students were academically able. Many teachers were observed to vary their discourse style during instruction. Most teachers spoke clearly, and half of the teachers gave adequate wait time, which can support code switching, and used nonverbal cues. Some teachers even encouraged choral responses from the class and maximized their teaching by changing their voice to make a point.

TAKING A CLOSER LOOK: COUNTERPRODUCTIVE PRACTICES

At first glance, it is encouraging that teachers are already implementing various techniques and activities associated with instructional and communicative scaffolding. However, the overall goal of literacy instruction for ESL students is one of constructed meaning and purposeful language use. Unfortunately, although many teachers are activating background knowledge and providing clear communication, the literacy events found in many classrooms do not focus ESL students on constructed meaning or purposeful language tasks. It seems that what teachers do, or do not do, is strongly influenced by how they define language proficiency and their understanding of second-language development.

For example, teachers in our study were able to categorize ESL students as having low, moderate, or high English proficiency, but used very different criteria. For one teacher, oral proficiency was extremely important and seemed to be the sole criterion for determining proficiency. Another teacher considered a combination of speaking, reading, and writing essential for English-language proficiency. All the teachers made comments suggesting that they believed oral proficiency should be a goal for their ESL students. In fact, lesson activities in all rooms were heavy with oral exercises (e.g., oral reading, oral question–answer periods, and teacher recitation). This may explain, in part, why activities focusing on student use of language for meaningful purposes were absent. It should be noted that we did not observe much comprehension instruction emphasizing use of the context, differentiated reading materials appropriate for students' reading levels, or comprehension strategy instruction. In some of the lessons observed, a purpose was set for reading, always by the teacher.

Needless to say, the lack of instruction focused on the construction of meaning is a cause for concern. But a closer inspection of other existing practices is equally disturbing. Although cooperative or collaborative learning was observed in most of the lessons, it did not necessarily result in the purposeful use of language for all group members, especially ESL students. In fact, some collaborative learning groups appeared to be void of both collaboration and learning for some group members. Consider Nadia's experience as described in the following excerpt from fieldnotes:

Teacher: "We've been studying about the people who came here. The first people were in the New England colonies. The second group of people who came were in the Southern colonies. Now today, we're going to be reviewing some of what we've already learned and also learning some new things." (Teacher distributes worksheets.)

Teacher: "Let's go through the questions so you know what you are looking for." (Goes over questions by having students read them aloud, paraphrasing them where necessary.) "Are there any questions about the questions?" (Pauses. No response.) "You need to read pages 114 to 119, and you need to work with your group. When you're done, I'm going to pull one paper and that will be the grade for your group. So what does that mean?"

Students: "We all have to do the work."

Teacher: "You all have to do the work." (Students move to various parts of the room with their groups. One group moves out into the hall. Teacher walks around from group to group, sitting with each group for a few minutes and working with them, answering questions, or listening in. Groups are all single-gender groups. Teacher helps a group of boys on how to work together after it becomes clear that the group is having trouble doing this.)

(Nadia is not an active participant in her group. She sits quietly and watches what the others are doing, but does not appear to be following along. She often looks away or down at the floor. The group's approach is to read the question aloud then look for the answer in the textbook. When someone finds the answer, she tells the others and reads it out. If the others agree, they all work together to rephrase the answer in original wording. If they do not agree, they might continue to look through the text or discuss it until the group is satisfied with the answer. Once the group has decided how to phrase the answer, they write it out on the worksheet. One girl, sitting to the left of Nadia shows Nadia her paper after she has finished writing. Nadia then copies the answer. This pattern continues until the end of the class period.)

In this example, Nadia is not engaged in the purposeful use of language, which is significant not only because of its implications for her literacy development, but also because of its implications for her ability to develop social relationships in the classroom. In addition, this scenario exemplifies the fact that collaborative and cooperative learning need not involve tasks that require higher level thinking. The lack of emphasis on meaning during literacy instruction for ESL students has been noted before (Bos & Reyes, 1996; Elley & Mangubhai, 1983; Fitzgerald, 1995) and is reflected in other aspects of the instruction we observed.

For example, linguistically heterogeneous groups that might have facilitated English-language vocabulary development often did not allow students to use language in substantive ways. In many cases, this grouping pattern was best described as a physical arrangement of chairs, not as an instructional strategy. Similarly, other strategies with the potential to scaffold vocabulary development were weakly utilized. For example, when teaching the meanings of individual words, teachers did not vary the depth of their instruction according to the conceptual difficulty of the new words. All words received the same treatment, usually a teacher-supplied definition.

The following example shows how one fifth-grade teacher defined key words during the content lesson:

Teacher: "Okay, what does 'distinguished' mean? 'Distinguished' means very well respected people. Can you imagine sitting around with your friends for days to discuss courage and honesty. Look at the second

Student: "Phil—" (Student struggles to say the word.)

Teacher: "Philosophic discussions—discussions that are based on philoso-phy. That's all that means. Turn to page 2 of your play." (Students seem restless. They are fidgeting and talking quietly.)

Teacher: "Zoology is the study of animals. Biology is the study of (inaudible). Botany is the study of plants. Okay, ready to begin?"

The preceding excerpt is devoid of a supportive context for the acquisition of new vocabulary. Teachers often forget that effective vocabulary instruction requires opportunities for children to experiment with words in meaningful ways and build their own word knowledge in relation to existing schemata. Failure to do more than provide an oral definition for a new word reduces the likelihood that students will learn it and apply the new word in new ways (Stahl & Fairbanks, 1986).

In a final example of how existing practices often fail to reach the ultimate goal of meaning and language use, we turn our attention to explicit communication. As noted previously, teachers may clearly state their expectations for success and participation in elementary classrooms. However, clearly stating expectations for success is not the same as holding high expectations for students. Tasks that students perform that do not require high levels of thinking or participation by all students will not propel ESL students forward. In addition, although making students aware of what they need to do to complete a particular exercise is an important aspect of clear communication, it may not benefit second-language learners unless the teacher facilitates that participation.

MOVING INSTRUCTIONAL PRACTICE FORWARD

Recognizing what teachers currently do well in their classrooms is important because these practices can serve as powerful scaffolds for the development of other practices that are pedagogically sound, but may be pursued less often or not at all. For example, with regard to instructional scaffolds, teachers did pay attention to vocabulary, although it was not the type of attention needed to enhance ESL students' vocabulary development. This is disturbing in light of Jiménez's (1997) finding that vocabulary knowledge is a distinguishing feature between ESL students who are successful readers in English and those who are not. Yet it is commensurate with Watts' (1995) findings regarding vocabulary instruction provided for native English speakers during reading instruction. A focus on more effective forms of vocabulary instruction, as a part of teacher development, would benefit all learners.

In terms of communication in the classroom, the data show a clear emphasis on being explicit with rules, routines, expectations, and directions. However, the information communicated clearly often was not socially constructed. Most lessons were teacher directed and teacher controlled with an emphasis on preplanned activities and structures. This positioned students as recipients of language and ideas rather than active participants in the construction of language and ideas.

Other practices will need to be introduced to teachers more fully because they do not yet exist in any form as a part of daily instruction. In our research, for example, we observed an absence of explicit consideration or acknowledgment of ESL students' native cultures and languages, which has been shown to be critical to the development of second-language literacy (Au, 1998; Collier, 1995; Igoa, 1995; Jiménez, Garcia, & Pearson, 1995; Moll, 1988). Students were not encouraged to use their literacy knowledge acquired in their native languages. Furthermore, this lack of attention to elements of students' native cultures make other recommended practices less powerful.

Finally, there were no opportunities for students to read texts at their own levels and no emphasis on comprehension strategy instruction, a finding that fits with Dole's (1997) assertion that despite the benefits of cognitive strategy instruction, it continues to be underutilized in schools. Other recommended practices absent from the lessons we observed were use of graphic organizers, hands-on models, changing facial expressions, gestures, or other symbols to support ESL students in their comprehension of discourse and their English-language acquisition. This suggests that teachers used techniques that could be preplanned, and implemented according to those plans, as opposed to techniques that required moment-to-moment decision making and responsiveness to unplanned, often unpredictable, input from students, according to the nature of true interaction.

Teacher training in effective literacy instruction for ESL students must assist teachers in identifying existing practices proved to be beneficial to ESL students and ways of incorporating less utilized pedagogical practices. Such teacher development must be viewed as just that—teacher development. If teachers are truly to develop their abilities to work in linguistically diverse settings, they require opportunities for problem solving, critical thinking, and reflection. Clair (1995) argued that many regular classroom teachers are ill prepared to support second-language learners because teacher education programs stress technical components of teacher competence rather than a stance toward critical thinking. She suggested that teachers need opportunities to reflect on ESL issues and must be encouraged to use what they know about language and children as they become responsive practitioners who understand why and how their classrooms are diverse. Stephen, the fourth-grade teacher, recalled during a focus interview with us:

> I don't think I've ever had any staff development. . . . It's basically ignored in undergraduate programs, and as a district, I think we still haven't (pause), you know, the need is there, the importance of ESL students still has not been put at the top. (focus group discussion, 5/8/97)

Promise lies in models of staff development wherein teachers learn about techniques that can be used in conjunction with, or as an extension of, what they already do in the classroom (Adger, 1996) as well as models that are contextually specific to the classroom community and responsive to the changes that occur as teachers begin to change their practices (Truscott & Truscott, 1997). Indeed, such opportunities could link teacher practices with teacher beliefs, a vital dimension of professional growth (Johnson, 1992).

The model presented here provides direction for contextually specific teacher development in which current behavior is used to scaffold the development of other desired behaviors. For example, the fact that teachers were explicit in communicating classroom rules and expectations could be used to explore ways for integrating ESL student language and culture into such communication. Similarly, the teachers' focus on new vocabulary could be modified to include more contextual information and strategy instruction.

CONCLUSION

We do not mean to imply that what we observed reflects general practice in these or other mainstream classrooms serving ESL learners. Nor do we want to minimize the complex nature of effective instruction in a linguistically diverse setting. A major premise of the model is that good literacy practices are important for all children. Some are more crucial than others for second-language learners. The model does not include strategies that would be supportive only for ESL students and not for native English speakers. This is the case because the large majority of second-language learners receive their literacy instruction in English-only mainstream classrooms. Also, research suggests that effective instruction may differ depending on the linguistic and cultural background of the student (Garcia, 1999, p. 237). Importantly, this study confirms our belief that teachers need to acknowledge that a "one size fits all" orientation minimizes the rich diversity that exists among learners in elementary classrooms, whereas an "if it fits, wear it" philosophy allows teachers to tailor instruction to meet the needs of all children.

ACKNOWLEDGMENTS

The authors thank their research assistants, Carrie Case, Kim Washington, and Norma Sciarra, as well as the teachers who generously participated in the study reported in this chapter. This study was supported in part by a grant from the Central Connecticut State University chapter of the American Association of University Professors, New Britain, CT.

REFERENCES

Adger, C. T. (1996). *Language minority students in school reform: The role of collaboration* (ED 400 681). Washington DC: ERIC Clearinghouse on Languages and Linguistics.

Athanases, S. Z. (1998). Diverse learners, diverse texts: Exploring identity and difference through literary encounters. *Journal of Literacy Research, 30,* 273–296.

Au, K. H. (1995). *Literacy instruction in multicultural settings.* New York: Holt, Rinehart, & Winston.

Au, K. H. (1998). Social constructivism and the school literacy learning of students of diverse backgrounds. *Journal of Literacy Research, 30,* 297–319.

Au, K. H., & Carroll, J. H. (1997). Improving literacy achievement through a constructivist approach: The KEEP demonstration project. *The Elementary School Journal, 97,* 203–221.

August, D., & Hakuta, K. (Eds.). (1997). *Improving schooling for language-minority children: A research agenda.* Washington, DC: National Research Council.

Bos, C. S., & Reyes, E. I. (1996). Conversations with a Latina teacher about education for language-minority students with special needs. *The Elementary School Journal, 96,* 203–221.

Clair, N. (1995). Mainstream classroom teachers and ESL students. *TESOL Quarterly, 29,* 189–196.

Collier, V. P. (1995). Acquiring a second language for school. *Directions in Language Education, National Clearinghouse for Bilingual Education, 1*(4), 1–10.

Constantino, R. (1994). A study concerning instruction of ESL students comparing all-English classroom teacher knowledge and English-as-a-second-language teacher knowledge. *Journal of Education Issues of Language Minority Students, 13,* 37–57.

Cummins, J. (1994). The acquisition of English as a second language. In K. Spangenberg-Urbschat & R. Pritchard (Eds.), *Kids come in all languages: Reading instruction for ESL students* (pp. 36–62). Newark, DE: International Reading Association.

Delpit, L. D. (1995). *Other people's children: Cultural conflict in the classroom.* New York: The New Press.

Dole, J. (1997, October). *Explicit versus implicit instruction in comprehension.* Paper presented at the Guy Bond Memorial Reading Conference, Minneapolis, MN.

Droop, M., & Verhoeven, L. (1998). Background knowledge, linguistic complexity, and second-language reading comprehension. *Journal of Literacy Research, 30,* 253–271.

Elley, W. B., & Mangubhai, F. (1983). The impact of reading on second language learning. *Reading Research Quarterly, 19,* 53–67.

Faltis, C., & Hudelson, S. (1994). Learning English as an additional language in K–12 schools. *TESOL Quarterly, 28,* 457–468.

Fitzgerald, J. (1995). English-as-a-second-language reading instruction in the United States: A research review. *Journal of Reading Behavior, 27,* 115–152.

Flatley, J. K., & Rutland, A. D. (1986). Using wordless picture books to teach linguistically/culturally diverse students. *The Reading Teacher, 40,* 276–281.

Flores, B., Cousin, P., & Diaz, E. (1991). Transforming the deficit myths about learning, language, and culture. *Language Arts, 68,* 369–379.

Gandara, P. (1997). *Review of research on instruction of limited English proficient students.* A report to the California legislature from the University of California Linguistic Minority Research Institute, Irvine, CA.

Garcia, E. (1999). *Student cultural diversity: Understanding and meeting the challenge* (2nd ed.). New York: Houghton Mifflin.

Garcia, E. E. (1992). *The education of linguistically and culturally diverse students: Effective instructional practices.* Santa Cruz, CA: National Center for Research on Cultural Diversity and Second Language Learning.

Garcia, E. E., & Padilla, R. V. (Eds.). (1985). *Advances in bilingual education research.* Tucson, AZ: University of Arizona Press.

Garcia, G. E., Montes, J., Janisch, C., Bouchereau, E., & Consalvi, J. (1993). Literacy needs of limited-English-proficient students: What information is available to mainstream teachers? In D. Leu & C. Kinzer (Eds.), *Examining central issues in literacy research, theory, and practice* (pp. 171–178). Chicago: National Reading Conference.

Garcia, G. E., Willis, A. I., & Harris, V. J. (1998). Appropriating and creating space for difference in literacy research. *Journal of Literacy Research, 30,* 181–186.

Heath, S. B. (1983). *Ways with words: Language, life, and work in communities and classrooms.* London: Cambridge.

Henry, A. (1998). "Speaking up" and "speaking out": Examining "voice" in a reading/writing program with adolescent African-Caribbean girls. *Journal of Literacy Research, 30,* 233–252.

Hough, R. A., Nurss, J. R., & Enright, D. S. (1986). Story reading with limited-English-speaking children in the regular classroom. *The Reading Teacher, 39,* 510–514.

Hudelson, S. (1984). Kan yu ret an rayt en inglés?: Children become literate in English as a second language. *TESOL Quarterly, 18,* 221–238.

Igoa, C. (1995). *The inner world of the immigrant child.* New York: St. Martin's Press.

Jiménez, R. T. (1997). The strategic reading abilities and potential of five low-literacy Latina/o readers in middle school. *Reading Research Quarterly, 32,* 224–243.

Jiménez, R. T., Garcia, G. E., & Pearson, P. D. (1995). Three children, two languages, and strategic reading: Case studies in bilingual/monolingual reading. *American Educational Research Journal, 32,* 67–97.

Johnson, K. E. (1992). The relationship between teachers' beliefs and practices during literacy instruction for nonnative speakers of English. *Journal of Reading Behavior, 24,* 83–108.

Krashen, S. (1981). *Second-language acquisition and second-language learning.* Oxford: Pergamon.

Lewis, A. C. (1991). Washington news. *Education Digest, 56,* 51–53.

Little, G., & Sanders, S. (1989). Classroom community: A prerequisite for communication. *Foreign Language Annals, 22,* 277–281.

Means, B., & Knapp, M. S. (1991). Cognitive approaches to teaching advanced skills to educationally disadvantaged students. *Phi Delta Kappan, 73,* 282–289.

Moll, L. C. (1988). Some key issues in teaching Latino students. *Language Arts, 65,* 465–472.

Moll, L. C., & Diaz, S. (1987). Changes as the goal of educational research. *Anthropology and Education Quarterly, 18,* 300–311.

Moll, L. C., & Gonzalez, N. (1994). Lessons from research with language minority children. *Journal of Reading Behavior, 26,* 439–156.

National Association for Bilingual Education (NABE). (1993). Census reports sharp increase in number of non-English-speaking Americans. *NABE News, 16,* 1, 25.

National Center for Education Statistics. (1997). *Are LEP students being taught by teachers with LEP training?* (Document No. 97907). Washington DC: National Center for Education Statistics.

National Center for Educational Statistics. (1995). *The condition of education.* Washington DC: U.S. Department of Education.

Nieto, S. (1996). *Affirming diversity: The sociopolitical context of multicultural education* (2nd ed.). New York: Longman.

Penfield, J. (1987). ESL: The regular classroom teacher's perspective. *TESOL Quarterly, 29,* 189–196.

Peregoy, S. F. (1991). Environmental scaffolds and learner responses in a two-way Spanish immersion kindergarten. *The Canadian Modern Language Review, 47*(3), 463–476.

Peregoy, S. F., & Boyle, O. F. (1993). *Reading, writing, and learning in ESL: A resource book for K–8 teachers.* New York: Longman.

Perez, B. (1998). Literacy, diversity, and programmatic responses. In B. Perez (Ed.), *Sociocultural contexts of language and literacy* (pp. 3–20). Mahwah, NJ: Lawrence Erlbaum Associates.

Raphael, T. E., & Brock, C. H. (1993). Mei: Learning the literacy culture in an urban elementary school. In D. Leu & C. Kinzer (Eds.), *Examining central issues in literacy research, theory, and practice* (pp. 179–188). Chicago: National Reading Council.

Reves, T. (1993). What makes a good foreign language reader? *English Teachers' Journal* (Israel), *46,* 51–58.

Reyes, M., & Molner, L. (1991). Instructional strategies for second-language learners in the content areas. *Journal of Reading, 35,* 96–103.

Rigg, P. S. (1989). Language experience approach: Reading naturally. In P. Rigg & V. G. Allen (Eds.), *When they don't all speak English: Integrating the ESL students into the regular classroom* (pp. 65–76). Urbana, IL: National Council of Teachers of English.

Roberts, C. A. (1994). Transferring literacy skills from L I to L2: From theory to practice. *Journal of Educational Issues of Language Minority Students, 13*, 209–221.

Schirmer, B. R., Casbon, J., & Twiss, L. L. (1996). Innovative literacy practices for ESL learners. *The Reading Teacher, 49*, 412–414.

Schumm, J. S., Vaughn, S., Klinger, C., & Haager, D. (1992). A content analysis of basal readers: Teaching suggestions for ESL/LEP students learning to read English. In C. Kinzer & D. Leu (Eds.), *Literacy research theory and practice: Views from many perspectives* (pp. 425–434). Chicago: National Reading Conference.

Stahl, S. A., & Fairbanks, M. M. (1986). The effects of vocabulary instruction: A model-based meta-analysis. *Review of Educational Research, 56*, 72–110.

Tedick, D. (1998, May). Interview on Minnesota Public Radio. *Learning English as a second language and the California decision to abolish bilingual education.*

Tikunoff, W. J. (1985). *Applying significant bilingual instructional features in the classroom.* Rosslyn, VA: National Clearinghouse for Bilingual Education.

Truscott, D. M., & Truscott, S. D. (1997). *Moving away from stand up and deliver: Constructing situated training for professional development.* Paper presented at the annual meeting of the American Educational Research Association, Chicago, IL.

Truscott, D. M., & Watts-Taffe, S. M. (1998). Literacy instruction for second language learners: A study of best practices. In T. Shanahan & F. Rodriguez-Brown (Eds.), *National Reading Conference Yearbook, Forty-Seven* (pp. 242–252). Chicago: National Reading Council.

Urzua, C. (1987). "You stopped too soon": Second language children composing and revising. *TESOL Quarterly, 21*, 279–304.

Valdés, G. (1998). The world outside and inside schools: Language and immigrant children. *Educational Researcher, 27*, 4–18.

Watts, S. M. (1995). Vocabulary instruction during reading lessons in six classrooms. *Journal of Reading Behavior, 27*, 399–424.

Weber, R. (1991). Linguistic diversity and reading in American society. In R. Barr, M. Kamil, P. Mosenthal, & P. D. Pearson (Eds.), *Handbook of reading research* (Vol. II, pp. 97–119). New York: Longman.

Wilkinson, C. Y., Courtney, Robertson, P., & Kushner, M. (1992). Promoting language development through the Graves writing workshop. *The Bilingual Special Education Perspective, 6*, 3–6.

Wong-Fillmore, L., & Valadez, C. (1986). Teaching bilingual learners. In M. C. Wittrock (Ed.), *Handbook on research on teaching* (pp. 648–685). New York: Macmillan.

Wood, D., Bruner, J. S., & Ross, G. (1976). The role of tutoring in problem solving. *Journal of Child Psychology and Psychiatry, 17*, 89–100.

10

Assessing and Assisting Performance of Diverse Learners: A View of Responsive Teaching in Action

Robert Rueda
University of Southern California

Erminda Garcia
San Francisco Unified School District

Recitation teaching has been found to characterize many educational programs for language minority students and low-achieving at-risk students, as well as those for students in general (Goodlad, 1984). This instructional approach features highly routinized and/or scripted interaction, teacher domination, and a focus on isolated and discrete skills. Recent research, however, suggests the efficacy of responsive teaching, especially in conjunction with culturally compatible activity settings (Au, 1993; McLeod, 1994; Tharp, 1989). Responsivity is used here to mean assisted performance provided to a learner that is within the learner's zone of proximal development (Dixon-Krauss, 1996; Tharp & Gallimore, 1989), that is, teaching adjusted to a level just above what an individual might accomplish independently. For teaching to fall within the learner's zone of proximal development, constant monitoring of the learner must take place.

In other words, in this assisted performance paradigm grounded in a sociocultural perspective on literacy (Anthony, Johnson, Mickelson, & Preece, 1991; Cambourne & Turbill, 1994; Garcia & Pearson, 1994; Valencia, Hiebert, & Afflerbach, 1994), assessment and instruction are closely linked in an inseparable fashion. Responsivity can be likened to the close monitoring of student or child output such as that found in "caretaker speech" (Ochs & Schieffelin, 1984). As Cambourne and Turbill (1994) noted, there is a clear parallel between the fundamental elements of responsive interactions in the everyday world, such as language learning, and responsive assessment in academic settings. Whereas traditional views often have conceptualized assessment as something that happens after an instructional episode, a sociocultural view sees it as intertwined conceptually and chronologically with instruction. In this light, interactive decision making (Au, 1993) that occurs during the course of classroom interactions can legitimately be seen as assessment that informs instruction.

In examining assessment from this perspective, previous work (Shavelson & Stern, 1981) suggests that an important consideration is the belief system or implicit theories that an individual teacher holds regarding such basic issues as the nature of literacy and learning. These theories and beliefs represent the store of knowledge that affects planning and decisions (Clark & Peterson, 1986), and can be expected to have a strong impact on responsive teaching interactions. A related aspect of teachers' thought processes is interactive decision making. Inquiry into interactive thoughts and decisions focuses on the extent to which teachers make decisions that lead them to change their plans or behavior "online," in other words, how they assess while they are teaching (Clark & Peterson, 1986).

With few exceptions (Cambourne & Turbill, 1994; Johnson, 1993), however, much of this research has not generally emanated from an assisted performance framework, and therefore the issue of responsive instruction has not been systematically incorporated. This also has resulted in an artificial distinction between assessment and instruction such that "interactive decision making" generally has not been seen as an aspect of assessment. Finally, student linguistic and cultural diversity has not been included in this work, although such differences might be expected to result in a more complex learning environment. Currently, there is a surge of interest in studying teacher belief systems (Pajares, 1992), but there is little information on teacher beliefs related to the assessment of language-minority students, particularly in the area of literacy. In spite of these weaknesses, the existing work provides a strong basis for examining responsivity during teaching and for reconceptualizing teachers' thoughts and decision making as assessment embedded in specific instructional contexts.

PURPOSE OF THE STUDY

Traditionally, research on literacy instruction and assessment has focused almost entirely on the child or on properties of the measures because of limitations associated with prevailing theories. A sociocultural research perspective (Tharp & Gallimore, 1989), however, shifts the unit of analysis from a narrow focus on the individual child to closer examination of the activity settings (the who, what, when, where, and why of everyday human interaction) in which literacy-related activities take place. In short, rather than an examination of the child in an isolated fashion, it is the child interacting with "more competent others" in a specific activity setting that needs to be assessed (Moll, 1990; Dixon-Krauss, 1996).

In this chapter, we present highlights from a study that examined responsivity in the context of reading lessons. Specifically, we investigated the beliefs and practices of six teachers in a particular learning community related to reading instruction and assessment as they worked collaboratively to develop more responsive teaching practices for the Latino students they served. A major goal of the study was to investigate the strategies and features of the interaction to which teachers attended while conducting responsive reading lessons with their students, and to see how these interactional strategies and features related to their beliefs and developing practices.

The specific questions investigated were the following: What are the teachers' beliefs related to literacy and reading, bilingualism and biliteracy, and assessment? How are these beliefs related to classroom practices? How well do these classroom practices capture the features of responsive instruction? While engaged in interactive reading lessons, to what features of the activity settings do the teachers attend? What strategies do they use to focus themselves and monitor students or other features of the activity setting in order to be responsive? The overall goal was to explore how teachers think about, monitor, and evaluate the complex teaching and learning processes related to literacy in their classrooms.

METHODS

The study was descriptive in nature. Data collection took place in a school wherein the second author had consulted and collaborated for approximately 2 years. The purpose of this school-initiated collaboration was to assist the teaching staff in moving toward more "responsive" teaching and assessment (Goldenberg, 1991). The actual data collection for the study took place during a 1-year period from January through January.

The School Context

Stevenson School is an inner-city school in a large California school district serving approximately 360 students. At the time of the study, about 88% of the entire population were of Latino background, and 77% were limited-English proficient. The remainder of the school population was Asian (3%) and White (9%). In the year before the study, the school as a whole implemented a program allowing all students to acquire literacy in two languages. The program was designed as a child-centered approach to learning emphasizing the development of fluency and literacy in both Spanish and English. All 12 classrooms in the school became bilingual classrooms.

We argue that the teachers and principal at this school represented a community of learners (Rogoff, 1994) because they worked as a group to reflect on their practice and develop professionally on a long-term basis. Part of the commitment to responsive teaching involved reflection on individual practice and an agreement to implement interactive journals, literature conversations or study, a writer's workshop, thematic teaching, paired readings, and portfolios.

We used a case study approach, focusing our efforts on six teachers in Grades K to 6. They were selected on the basis of their interest in responsive teaching and in the study itself, and also because they represented a range of grade levels. A brief profile of each teacher follows.

Focal Teachers

Sarah (kindergarten).   Sarah had been a student teacher with one of the other teachers (Lucy) in the study. After receiving her bilingual credential, she assumed teaching duties at the kindergarten level. She began as a traditional teacher, relying on scripted basal lessons and worksheets, and modeling much of what she did after her master teacher. However, she was very inquisitive about both her own teaching and the teaching demonstrations she observed, and was working toward less dependence on commercial materials. She occasionally engaged in responsive teaching, but not consistently.

Lourdes (first grade).   Lourdes had a bilingual credential and was in her third year of teaching. She spent her first year "trying to get through day to day" because of all the unfamiliar demands. Her first year was in a K–1 combination classroom. She was observed to be responsive with small groups of six to eight students, although at the beginning of the study, she was "transitional," that is, in the process of adapting her traditional ways toward more responsive practices. She often questioned whether her kids were learning, and was concerned with how they scored on large-scale assessments.

Lucy (grade 2–3 combination). Lucy had a bilingual credential and had taught for about 4 to 5 years. Although she initially taught kindergarten, she moved to second grade and found the transition to a higher grade level exceedingly difficult. She sometimes felt that teaching was very hard and took an excessive amount of time. She attended a lot of conferences for new ideas, but complained that she had not put her learning into an overall "schema." She was observed to engage in very responsive interactions with small groups of students, but often was concerned with the mechanics of lessons such as correct pronunciation rather than comprehension. She was much less concerned with the "why" of instruction and sometimes expressed real concerns about her kids "getting it."

Ana (third grade). Ana had a bilingual credential and had taught for 5 years. All her experience had been in second or third grade. She was very willing to replicate new teaching ideas demonstrated, but asked few reflective questions. She was interested in thematic teaching, but still questioned how well her students were doing compared with "basal" kids.

Amy (fourth grade). Amy had taught for 2 years, and before that had been a student teacher in the classroom of another teacher (Christina). She used literature in her classroom, but still held on to reading basals because she was not confident she could structure time adequately without them. Although she did not appear to have a well-articulated theory of biliteracy, her classroom was literally filled with print, and the pursuit of literacy in both Spanish and English was evident. She was a natural leader, having assumed the position of grade level leader after only 2 years. She asked a lot of questions, and her teaching often involved responsive interactions with students.

Christina (sixth grade). Christina had taught for about 10 years. She came to the school at the invitation of the principal to support the bilingual education program because of her reputation as an excellent teacher in the district. She believed strongly in literature as a vehicle to engage students, took a great deal of time to organize thematic teaching, and encouraged a lot of student talk about books. She continually reflected and asked questions, and was very confident in both her teaching and her mentoring of other teachers.

Data Collection

Data sources for this study included the following: an interview of teacher belief systems about reading and literacy, literacy assessment, and bilingualism–biliteracy; a survey of reading instructional practices; a sur-

vey of reading instructional materials; a survey of reading assessment
practices; and videotapes of reading lessons. Additionally, there were
stimulated recall interviews using these videotapes, informal interviews,
and classroom observations. These measures and procedures are described in detail in Rueda and Garcia (1995).

For the belief systems interview, which led the data collection, teachers' views were placed along a continuum for each of the three domains
examined via that instrument. In the reading and literacy domain, the
continuum ranged from a constructivist–interactionist orientation at one
end to a transmission orientation at the other end. In the literacy assessment domain, the orientations ranged from a constructivist–interactionist to a discrete-skills orientation. In the bilingualism–biliteracy domain,
the continuum spanned from an additive to a subtractive perspective.
The following section presents some key patterns from the teacher belief
interviews. These are followed by findings from the stimulus recall interviews.

FINDINGS

Teachers' Beliefs and Practices

Two trends were evident in the analysis of teachers' beliefs in the areas
examined. First, despite the relatively homogeneous goals of these teachers and their apparent consensus on general instructional principles,
there was a significant amount of variance in their teaching beliefs. Second, among individual teachers, beliefs tended to be mixed or eclectic in
sometimes seemingly contradictory ways. Each of these is illustrated in
the following discussion.

Reading and Literacy.   In general, teachers held different views
about reading and literacy. Some believed that skills and phonics should
play an important role in literacy instruction. For example, when Amy
was asked how she thought fourth graders should be taught to read, she
said: "I've been trying to figure that one out (laughs). I believe phonics is
a good way to learn, . . . to get a good start."

Although Amy had begun to question the wisdom of teaching phonics
and skills out of context, the primacy of phonics and skills in her beliefs
about literacy was evident. Conversely, Christina leaned more toward a
constructivist orientation, especially regarding how to help children having difficulty learning:

Christina: "I strongly believe that every child can succeed no matter what. That is my philosophy that I have had. So what I do in the room [is] I provide them a lot of developmental activities. For example, if we read a novel, I have a child that is maybe reading at third grade, but he is reading and is understanding what is happening in that novel at sixth grade. So, we do a lot of activities, mainly; today what they had to do was a Most Wanted Poster. We had to analyze one of the characters. You are going to have different levels there, but I let them create what they want. They know what my objective is. . . . They design it and develop it, and they are always asking, 'What should it look like?' Whatever you do is what is right."

Despite the relatively constructivist goals on which the teachers as a whole had agreed, the emphasis on specific skills and prerequisite skills was much more characteristic of Amy's beliefs than Christina's.

Literacy Assessment. In general, there also was variance among the teachers concerning literacy assessment. Sarah, for example, had begun to think about performance assessment and portfolios in her class, but was still concerned with skills:

Sarah: "In my portfolio, what I have is the checklist for kindergarten, which isn't really important anymore by what I use. It is just for me. Then I have their tests, math tests in there. Then, interactive journals, I put that in there, so parents can see their progress, and also the teacher who is going to have them."

Although Sarah had begun to think about assessment in a more constructivist framework, she relied heavily on a skills-based checklist to inform herself. In contrast, the students' journals were used more to inform parents and their succeeding teacher. This eclectic mixing of beliefs and practices from different theoretical perspectives was a pattern found to hold for virtually every teacher in the study.

Ana appeared to be more constructivist in her orientation to assessment. When asked how she knew when some particular aspect of instruction was working, she cited several means she could use to inform herself: "Well, I see evidence in the children's writing, their monthly samples, their interactive journals, their readings, and the books that they are choosing to read."

Although Ana was concerned about skills, she was much more amenable to evaluating performance in the context of ongoing classroom activities. As in the domain of reading and literacy, there was a tendency among the focal teachers to express beliefs that mixed aspects from both ends of the instruction-assessment continuum.

Bilingualism and Biliteracy.   Interestingly, there was much less variance among the teachers with regard to bilingualism and biliteracy, as compared with the other dimensions. The teachers overwhelmingly tended to express beliefs consistent with an "additive" approach to bilingualism and biliteracy (Rueda & Garcia, 1996). This is illustrated in the following segment of the interview with Lourdes:

Interviewer:	"In what ways do you think language-minority students differ from non–language-minority students in the classroom?"
Lourdes:	"Academically, they are the same. Behavior-wise, they are the same. You know, as long as a parent is involved, the child is doing fine. But once the parent doesn't get involved, then that is when you have some of your behavior problems. Whether they're Spanish speakers or not, minorities or not, I can't see any difference."
Interviewer:	"In your opinion, is it [the bilingual program] successful?"
Lourdes:	"I think for the most part, like I said, 95% to 99% of it works. I see the benefits. At the beginning of the year, I have English speakers that come in here and they don't understand the word. At the end of the year, they are maybe not talking to me in Spanish, but I hear them talking outside on the playground, you know, saying 'Es mi pelota,' (It's my ball), or 'Maestra, ésto es mío,' (Teacher, this is mine), and it is just great."

This view of bilingualism as an asset, for both English-speaking and Spanish-speaking students, was a common belief among the focal teachers. The variance in beliefs about literacy and literacy assessment was not reflected in their beliefs about bilingualism, suggesting the independence of these domains. As mentioned earlier, however, according to the interviews, none of the teachers held uniform beliefs about literacy instruction and assessment, but tended to mix elements of different traditions to some extent.

Monitoring Interactive Teaching: A View Into Responsivity

The sources of data used to examine patterns of teacher monitoring or behaviors and cognition associated with attempts to be responsive included the beliefs interview as well as two stimulated recall interviews and other informal interviews conducted during and after teachers watched their tapes. A number of clear patterns emerged when the data from these other interviews were considered. These patterns are discussed in the following sections. After this, a comparison between two of the teachers in the group is presented that highlights the divergence of views encountered in the study.

Reading Was Distributed.   Although all the teachers conducted what might be called reading groups, they tended to conceptualize reading as permeating a much wider range of classroom activities. Lucy, for example, talked about a distribution of reading across the day:

Lucy: "I think it [reading] goes on in everything that we do. In the beginning of the day, in the opening I write on the board, and we do reading together during our language arts time. During math, we do a lot of writing out things instead of just numbers, and journals we do reading back and forth interactively. I would say in every subject that we do reading is involved in it. So I really can't pinpoint it just in certain areas."

This pattern clearly reflects recent conceptualizations of reading and literacy (McLeod, 1994) as an all-encompassing feature of the classroom rather than a discrete subject area.

Student Features Figured Prominently.   When teachers described their attempts to be responsive in their lessons, by far the most common feature they reported attending to involved student characteristics, including body language, facial expression, and verbal output. An example of focusing on body language is found in the following exchange:

Interviewer: "Are there certain things you pay attention to in the kids' behavior?" (Referring to the videotaped segment).

Christina: "I look at the body language a lot. . . . I look at their body language. What are they communicating to me? I think that's important. And I just, you know, I always look at my kids and just watch—'What are they doing? What are they telling me?' If they're not grasping it, how am I going to come up with another type of question?"

Often all three of these features were processed simultaneously:

Lucy: "I think it [the lesson] is working because everyone is partici-
                 pating, everyone's enjoying."

Interviewer: "You judge that by how much they talk?"

Lucy: "Yeah, by how much they're verbalizing what they're thinking.
                 Just by the looks on their faces they seem to be enjoying some-
                 thing. I know it's working. There's one point in the lesson
                 where I think I'm asking too many questions, and they're like
                 'Uhhhhhhhh.' That kind of told me that I'm talking too much
                 and they're ready to move on."

In short, the teachers frequently focused on students' externally observable characteristics to adjust their teaching.

Monitoring Strategies Reflected Shortcomings.   In general, the
teachers could not describe well-defined, organized strategies that they
use to maintain responsivity during a lesson. Although they often used
identifiable strategies, these did not appear to be systematically, consistently, or consciously used. For example, when Sarah was asked how she
knew when her teaching was working or not, she could only describe
some rudimentary ways of knowing this:

Sarah: "I see the students hesitate, and if I see that they don't under-
                 stand, or have a grasp of what I am asking them to do, then I
                 check myself and I try to go through a whole different process
                 in a way to explain it to them. Because if I can see in their faces
                 that there is no way they understand what I am saying, I have
                 to make sure that the children understand."

Sometimes the teachers could describe strategies for monitoring the
responsivity of a lesson. However, they were unable to provide the variety
or level of details found in more formal assessments of responsivity, such
as the components of the instructional conversation or Mediated
Learning Environment Scales (Lidz, 1991; Rueda, Goldenberg, & Gallimore, 1992).

Teachers Relied on Intuition.   Every single teacher made reference
to the fact that "knowing" about a student's performance at a given point
in time is partly or even largely intuitive. Lourdes's expression of such a
sentiment in one of the interviews typified her colleagues' responses:

Lourdes: "I think I see my job as a mother's job—intuition. You know
                 when something is not going right. . . . But as far as telling a

> new teacher, I would just say, 'Go with your feelings, your gut feelings, because you're usually right and if you're not right, well, then, you made a mistake and you go on.' " [stimulated recall interview 2]

Christina used the metaphor of "sixth sense" to describe this aspect of her teaching:

> "So, when something I know goes right, I have that feeling. I don't know. It is hard to explain, because, I guess it is a sixth sense you make up." [teacher beliefs interview]

Teacher experience appeared to be an important factor in evaluating the relative weight that should be attached to test scores versus observations based on such intuition. At times, there was a discrepancy between the intuition, which all the teachers felt to be so important, and students' actual behavior or test scores:

Amy: "I'm so unsure of everything at this point that I need something solid for me to look at and have, so I have my notes and my gradebook, plus I give them a test just to make sure that I know, so that my gut is assured."

Interviewer: "Are there times when there's a disagreement between what you feel and what the book says?"

Amy: "A very shy student came up to read with me. He didn't read at all and so I thought, 'His reading scores are really low.' But I had one of the helpers have him read into a tape recorder, and when I went to the tape recorder and listened to it, he was doing beautiful. I think it was first quarter, 3 weeks after the school year started, so I think he was just real nervous around me and he couldn't read. So that one, I really got a shock when I found out he's one of my stronger readers."

The teachers in the study articulated somewhat mixed beliefs about the origin and trainability of this intuitive sense. Some felt that one is simply born with such intuition, whereas others thought that one could acquire it with training and experience. However, all believed an intuitive sense was critical for good teaching.

"Mental Portfolios" Were Used.   Assessment information on the performance of individual students was part of a teacher's mental record-keeping system. This feature of classroom monitoring, that is, using a

"mental portfolio," was described in similar ways by the teachers. The following excerpt is typical of their responses:

Lourdes: "I don't have time to write down everything, but I think we're like a computer and we know where everything is."
Interviewer: "I want to know what your 'computer' is like."
Lourdes: "It's hard to explain, but you know, you ask me, 'Where is this child?' And I can tell you whether he's doing fine and what numbers he needs to work on or what level he is. And it's not something that I need to write down. I know it because I see their work every day."

These mental portfolios appeared to be dynamic in the sense that they were constantly being added to, and they often were used to check the current performance of an individual student. An important feature of mental portfolios was the use of student writing to monitor understanding and comprehension. Several teachers relied on students' writing either during or after a lesson as a way of monitoring comprehension, and these written products appeared to play an important role in the mental portfolio as well as in the teachers' thinking about responsive instruction.

Opportunities for Responsive Teaching Were Missed. In some cases, we identified instances in which teachers attempted to be responsive, but did so in ways that were unsuccessful. For example, one unsuccessful pattern was to attend to low-level or inappropriate features of the lesson. An example of this was revealed during an interview with Lourdes:

Interviewer: "When you're at the head of this small reading group, what goes through your mind? What are you telling yourself?"
Lourdes: "Well, I'm asking myself, "Okay, let's see if he's going to get the words like the sight words 'the' and 'it.' And if he doesn't, then I think, 'Oh, . . . I have to go back and do this. Because if he's the only child, that's not getting it, then I can't put the whole class back.' "

In other cases, teachers monitored students in a manner consistent with responsive teaching, but failed to act on the information they obtained. In some cases, this failure could be traced to implicit beliefs about reading and the consequent need to "do the lesson" and follow a predetermined plan:

Lucy:	"After viewing the lesson, I started thinking, 'What could I have improved or done differently?' First of all, I think the lesson is too long. I shouldn't have asked so many questions. I just think it dragged on and the kids were starting to get bored, a little antsy. So I would have shortened it."
Interviewer:	"Did you feel that way while you were doing the lesson?"
Lucy:	"I did, but like I said, I was determined to finish my lesson plan. Yeah, but now that I'm looking at it, I would have definitely have changed."

Although the preceding patterns characterized the group of teachers as a whole, there were some intriguing differences among teachers as well. To illustrate these differences, we examine more closely the interview responses of two teachers in the following section.

A Comparative Analysis: Christina and Sarah

The data on Christina suggested a strong constructivist orientation to instruction and assessment. Her description of her teaching is very close to what is found in the literature on instructional conversations (Goldenberg, 1992/93; Rueda et al., 1992):

| Christina: | "I try to limit my talking. I try to do more of a Socratic seminar in a way. But my kids haven't reached that point yet. They're able to join in when they want to say something, and I try not to be the only one talking because I want to get a feel for whether they understand. That's my rule. That's my method. Are they comprehending it? If they're not comprehending, how am I going to help them?" |

In describing a lesson, Christina made it plain that she had an overall goal but was not tightly wed to an inflexible script:

| Interviewer: | "When you were planning, how did you go about it?" |
| Christina: | "I didn't think about it. I just . . . I didn't even know who exactly was my group until we got together. So I didn't even have, you know, 'I'm going to ask this kid this question.' No, I just knew what I was going to ask. I knew I had an outcome. But it wasn't, 'Okay, I'm gonna ask Chris this question.' No." |

Another important part of Christina's lessons was making connections to children's background knowledge, a key feature of instructional conversations:

Christina: "I structure it (the lesson). Basically, I always have an objective every time I meet with the kids. This day it was, I want to know: Are they really understanding the setting (of the story) and how the setting is important to the plot of the book? So, we had to talk about the way of life, how it was before. We've researched early man, we've gone into *National Geographic*, because I really want them to get the idea in their head that it's not going to Von's if I'm hungry or going to McDonald's to buy something—it's a whole different way of life. I wanted to know exactly if they're able to, you know, take that information visualizing. And if they're not, how am I going to help them do it?"

How do all these features translate into responsivity during teaching? The following example shows how Christina changed an aspect of a lesson as a result of monitoring:

Interviewer: "Samuel hasn't said anything this whole time." (referring to a student on the videotape).

Christina: "He's usually very verbal, but he's more confident in Spanish. So I'm thinking, 'Okay, I notice he's not answering. What am I going to do to get him to answer or to participate in the conversation?' "

Interviewer: "And what did you work out?"

Christina: "I reformulated a question, and someone brought something up, and I said something, and all of a sudden he got into the group. But, see (at the beginning) how he's just rubbing his face and kind of like, 'Don't call on me.' "

A different pattern was found for Sarah. Interview data suggested that hers was a "mixed" or eclectic orientation. In contrast to Christina, Sarah did not have a well-developed schema for monitoring the responsivity of her lessons, stating: "I'm not sure what I think. I think I worry that the students will not grasp what I want them to grasp." In addition to a relatively more limited awareness of self-monitoring, Sarah's interview showed a concern with managing students' behavior and having students "get it."

In describing how she organized the curriculum in her classroom, Sarah leaned toward a prespecified curriculum and product-based assessment. Unfortunately, these two tendencies apparently led to fewer opportunities for students to engage in instructional conversations and thus fewer opportunities for Sarah to be responsive:

Sarah: "What I do is all that information in the (California state curriculum) Frameworks, especially for language arts, I follow that, and I make sure the students start to read from left to right and they see that constantly. I always read from left to right, and I model so it's becoming like they even do it themselves, and I motivate them to do it. Every time I see one (student do it), I praise him, so everybody wants to do it. So I just follow the framework and the (district) checklist that we have for the kindergarten. And if I see that they're doing it, I usually mark it. So, I have a checklist that I mark for every student and I comment for every student."

Juxtaposition of the data for Christina and Sarah inevitably raised the question what was behind the differences in the thoughts and practices of these two teachers? One intriguing possibility surfaced in Sarah's discussion of her own education:

Sarah: "I went to Mexican schools. It was really hard because they would assess you with exams and it was a lot of like . . . they would give you poetry and you had to write the poetry, memorize the poetry, by not just dictation, but you also had to learn ortografía (spelling). The punctuation had to be perfect, exact, and if you did not do that, it was not your best. It was mostly copy, copy, copy. That was my literacy."

This recitation style of education surfaced later in Sarah's own assessment practices with her students:

Sarah: "I usually test them Mexican style—that's every two chairs and there's no copying, and it's really, I mean it's scary. But I want them to be ready when they go to first grade and they take that (state mandated) test, I want them to be ready for that, and the kids don't do good."

In short, the relatively well-developed schema for monitoring responsivity exhibited by Christina contrasts with the more diffuse and less recognizable schema demonstrated by Sarah. In addition to the fact that she is much less experienced than Christina, Sarah's beliefs appear to be more mixed.

DISCUSSION

The teachers we studied had been engaged in a long-term reflective process regarding their practices, but in many ways they were still at a "transitional" state. Practices seemed to be based not only on theoretically based principles, but also on a combination of relatively theory-free beliefs about "what works" drawn from both intuition and experience.

Why does it appear so difficult to be responsive in teaching interactions? Although most parents interact responsively with their children, Tharp and Gallimore (1989) and others have noted how difficult it is to transfer this style of interaction to the classroom. In comparing home and school classroom teaching styles, Johnson (1993) provided some hints about the difficulties related to teaching responsively:

> First, responsive teaching in a classroom of 30 is much more demanding than responsive teaching with a single child in the home. Given the typically large number of students, the constraints of time and curriculum, and the multiple roles of the classroom teacher, responsive teaching requires exceptional teacher effort. Second, because responsive teaching is more complex in a classroom than in a home, teachers should be formally prepared in the process. Responsive teaching does not evolve naturally and is more difficult to learn than more direct styles of teaching. Finally, recitation, the predominant direct style of teaching, is less psychologically demanding for the teacher (pp. 149–150).

Future research might seek to clarify the factors that mediate practice, such as the type and amount of experience and receptiveness to new ideas, among other factors.

As the interview and other data suggested, all the teachers had positive views of bilingualism and biliteracy. Interestingly, the teachers did not explicitly describe special accommodations for the language-minority students they taught, although all did accommodate language needs in their instruction. In the interviews, there was less variance in this dimension than in other dimensions such as literacy and reading. Perhaps this was because the teachers remained at the school only if they shared the prevailing value system.

We found that the teachers varied in their ability to describe and access their knowledge of the processes they used to monitor their teaching and their students' understanding. In some cases, the teachers appeared to use a template (Faltis, 1990) to monitor their lessons. Although all recognized the desirability of providing responsive learning environments and the need to monitor student learning on an ongoing basis, it was difficult to elaborate a well-articulated strategy or scheme for doing so. Student body language, facial expressions, and answers to questions seemed to be the primary factors that teachers used to gauge student comprehension, understanding, and interest. In almost all cases, the teachers used a "mental portfolio" (Faltis, 1990) to monitor their lessons and evaluate the behavior of individual children.

This attention to student characteristics is in contrast to what Clark and Peterson (1986) have reported in summarizing earlier studies. It may be that this strong tendency to focus on students is related to the fact that these teachers were attempting to practice according to an assisted performance model, albeit imperfectly. That is, these teachers were deliberately trying to be responsive, whereas other teachers in earlier studies were not. This issue remains to be investigated and clarified.

One aspect of responsive teaching is the close monitoring required to assist performance within the learner's zone of proximal development. Although normally not recognized as such, this form of assessment is on-line, ongoing, and intimately tied to instruction. Whereas other studies have examined teachers' thoughts during interactive teaching, none have approached this issue from an assisted performance framework, and none have examined teachers who were systematically trying to become more responsive. This factor may account for the finding that, unlike what has been reported in earlier studies, the teachers in this study were overwhelmingly focused on characteristics of the students and not on pre-planned curricular goals or other factors.

An additional finding was that teachers could not readily describe the strategies or a general "schema" for how monitoring took place in their lessons. It may be that this was because the teaching we observed was for the most part in the middle to low middle range in terms of responsive features. Whereas this is consistent with what we think reflects the reality of much classroom practice, a different view might be obtained by examining only teachers who consistently exhibit highly responsive lessons (Johnson, 1993). Alternatively, it may be that this type of knowledge, by its very nature, is implicit and difficult to access.

Because reading was so distributed in these classrooms, it may have been limiting to focus this study only on responsivity in one type of activity setting, namely small group reading lessons. A more comprehensive study would look at a variety of activity settings. Given the desirability of fostering responsive activity settings for language-minority students, this issue merits further study.

One especially important question has to do with how to foster responsive teaching. Experience in this community and review of the literature suggests that the process is long term and difficult, requiring extensive resources and assisted performance. Others have noted the ineffectiveness of short-term professional development efforts (Cochran-Smith & Lytle, 1992; Darling-Hammond & Ancess, 1996; LaBoskey, 1994; Lieberman & Miller, 1991). Answers to these questions will be critical as schools seek to address more vigorously the educational needs of English-language learners and other students.

ACKNOWLEDGMENTS

This work was prepared with funding from the Office of Educational Research and Improvement (OERI) of the U.S. Department of Education, under Cooperative Agreement No. R117G10022, through the National Center on Cultural Diversity and Second Language Learning at the University of California at Santa Cruz. In addition, part of the writing of this document was supported under the Education Research and Development Program, PR/Award No. R306A60001, The Center for Research on Education, Diversity, and Excellence (CREDE), as administered by the Office of Educational Research and Improvement (OERI), National Institute on the Education of At-Risk Students (NIEARS), U.S. Department of Education (USDOE). The contents, findings, and opinions expressed here are those of the authors and do not necessarily reflect the positions or policies of OERI, NIEARS, or the USDOE. The authors express their appreciation to all the teachers who gave their valuable time in the work reported here, and to Cecilia Fernandez, Simon Kim, Pete Menjares, Lucy Tse, and Jeff McQuillan who helped in data collection and analysis.

REFERENCES

Anthony, R. J., Johnson, T. D., Mickelson, N. I., & Preece, A. (1991). *Evaluating literacy: A perspective for change.* Portsmouth, NH: Heinemann.
Au, K. H. (1993). *Literacy instruction in multicultural settings.* Fort Worth, TX: Harcourt Brace Jovanovich.

Cambourne, B., & Turbill, J. (1994). *Responsive evaluation: Making valid judgements about student literacy*. Portsmouth, NH: Heinemann.

Cazden, C., & Mehan, H. (1990). Principles from sociology and anthropology: Context, code, classroom, and culture. In M. Reynolds (Ed.), *Knowledge base for the beginning teacher* (pp. 47–57). Washington, DC: American Association of Colleges for Teacher Education.

Clark, C. M., & Peterson, P. L. (1986). Teachers' thought processes. In M. C. Wittrock (Ed.), *Handbook of research on teaching*. (3rd ed., pp. 255–296). New York: Macmillan.

Cochran-Smith, M., & Lytle, S. L. (1992). *Inside/outside: Teacher research and knowledge*. New York: Teachers' College Press.

Darling-Hammond, L., & Ancess, J. (1996). Authentic assessment and school development. In J. B. Baron & D. P. Wolf (Eds.), *Performance-based student assessment: Challenges and possibilities*. The Ninety-Fifth Yearbook of the Society for the Study of Education, Part II (pp. 52–83). Chicago: University of Chicago Press.

Dixon-Krauss, L. (1996). *Vygotsky in the classroom: Mediated literacy instruction and assessment*. White Plains, NY: Longman.

Downie, R. S., & Telfer, E. (1970). *Respect for persons*. New York: Schocken Books.

Faltis, C. (1990). New directions in bilingual research design: The study of interactive decision making. In R. Jacobson & C. Faltis (Eds.), *Language distribution issues in bilingual schooling* (pp. 45–57). Clevedon, England: Multilingual Matters.

Florio-Ruane, S., & deTar, J. Conflict and consensus in teacher candidates' discussion of ethnic autobiography. *English Education, 27*(1), 11–39.

Garcia, G. E., & Pearson, P. D. (1994). Assessment and diversity. In L. Darling Hammond (Ed.), *Review of research in education* (Vol. 20, pp. 337–391). Washington DC: American Educational Research Association.

Garmston, R. (1991). Staff developers as social architects. *Educational Leadership: Journal of the Department of Supervision and Curriculum Development, N.E.A., 49*(3), 64.

Goldenberg, C. (1991). *Instructional conversations and their classroom application*. (Educational practice report #2, Center for Cultural Diversity and Second Language Learning). Washington DC: Center for Applied Linguistics.

Goldenberg, C. (1992/93). Instructional conversations: Promoting comprehension through discussion. *The Reading Teacher, 46*, 316–326.

Goodlad, J. (1984). *A place called school*. New York: McGraw-Hill.

Johnson, L. N. (1993). On becoming a responsive teacher: A self-observational process analysis. In M. J. O'Hair & S. J. Odell (Eds.), *Diversity and teaching: Teacher Education Yearbook I* (pp. 138–151). Fort Worth, TX: Harcourt Brace Jovanovich.

LaBoskey, V. K. (1994). *Development of reflective teacher practice: A study of preservice teachers*. New York: Teachers' College Press.

Lidz, C. S. (1991). *Practitioner's guide to dynamic assessment*. New York: Guilford Press.

Lieberman, A., & Miller, L. (1991). *Staff development for education in the '90s: New demands, new realities, new perspectives*. New York: Teachers' College Press.

McLeod, B. (1994). *Language and learning: Educating linguistically diverse students*. Albany: State University of New York Press.

Moll, L. C. (Ed.). (1990). *Vygotsky and education: Instructional implications and applications of sociohistorical psychology*. New York: Cambridge University Press.

Ochs, E., & Schieffelin, B. B. (1984). Language acquisition and socialization: Three developmental stories and their implications. In R. Shweder & R. LeVine (Eds.), *Culture theory: Essays on mind, self, and emotion* (pp. 276–320). New York: Cambridge University Press.

Pajares, M. (1992). Teachers' beliefs and educational research: Cleaning up a messy construct. *Review of Educational Research, 62*(3), 307–332.

Rogoff, B. (1994). Developing understanding of the idea of communities of learners. *Mind, Culture, and Activity, 1*(4), 209–229.

Rueda, R., & Garcia, E. (1995). *Responsivity and assessment: A study of one community of practice (final report)*. Santa Cruz, CA: National Center for Cultural Diversity and Second Language Learning.

Rueda, R., & Garcia, E. (1996). Teachers' perspectives on assessment and instruction with language-minority students: A comparative study. *Elementary School Journal, 96*(3), 311–332.

Rueda, R., Goldenberg, C., & Gallimore, R. (1992). *Rating instructional conversations: A guide.* (Educational Practice Report #3, Center for Cultural Diversity and Second Language Learning). Washington DC: Center for Applied Linguistics.

Shavelson, R. J., & Stern, P. (1981). Research on teachers' pedagogical thoughts, judgements, decisions, and behavior. *Review of Educational Research, 51*, 455–498.

Sleeter, C. E. (1987). Definitions of learning disabilities, literacy, and social control. In B. Franklin (Ed.), *Learning disability: Dissenting essays* (pp. 67–87). Barcombe, England: Falmer Press.

Sprague, M. M., & Makibbin, S. S. (1994). Study groups: A conduit for change in education. *Contemporary Education, 2*, 99–103.

Tharp, R. (1989). Psychocultural variables and constants: Effects on teaching and learning in schools. *American Psychologist, 44*, 349–359.

Tharp, R., & Gallimore, R. (1989). *Rousing minds to life: Teaching, learning, and schooling in social context.* New York: Cambridge University Press.

Trueba, H. (1987). *Success or failure?: Learning and the language minority student.* New York: Newbury House/Harper & Row.

Valencia, S. W., Hiebert, E., & Afflerbach, P. (Eds.). (1994). *Authentic reading assessment: Practices and possibilities.* Newark, DE: International Reading Association.

11

The Implementation of a Multicultural Literacy Program in Fourth- and Fifth-Grade Classrooms

Margaret A. Moore-Hart
Barbara J. Diamond
John R. Knapp
Eastern Michigan University

I have two students this year who were nonreaders when they entered the class. Now look at them; they both are reading on a fourth-grade level. I can't keep these books out of their hands. . . . It's like the secret to reading has been unlocked. This program is really working.

This is a quote from a teacher who is participating in a multicultural literacy program in Southeast Michigan. He perceives a dramatic improvement in his African American students' reading and writing performance, which he links to this multicultural program. Many teachers and parents, however, continue to see evidence of widespread patterns of failure among students in poverty. Others are concerned that the gap between the school literacy achievement of students who are culturally and linguistically diverse and those who are European American has widened (Au, 1998; Ladson-Billings, 1994). As the number of these students increases in our schools, the expectation that our educational system will meet their needs also increases significantly. In their article, Reyhnor and Garcia (1989) accentuated the issue:

For more than two centuries people from divergent cultures and nations have migrated to the United States seeking the promise of opportunity. Now children from divergent cultures and languages come to our classroom seeking the self-same promise of opportunity. (p. 85)

223

Helping these students become successful readers and writers remains one of the greatest challenges schools face.

In addition to these challenges, educators are confronted with the need to help tomorrow's citizens acquire the knowledge, skills, and attitudes critical to functioning and interacting with people from varied cultures and backgrounds in our global society. Banks (1994) emphasized that education should encourage students to accept and be sensitive to cultural diversity, to understand that similar values frequently underlie different customs, to have quality contact with people from other cultures, and to role play experiences involving people from other cultures.

MULTICULTURAL LITERACY: WHAT RESEARCH SAYS

Many educators are realizing the need to address these complex issues as the demographics of our classrooms begin to shift in schools throughout our nation. The Holmes Group (1990) asserted that "schools need to do a much better job of building on students' own cultural capital" (p. 11). This group stresses that teachers must become more thoughtful about culture, "cherishing and building on the webs of meaning and value and community that students bring to school" (p. 11). Schools are seen as building bridges between traditional academic culture, the culture of students, and world culture.

Other researchers have suggested that there is a link between culture and achievement. Their studies emphasize that improvements in learning, including basic skills, can be expected when instruction is compatible with home culture patterns (Au, 1993; Banks, 1994; Delpit, 1995; Vogt, Jordan, & Tharp, 1987). Cummins (1986) and Campos and Keatinge (1984) reported that the extent to which students' language and culture are incorporated into the school program constitutes a significant predictor of academic success. In reading instruction, for example, students' life experiences and cultural background knowledge influence the degree of comprehension and memory that they achieve (Lipson, 1983; Steffensen, Joag-Dev, & Anderson, 1979). The essence of students' prior experience and culture—their ways of interacting, communicating, celebrating and experiencing life—combines to form their initial understanding of the world.

Creating cultural compatibility requires schools to provide curricula that reflect the diverse racial and cultural groups in our society (Au, 1993; Banks, 1994; Delpit, 1995; Hoffman, 1996; Sleeter & Grant,

1994). According to the claim of several researchers, when students encounter literature that includes characters, settings, and themes that resonate with their prior experiences, they attain higher levels of reading and writing performance (Bishop, 1987; Moore & Diamond, 1990). Similarly, once students perceive connections between their own histories, experiences, and the curriculum, their ability to relate to new subjects is improved (Au, 1993, 1995; Beiger, 1995/1996; McDiarmid, 1993). Bishop (1987) further claimed that multicultural reading materials improve the self-esteem of culturally diverse students as they discover and develop pride in their cultural heritage.

Importantly, Bishop (1987, 1992) added that multicultural reading materials sharpen students' sensitivity to the commonalities of human experience. Once learners become aware of other cultures, their understanding and appreciation of their own culture and its relation to other cultures becomes heightened (Au, 1995; Florez & Hadaway, 1986; Norton, 1991; Purves, 1994). Thus, a starting point for understanding and appreciation of the varied cultures that comprise our society emerges from multicultural literature. One avenue for exploring cultures in more depth and broadening cultural knowledge is through the content areas such as history, geography, or science (Diamond & Moore, 1995).

To create a deep, reflective understanding of culture, Hoffman (1996) and Banks (1994) cautioned that culture should not be artificially inserted into the curriculum. Students need to acquire a knowledge base from which to look at culture through genuine learning experiences. Hoffman (1996) also emphasized that there is a need to develop culturally responsive teaching activities and to identify source materials so teachers can form a basis for learning together with culturally diverse students.

Other researchers (Cohen & Swain, 1976; Cummins, 1986; Diamond & Moore, 1995) have suggested that the social organization of teaching, learning, and performance play an important role in the achievement of economically challenged and culturally and linguistically diverse students. They have stated that schools need to reconsider their traditional ways of structuring classrooms and opportunities for learning. Small group arrangements, which encourage interaction and cooperation while deemphasizing competition, appear to improve reading and writing performances of many racially and culturally diverse students. Still other researchers (Cohen, 1987; Stevens & Slavin, 1995; Stevens, Slavin, & Farnish, 1991; Stevens, Madden, Slavin, & Farnish, 1987) have found that students achieve better in cooperative learning environments that include mixed ability levels. Studies also have suggested that reading and writing instruction that permits students to collaborate, discuss, and interpret texts results in dramatic improvements in both reading and verbal intellectual abilities (Au, 1993, 1995; Cummins, 1986).

If we are to address the needs of linguistically and culturally diverse students, we need to redefine our educational systems and the roles of our educators (Au, 1993; Cummins, 1986). In his investigation of programs designed to reverse the pattern of school failure among culturally and linguistically diverse students, Cummins (1986) reported that intervention programs do not consistently demonstrate patterns of success for these students. Supplying teachers with new curricula developed by national experts or offering periodic in-service workshops seldom leads to substantial long-term improvement (Pisano & Tallerico, 1990). In fact, researchers have reported that instructional programs often are not faithfully implemented (Alvermann & Ridgeway, 1990; Hall, 1979; Routman, 1994).

In their review of staff development programs, Sparks and Simmons (1989) emphasized that teachers need to know more than how to use particular strategies; they need to know how to modify the strategy to meet the diverse needs of their students. Other researchers have stressed the importance of (a) a supportive context or environment that identifies the needs and concerns of teachers, and (b) support, guidance, and assistance to overcome these needs and concerns (Conley & Tripp-Opple, 1990; Hall, 1979).

The Concerns-Based Adoption Model (CBAM) provides an effective evaluation tool for monitoring program implementation and staff development. The CBAM defines program components by identifying teachers' concerns and needs (Diamond & Moore, 1995; Hall, 1979; Hall & Hord, 1987; Hall & Loucks, 1977; Hord, Rutherford, Austin, & Hall, 1987). After a framework has been constructed for program implementation, ongoing evaluation procedures become tools for modifying and changing the program to meet the ongoing needs and concerns of the community, classroom, and students. By using diagnostic tools, including tools to determine teachers' needs and concerns (Stages of Concerns Questionnaire) (Newlove & Hall, 1976) and their level of use (Levels of Use Interview) (Loucks, Newlove, & Hall, 1975), personnel can decide how to use resources and how to provide intervention strategies that smooth the implementation process, accommodate ongoing needs and concerns, and minimize innovation-related frustrations (Hall & Hord, 1987; Hord et al., 1987). Monitoring implementation of the program is critical if changes in students' behaviors are to be attributed to the treatment condition (Hall, 1979; Hord et al., 1987). According to Hall

(1979), gains in student achievement cannot be expected if a program is not being implemented as designed.

Currently, only a few existing programs have been designed specifically to achieve cultural compatibility and cultural understanding and appreciation. Despite growing support for educators to address the achievement gap of culturally and linguistically diverse students and those who live in poverty, only a few researchers have evaluated the effects of these programs on literacy learning. To address these critical issues, as university professors, we collaborated with public school teachers in two school districts to implement a multicultural literacy program. Specifically, we designed the program to (a) improve the educational achievement of culturally and linguistically diverse learners and students who live in poverty, (b) heighten the cultural awareness and understanding of all students, and (c) provide enrichment opportunities for all students.

OVERVIEW OF THE MULTICULTURAL LITERACY PROGRAM

The multicultural literacy program (MLP)[1] is based on current literacy research that highlights the need to foster compatibility between students' cultural and linguistic backgrounds and their academic achievement (Au, 1993; Banks, 1994; Hoffman, 1996). We designed the program to provide a variety of literacy experiences that emerged from our students' language and cultural backgrounds. The program components, implemented in fourth- and fifth-grade classrooms included the use of multicultural literature as reading instructional materials and a whole language perspective on teaching, using varied grouping patterns, an integrated curriculum approach, instruction that moves from whole to part to whole, and reading and writing as constructive processes. We defined multicultural literature as literature that focuses on specific cultures by highlighting and celebrating historical perspectives, traditions and heritage, language and dialects, and experiences and lifestyles (Diamond & Moore, 1995).

The MLP was implemented by teachers 2 days a week for 90 minutes during the allotted reading time, for a total of 180 minutes per week, beginning in September and culminating in May. To assist teachers in lesson development and implementation, we provided them with an MLP Manual, which included lesson guidelines, cultural resources, project in-

---

[1]The MLP was funded through the Fund for the Improvement and Reform of School and Teachers (FIRST), United States Department of Education for 3 years. The program later became part of the National Diffusion Network, United States Department of Education.

formation, and a core classroom set of 20 multicultural books (see list in Appendix A). In addition, we established a library of multicultural books at the university, available to teachers on request. To support a positive environment for diverse learners, the instruction context for the MLP was whole class instruction, cooperative learning, and paired configurations. The traditional reading program, as prescribed in the teachers' reading manuals, was used during the remaining 3 days of instruction.

More specifically, in both fourth- and fifth-grade classrooms, the teachers implemented the MLP using the following procedures:

- Teachers read a multicultural literature selection from their classroom library collection of books or the MLP library at the university. As teachers read the book interactively, they engaged students in discussions by drawing on their personal and cultural experiences and their background knowledge and by highlighting specific cultural themes embedded in the text. In cases wherein students read the selections themselves, teachers used modified models of cooperative learning in which students of varying abilities read together. Importantly, students read real literature instead of reading stories in their basal readers or merely completing skill sheets.

- Teachers assisted students in developing vocabulary skills, language skills, fluency, comprehension strategies, and cultural knowledge through modeling and interactive discussions about the text and its cultural elements. They linked these skills to meaningful, purposeful reading and writing activities linked to the culture and linguistic backgrounds of students.

- Teachers engaged students in multicultural literacy activities to reinforce learning through writing process activities, as well as paired and repeated reading activities, dramatic and choral reading activities, and storytelling activities.

- Teachers highlighted cultural understanding through written, oral, and artistic expression activities. They led discussions about the text and its cultural elements, highlighting connections between students' life experiences and those of characters in the text.

- Teachers integrated multicultural reading and writing activities with mathematics, art, science, social studies, and music so that students might see the relations among literacy learning, their daily life, and their cultural heritage.

- Teachers provided opportunities for students to interact with poets, musicians, artists, and storytellers in the community from diverse backgrounds.

Finally, to achieve the goals of the MLP, teachers attended five in-service workshops to acquire specific methods for implementing the MLP in their classrooms. We also scheduled classroom visitations with our teachers twice a month to support them in the implementation of the program.

PURPOSE OF THE STUDY

In this chapter, we examine the implementation of a multicultural program and its effect on reading and writing performance, and on attitudes toward reading, writing, and other cultures during two academic school years. The major objectives of our study were twofold. Our first objective was to determine whether the MLP was being implemented as designed. Our second objective was to determine whether students using the program improved their attitudes toward their culture and the cultures of others, and improved their reading comprehension and vocabulary more than students using traditional reading programs. Specifically, our research questions included the following:

What are the levels of use (Loucks, Newlove, & Hall, 1979) of the multicultural program for the treatment teachers?

What are the stages of concerns (Newlove & Hall, 1976) of the multicultural program for the treatment teachers?

Do groups of students using a multicultural literature program improve their attitudes toward their culture and the culture of others more than groups of students using traditional reading texts?

Do groups of students using a multicultural literature program improve their reading comprehension and vocabulary achievement scores more than groups of students using traditional reading texts?

STUDY METHODS

Profiles of the Two Participating School Districts

The population for the study consisted of fourth- and fifth-grade students and their teachers from two school districts in southeast Michigan. School district A was a racially balanced, economically varied population whose academic performance was diversified, with a large number of below average students. Specifically, 48% of the students were African

American; 50% were European American; and 2% were from other cultures. The school district further reported that 36% of the students received free or reduced lunches. Results from the California Achievement Test (CAT) indicated that 32% of the students fell at or below the 25th percentile in reading achievement.

In contrast, School district B was a predominantly European American, economically sufficient population whose academic performance was ranked as educationally advantaged, with a small number of below average students. Specifically, 86% of the students were European American; 9% were African American; and 5% were from other cultures. The school district further reported that 8% of the students received free or reduced-price lunches. Results from the CAT indicated that 8% of the students fell at or below the 25th percentile in reading achievement.

To paint a more complete picture of how the MLP affected student attitudes toward culture, we obtained a subsample of students to be studied in more depth. Teachers in the treatment group selected three students from their class to represent high-, average-, and low-ability students.

Design of the Study

We followed a pretest–posttest, quasi-experimental design. For the study, 20 fourth- and fifth-grade classes and their teachers were assigned to a treatment or comparison group using standard techniques for matching classes. Specifically, we followed the following steps:

1. Through interviews with administrators, principals, and teachers, we identified specific classes and the teachers to compose the treatment group.

2. To minimize treatment diffusion, the specific classes and teachers in the treatment group were located in different schools than the classes and the teachers in the comparison group.

3. We next identified the specific classes and their teachers to form the comparison group. With the assistance of school administrators, we established comparability of the groups on the following critical variables: (a) achievement level as measured by the mean scaled score of the CAT Total Reading Performance subtest, (b) grade level of the students, (c) number of years of experience of teachers, (d) percentage of students receiving federally subsidized school lunch programs, and (e) percentage of culturally diverse students.

Significantly, comparison group teachers from year 1 became part of the expanded treatment group during year 2. New teachers were added to the comparison group using the aforementioned process. These teachers could then become part of the expanded treatment group during year 3.

Working With the Treatment and Comparison Group Teachers

During years 1 and 2 of the study, fourth- and fifth-grade teachers in both the treatment and comparison groups received in-service instruction on current reading and writing strategies by district personnel or consultants.

In-service Sessions for the Treatment Group Teachers. During year 1, 10 pilot teachers in the treatment group received 5 days of in-service instruction spaced throughout the school year to meet teachers' ongoing concerns, needs, and interests. Our in-service sessions focused on the development of teachers' understanding of cultures; the undergirding principles, goals, and philosophy of the MLP; and methods and techniques of integrating multicultural literature and specific literacy activities into the reading program.

After the first day of in-service instruction, teachers began implementing the MLP in their classrooms, guided by the information gained from the in-service sessions and the MLP Manual, which included lesson guidelines, cultural resources, and project information. In addition to the five in-service days, we scheduled bimonthly visits to teachers' classrooms, beginning in October and culminating in May of each year, at times convenient to the teachers. We designed the visits to provide teacher assistance, guidance, and constructive feedback as they implemented the project activities in their classrooms. During these visits, we modeled and demonstrated lessons they wanted to see firsthand, or we cotaught lessons with the teachers, coaching them about various classroom management strategies and instructional techniques that incorporate cultural themes, heighten cultural understanding, or optimize literacy learning. Over time, we collaborated with our teachers, planning lessons to correlate with their curriculum and working together as a team to implement multicultural activities in their classrooms.

Similarly, during year 2, 29 new teachers in the treatment group received 5 days of in-service instruction and bimonthly visits to their classrooms. Brief descriptions of the in-service sessions are included in the following sections:

First In-service Session. We introduced teachers to the principles of the program and provided opportunities for them to learn about each other through an interview process using biopoems. After these activities, we shared multicultural books that affirmed all people and shared additional books and literacy activities that highlighted cultural themes (*Cornrows* and *Flossie the Fox*). Data from teachers also were collected, using the Stages of Concern Questionnaire, which is part of the CBAM.

Second In-service Session.   We focused on ways to promote cultural understanding by modeling how to compare several books that had similar themes, but were from different cultures. We also provided opportunities for teachers to express their concerns and successes in program implementation. Teachers further learned how to promote student fluency by using readers' theater and choral readings with several books. Finally, we focused on methods for integrating biographies of figures from various cultural backgrounds into the social studies and science curricula.

Third In-service Session.   At the beginning of the session, working in small groups, teachers shared the progress they had made toward project goals. Next, we modeled strategies for cooperative learning and ways to manage group activities within the framework of the program. For the literacy activity, we demonstrated how to highlight character and plot development and how to integrate reading, writing, discussion, and notetaking with the social studies curriculum using multicultural literature. Finally, a Chinese American from the Chinese Cultural Center provided information and resources about her culture. After her presentation, we discussed how the teachers might invite culturally diverse parents, poets, musicians, or artists to their classrooms to help students increase their cultural knowledge.

Fourth In-service Session.   In this session, we refocused on the principles of the MLP and provided cultural knowledge about specific cultural groups (African American, Hispanic American), reinforcing the idea that teachers should use this knowledge to highlight themes in multicultural literature selections. We also modeled the revision process and other writing activities that could be incorporated into the program.

Fifth In-service Session.   After teachers shared the knowledge they had gained from program implementation during the year, we reflected on modifications to be made in the program for the next year. Following this discussion and reflection, we highlighted ways to use storytelling and poetry to promote cultural understanding. Finally, teachers brainstormed ways to organize the program to meet their teaching styles and the needs of their students.

Year 2 In-service Sessions for the Pilot Teachers. To help pilot teachers implement the program successfully during the second year, we planned three in-service sessions over the year. These in-service sessions gave teachers opportunities to share and collaborate with one another as they extended and developed the program in their classes. Two teachers, for example, shared how they were integrating a Native American thematic unit across the content areas. We also modeled additional reading and writing strategies that could be used with the multicultural books to extend students' cultural knowledge. Finally, we invited culturally diverse people to our sessions to share their cultural heritage and traditions with the teachers. Importantly, pilot teachers received monthly visits to their classrooms.

In-service Sessions for the Comparison Group Teachers. In contrast, teachers in the comparison group received 3 days of in-service instruction conducted by district personnel and consultants on current reading and writing strategies, including the whole language philosophy. Informal observations by the researchers and consultations with district administrators and principals showed that most of the comparison teachers followed the traditional basal-oriented reading program 5 days a week. Typically, teachers provided instruction in phonics, comprehension, or word recognition skills by following the teacher's manual that accompanied the basal reading program. They further guided the oral reading of a story, asked questions about the story, and assisted students as they completed worksheets or workbook activities, which were part of their basal reading program.

A few teachers also used literature with their reading program. These teachers usually read a novel as a class. The students then completed work sheets, which were usually materials prepared commercially to accompany the selected novel. The worksheets focused primarily on skills and comprehension questions. A few teachers used multicultural literature, but only to the extent that it was included in their reading series. If writing instruction was provided during the language arts program, it evolved from exercises in the spelling manual or grammar manual. Students seldom wrote creative stories or poems. Journal writing was seldom used, and the writing process was not emphasized.

Grouping procedures used by these teachers primarily included whole class and homogeneous ability groups. In some schools, students from each grade level were grouped into three groups (high, medium, and low ability groups) within their class. In other schools, students were grouped according to ability within their grade level. Students of similar abilities then met with an assigned teacher during the reading block.

The comparison group teachers, however, were not given instruction on ways to integrate multicultural literature with their traditional, basal-oriented reading program or strategies to promote cultural understanding or extend cultural knowledge.

Instructional Materials

The materials for the MLP included multicultural books (see Appendix A for a selected sample of multicultural books), the MLP Manual, and reading texts. The MLP Manual included various literacy activities that we developed to be used with the multicultural books (see Appendix B for an example). We designed these activities, which were modeled and practiced during the in-service sessions, to serve as a catalyst or source for new ideas that teachers could develop with other multicultural books.

Viewing multicultural literature as literature about groups who typically are underrepresented or inaccurately or negatively portrayed, we identified specific multicultural books as primary to the collection of books used in the program. Therefore, the multicultural books included selections from the African American, Arab American, Asian American, Hispanic American, and Native American cultures, as well as books from the homelands of these cultures, whenever appropriate. In addition, we included a small collection of books from the European American culture for cultural comparison purposes. We further developed guidelines for selection of multicultural books based on authenticity of cultural representation as identified by characters, settings, themes, and language patterns (Diamond & Moore, 1995) and other noted sources of multicultural bibliographies (Bishop, 1992; Harris, 1991; Norton, 1991).

Data Sources

The data collection period extended from September 1989 to May 1991. Program implementation measures included Levels of Use Interview (Hall & Loucks, 1977; Loucks, Newlove, & Hall, 1975), CBAM Questionnaire (Newlove & Hall, 1976), and informal observations.

The cultural attitude measures included (a) student interviews conducted in April, 1990 and April, 1991, and (b) pre- and postculture attitude measures (We obtained pretest measures in September, 1989, and posttest data in May, 1990 and May, 1991.) Because a review of related research did not reveal an existing cultural attitude survey, we designed the cultural survey, which consisted of 19 items to which the participant responded, using a 4-point rating scale: 1 (never), 2 (hardly ever), 3 (sometimes), 4 (often). Items were summed to yield a total score. Coefficient alpha based on the data was found to be .77, an acceptable level of internal consistency. Questions included such examples as "I enjoy talking about how people from other countries think and feel"; "I need to learn about the ideas and beliefs of people from different ethnic and racial backgrounds"; and "I get upset when I read about people from other countries and cultures."

Specific literacy measures included pre- and postreading as well as pre- and postvocabulary CAT measures. We obtained pre- and posttest data on reading and vocabulary CAT measures in April of each school year. (Pretest data in 1989 were obtained before the study in April, 1989.)

EVALUATION OF THE MULTICULTURAL LITERACY PROGRAM

Investigating the Processes of Program Implementation: Years 1 and 2

To determine the extent to which the innovative program was implemented as designed during years 1 and 2, we examined the behaviors and characteristics of the teachers involved through Levels of Use Interview, CBAM Questionnaire, and informal observations.

Teachers' Implementation of the MLP.   The results of the teacher Levels of Use Interview conducted by a trained consultant showed that at the end of year 1, nine of the ten pilot teachers were at Level IVA, a Routine Level of Use (at which users are comfortable with the program, but make few changes in the innovation), and one teacher was at Level IVB, a Refinement Level of Use (at which users vary the innovation to increase its impact on student learning). Specifically, nine of the teachers were comfortable with the program, making minimal changes or modifications in the program to improve students' performance. They followed the lessons in the manual without making adjustments to match the needs of their students or their classrooms. In contrast, the teacher who was at the Refinement Level of Use began to adjust the program to increase her students' learning. For example, she shared the following:

> I don't feel like if I decide to do something that they have suggested in the manual that I have to follow every little step in there. I can make any changes in this . . . knowing my own classroom. There are certain things that they may suggest to do—something I know is not going to work. Sometimes I can see that something else will work better.

In his report, the consultant further added that all the teachers were very enthusiastic and comfortable with the program.

At the end of year 2, the findings indicated that five of the nine pilot teachers (one teacher retired at the end of year 1) were at Level IVA, a Routine Level of Use, and four teachers were at Level IVB, a Refinement Level of Use. Teachers at the refinement level made the following comments:

> The strength of the program is learning all different kinds of strategies and being able to use them not only with multicultural books, but any books I open up and read in my class.

> This multicultural program has allowed us to not only be exposed to a structured program, but also allowed us to be creative, and also allowed our students to be creative, and they really enjoy this program.

The consultant also explained that although it was premature to rate some of the teachers at Level V, Integration (at which users plan specific actions to share the innovation with others), many teachers were beginning to share the program with others in their school, and to encourage others to become involved across their school district.

In addition, the findings suggested that 21 of the 29 teachers new to the program this year were at Level IVA, and that 8 of the new teachers were at Level IVB. The consultant further commented:

> In the 15 years, I have been interviewing over 200 teachers across the country who have implemented over a dozen different innovations, I have never encountered the level of enthusiasm, understanding, and commitment to a project as I have with this multicultural program. . . . In addition, teachers believe that their students are improving their reading speed and comprehension, reading more, enhancing their writing performance, and gaining greater understanding and appreciation of other than Euro-American culture.

Teachers' Comfort With the MLP. The results of the CBAM Questionnaire showed that the pilot teachers progressed from Personal and Informational Stages of Concern in the fall of 1989, to Management and Consequences Stages of Concern in the fall of 1990, to Management, Consequences, Collaboration, and Refocusing Stages of Concern in the fall of 1991. Specifically, at the beginning of the year, teachers had many self-concerns at the Informational and Personal Stages of Concern. Examples of comments reflecting self-concerns included the following: "My self-confidence is low. Please help"; "I would like to see some modeling before I try it myself"; and "I am concerned about learning how to implement a good MLP that includes both the reading and writing involvement." A few teachers also had task and management concerns. For example, they stated: "I feel a lack of materials for use in the classroom," or "Time and materials are a problem."

At the beginning of year 2 (fall, 1990), the concerns shifted to the Consequence Stages of Concern (concerns related to the impact of the innovation on student learning). Examples of impact-related concerns included the following: "I am hoping my students will make great gains from using this program," and "I am concerned about leaving out a culture that might be beneficial to my students."

The following fall (1991), teachers' concerns progressed to the Collaboration (a focus on ways to share the innovation with others) and Refocusing (a focus on modifying the innovation) Stages of Concern. For example, teachers were interested in collaborating with others in their school or school district. They commented, "I am concerned that the program will not be continued in the next grade," or "It would be very helpful to categorize the books per grade level by the different cultures." Other concerns included ideas for refining or modifying the program at the Refocusing Stage of Concern. For example, one teacher said, "I am concerned about putting the computer into use with the multicultural program more."

Table 11.1 displays the number of responses at each Stage of Concern for the pilot teachers and new teachers during years 1 and 2 of the MLP. The findings showed that the 29 new teachers in year 2 progressed from Personal, Informational, and Management Stages of Concern in the fall

TABLE 11.1
Number of Unit Responses at the Time of Administration
for Pilot and New Teachers at Each Stage of Concern

| Stages of Concern | Time of Administration | | | | |
| | Fall 1989 | Fall 1990 | | Fall 1991 | |
	Pilot	Pilot	New	Pilot	New
Awareness	0	0	0	0	0
Informational	4	0	6	0	0
Personal	7	0	35	0	0
Management	8	5	28	4	15
Consequence	4	12	10	10	30
Collaboration	0	1	0	3	4
Refocusing	0	0	0	2	9

of 1990, to Management, Consequences, and Collaboration Stages of Concern in the fall of 1991. Interestingly, many of the second-year teachers progressed to higher stages of concern more quickly than the pilot teachers. Their self and management concerns shifted from "I need to learn more about the cultures," or "How much time out of the classroom will this program entail?" to impact-related and collaborative concerns in the fall of their second year. Examples of their concerns in the fall of 1991 included the following: "I am concerned about helping my students to learn and appreciate the differences between people," or "When I think about the MLP, I am concerned that not enough people are exposed."

Informal Observations of Teachers. To gain more information about teacher implementation of the MLP, informal observations were obtained from multiple sources including the authors, principals, curriculum supervisors, and project staff. Data consistently showed that teachers were implementing the MLP in their classrooms and using the strategies and activities modeled during their in-service sessions. In one classroom, after reading several Japanese folk tales, a teacher invited her sister-in-law to her class to share Japanese artifacts, clothing, and food with her students. Two days later, another friend visited her class to show the children how to write their names in Japanese.

As the school year continued, teachers brought examples of activities they were doing in their classrooms to the in-service sessions. This inspired others to try similar cultural activities in their own classrooms. For example, after two teachers shared how they had developed a thematic unit on Native Americans, we saw other teachers using the ideas to begin a similar thematic unit in their classrooms.

As teachers continued to design multicultural activities in their own classrooms and to share their ideas with others at our in-service sessions, their understandings of the purpose and need for a multicultural program seemed to increase. In visiting their classrooms, we saw them using note-taking strategies more frequently with their students while reading informational stories about Kenya, China, or the Navajo people. We saw other teachers leading students in discussions that compared and contrasted their own culture with the cultures of stories they read. Together, teachers and students in many classrooms investigated the cultural histories and traditions of others in more depth, using informational books, films, or videos. Teachers also began to explore the cultures of others through dramatizations or artistic and musical avenues by inviting culturally diverse musicians, poets, or artists to their classes.

Over time, teachers grew in their understanding of how to work with students from diverse cultures. For example, they became more comfortable using cooperative learning activities as students chorally read multicultural stories or practiced a reader's theater. Many teachers used paired reading activities. One teacher even had her students use paired reading to practice the reading of stories with first graders the next week.

Principals and curriculum supervisors also visited the classrooms of teachers participating in the MLP. They were impressed by the teachers' enthusiasm with the program, noting that the teachers were learning to innovate, adapt, and determine teaching lessons that met the diverse needs of their students. While visiting a school, one principal exclaimed, "The program is having a tremendous impact on our students. They are reading and writing more." They further commented that the classroom visits seemed to help teachers feel more secure and comfortable with the teaching strategies and to reinforce their understanding of how to implement the strategies. Without these visits, they speculated that teachers might continue using traditional teaching practices.

Principals also commented that teachers were beginning to share the strategies and activities with other teachers in their building. Some principals reported that the MLP teachers conducted in-service sessions in their own schools during the second year. For example, one principal commented: "The response by the teachers has been tremendous. They have been excited and frequently shared their experiences informally with other teachers and through presentations to building staff and at conferences." Curriculum supervisors similarly noted that teachers presented multicultural activities designed by them at local, state, and national conferences during year 2. One supervisor explained, "I have not observed a program with more potential than the multicultural literature reading program. It is having a long-lasting impact on the way people teach in our elementary schools."

Investigating the Impact of the MLP on Student Behaviors

To examine the effects of the MLP on students' cultural attitudes, reading comprehension, and vocabulary development, we used analysis of variance (ANOVA) techniques on the gains from pretreatment to posttreatment scores. (This is equivalent to a two-factor ANOVA, with groups being a between factor and occasions being a repeated measures factor.) We combined the cultural attitude data from the two districts, but because the districts differed markedly in the literacy achievement measures, we analyzed these measures separately for each district.

It should be noted that sample sizes for the various analyses varied because only participants who had both pre- and postmeasures were used. It also is important to note that the treatment condition for year 2 contained students who participated in the MLP during year 1 and new students who participate in the MLP during year 2. Similarly, the comparison condition for year 2 contained students who were in the comparison group during year 1 and new students who were in the comparison group during year 2.

Impact of the MLP on Student Cultural Attitudes. Analysis of the data comparing treatment and comparison conditions indicated that more favorable attitudes toward culture increased in the treatment group, but decreased in the comparison group, leading to a significant treatment effect ($F[1, 296] = 4.95$; $p < .03$) during year 1 of the program. The results of the analyses did not suggest, however, significant differences in the gain scores in year 2, although the gain scores for students using the multicultural program were higher than for those using the traditional reading program (Table 11.2).

To provide a richer, more descriptive source of data, and to gain more insight into the impact of the program on students' cultural knowledge and understanding in the two school districts, student interviews ($n = 30$) were administered to high-, middle- and low-ability students in the pilot classrooms in April, 1990, and April, 1991. Responses to each question were read and reread. Similar responses were clustered and categorized. The students' responses clustered into five categories: 1 (don't know), 2 (everyday living activities), 3 (thoughts, feelings, and beliefs), 4 (differences between their own culture and the culture of others), and 5 (general knowledge about a culture). Responses in 1990 were short and

TABLE 11.2

Posttest and Gain Score Means (M) and Standard Deviations (SD)
on Cultural Attitude Measures for Years 1 and 2

	Treatment		Comparison	
	Posttest	Gain	Posttest	Gain
Year 1	(n = 150)		(n = 148)	
M	64.49	1.43	62.89	−0.62
SD	7.67	7.87	7.45	8.01
Year 2	(n = 658)		(n = 132)	
M	64.99	5.6	63.39	4.52
SD	8.08	11.10	6.62	9.41

Note: The large number of treatment students in year 2 is explained by the fact that the comparison group teachers in year 1 and their new students in year 2 became part of the treatment group.

superficial. Some students merely responded, "Don't know," whereas others replied, "To learn about others."

Responses in 1991 consistently showed more in-depth replies, including more details and examples, demonstrating that students' cultural knowledge and understanding expanded and developed over time. The responses from the second year further indicated a decrease in the number of students responding, "Don't know," and an increase in the number of students providing details about their understanding of cultures. In addition, students were able to articulate their knowledge about the thoughts, feelings, and beliefs of people of other cultures. Representative comments included the following: "I learned about Ghana and Egypt, countries in Africa, and a fruit called papyrus and how they learned how to make paper from it"; "I like talking about Black people and how my family lived back then"; "We learned about Japan when we read *Sadako and the Thousand Paper Cranes*. We learned that a lot of things are different there. They put good luck signs on their doors; they leave food for the spirits. The people that died from the atom bomb, that's a lot different (celebration) than we do here on Memorial Day"; or "The stories in my reading book don't tell me about different cultures, and the ones from the cultural program tell you a lot about your culture and that helps me . . . like we had a project in which we had to find out what our names mean, and that helped me a lot. My name means love."

Comparisons of students of different ability levels on the 1990 interviews indicated that students' responses at all ability levels showed a heightened awareness of diverse cultures. The responses of lower ability students, however, reflected generalized statements about cultures, whereas the responses of higher ability students exhibited more details and more insightful understanding of cultures. For example, when asked why it is important to learn about cultures, one lower ability student commented, "To know things they do and stuff." Responding to the same question, a higher ability student shared, "If you don't know their culture, just say a person from Mexico came to live at your house, you wouldn't know how to talk to them or treat them because you want to make them feel at home."

At the end of the second year, responses for both ability levels showed the use of more details and examples. Similar to the findings for the first year, the responses of higher ability students exhibited more details and examples and more perception about the issues related to cultures. Representative comments of higher ability students included the following:

So you know about them and so you don't go off in life and say they are dumb because they are not like us. They have their own culture and were brought up a different way. They shouldn't feel bad about it because they have many talents.

So when you're older you won't be prejudiced. Like if they miss school for a couple of weeks or monthly you'll understand why because it has to do with one of their religions and be able to respect them and their cultures.

Well, I learned about the Chinese culture and Indians . . . Native Americans and Indian and Japanese . . . and I think African. I learned what their stories are . . . their background and some of how they are today, what they believe in . . . what their beliefs are.

In comparison, representative comments of lower ability students included the following:

Because you might learn about another person who is in that other culture, to know how to treat them.

So people won't think you're just stuck on your culture.

I can learn more about my race and my heritage.

Impact of the MLP on Literacy Measures for the Students in School District A.   Table 11.3 presents the means and standard deviations for posttest and gain scores on reading and vocabulary measures for District A. For year 1, there were no significant differences on the gain scores for students using the multicultural program, as compared with the gain scores for students using the traditional reading program. Whereas the gain scores for students using the multicultural program were higher than for those using the traditional reading program, the extremely large standard deviations associated with the gain scores greatly reduced the statistical power associated with the test of the treatment effect.

Results from the analysis of the data for year 2, however, indicated significant differences on the gain scores on the measures of vocabulary development and total reading performance ($F[1, 371] = 12.25$; $p < .0005$ and $F[1, 371] = 8.35$; $p < .0004$, respectively). The gain scores on the reading comprehension measure were not different, although greater gains were obtained for the treatment condition, as shown in Table 11.3.

We performed additional analyses to determine how ethnic group (African American vs. European American) was related to changes in reading performance. The results did not indicate a significant main effect for ethnicity nor a significant interaction. Therefore, we cannot conclude

TABLE 11.3

Posttest and Gain Score Means (M) and Standard Deviations (SD)
on California Achievement Test Measures of Reading Comprehension,
Vocabulary, and Total Reading for School District A for Years 1 and 2

		Treatment		Comparison	
		Posttest	Gain	Posttest	Gain
Year 1		(n = 94)		(n = 108)	
Reading comprehension	M	700.8	14.2	687.3	5.7
	SD	40.3	39.6	57.0	40.6
Vocabulary	M	707.6	16.2	688.6	15.2
	SD	44.4	35.1	56.0	31.8
Total reading	M	704.3	14.9	687.9	10.13
	SD	40.4	30.5	53.7	28.5
Year 2		(n = 282)		(n = 91)	
Reading comprehension	M	713.9	6.7	703.1	11
	SD	46.4	37.9	55.8	38.3
Vocabulary	M	717.0	16.9	701.7	14.0
	SD	46.0	27.8	64.3	34.1
Total reading	M	715.4	21.8	703.9	12.6
	SD	43.9	25.1	58.0	27.8

Note: The large number of treatment students in year 2 is explained by the fact that the comparison group teachers in year 1 and their new students in year 2 became part of the treatment group.

that there was greater gain for the African American students. However, the difference in means and gain scores between the treatment and comparison conditions was consistently greater for the African American students than for the European American students (Table 11.4).

Impact of the MLP on Literacy Measures for the Students in School District B. Table 11.5 presents the means and standard deviations for posttest reading and vocabulary scores and the gains for District B. Analysis of the data for school District B did not indicate significant treatment effects on the gain scores for reading comprehension, vocabulary development, or total reading performance for year 1 or year 2. Examination of Tables 11.3 and 11.5 discloses substantial differences in achievement levels between the two school districts. School District B was characterized by high levels of academic achievement, which might have attenuated the treatment effect associated with the MLP. On the other hand, treatment means and gain scores in this district were greater than the corresponding means and gains of the comparison group on each measure of achievement.

TABLE 11.4

Posttest and Gain Score Means (M) and Standard Deviations (SD) by Group and Ethnicity on California Achievement Test Measures of Reading Comprehension, Vocabulary, and Total Reading for School District A for Year 2

| | | Treatment | | | | Comparison | | | |
| | | African American (n = 92) | | European American (n = 152) | | African American (n = 23) | | European American (n = 57) | |
		Posttest	Gain	Posttest	Gain	Posttest	Gain	Posttest	Gain
Reading comprehension	M	701.9	20.9	723.9	14.1	677.7	11.9	714.9	10.4
	SD	46.7	39.8	45.9	37.4	46.7	42.3	49.5	38.3
Vocabulary	M	704.3	31.6	729.4	24.7	673.8	16.8	723.1	13.2
	SD	45.8	27.4	44.5	28.6	55.4	42.7	50.3	28.6
Total reading	M	703.1	26.3	726.6	19.5	675.8	14.4	719.0	11.8
	SD	44.4	27.7	42.5	23.8	47.7	26.5	48.2	29.5

TABLE 11.5
Posttest and Gain Score Means (M) and Standard Deviations (SD)
on California Achievement Test Measures of Reading Comprehension,
Vocabulary, and Total Reading for School District B for Year 2

		Treatment (n = 42)		Comparison (n = 38)	
		Posttest	Gain	Posttest	Gain
Reading comprehension	M	757.9	24.9	745.5	19.9
	SD	33.8	31.4	39.2	22.7
Vocabulary	M	761.9	19.9	759.9	17.5
	SD	45.9	26.1	45.2	26.0
Total reading	M	760.0	22.8	752.7	18.4
	SD	38.0	21.1	40.5	17.3

REFLECTIONS ON PROGRAM IMPLEMENTATION AND ITS IMPACT ON STUDENT BEHAVIORS

Cherishing and building on the cultural heritages of students through multicultural literacy experiences was becoming part of the students' school experience in many schools within these two school districts. Determining what factors influenced this change and how this change influenced student behaviors may be helpful to others.

Teachers' Implementation of the MLP

The multiple data sources (Levels of Use Interview, CBAM Questionnaire, and informal observations) all showed that the teachers not only were implementing the program, but also that they were comfortable and enthusiastic about the program. Some teachers further modified instructional strategies to meet their students' needs. Others developed new instructional strategies, seeking ways to integrate the program with their social studies and science curricula.

One possible explanation for this degree of comfort with the multicultural program might be our in-service sessions and bimonthly classroom visits. Consistent with the recommendations of Hall (1979) and Hord et al. (1987), we designed the in-service sessions to match the teachers' stages of concerns as they evolved. At the beginning of the year, teachers wanted to know more about the multicultural program and its components. They wanted to become familiar with multicultural literature and how to use it.

The first two in-service sessions were organized to meet these concerns. The classroom visits provided the teachers with additional guidance and support as they tried the strategies in their classrooms.

As the year continued, we began addressing the teachers' concerns about time and classroom management strategies during our in-service sessions by modeling the use of cooperative learning and paired reading, the writing process, and thematic learning. Throughout all these in-service sessions, we also modeled cultural activities designed to heighten students' and teachers' knowledge of culture and cultural groups. Over time, classroom visits changed from demonstrations to collaborative teaching opportunities, in which teachers experimented with the strategies modeled during in-service sessions. These changes in teachers' behaviors might be attributed to our ongoing support, which helped them feel more secure with us and with exploring new teaching strategies. The visits seemed to reinforce the teachers' understanding of the teaching strategies and to prevent them from sliding back into traditional teaching practices.

As the pilot teachers continued to implement the program during year 2, they began to advance to a higher level of use, the Refinement Level. Seeing that their Stages of Concerns were at the impact-related and collaborative stages, we provided teachers more opportunities to collaborate and share with one another during the in-service sessions. These interactions seemed to inspire teachers to refine and modify the program to match the needs of their students. In particular, teachers began to see ways to integrate the program with their social studies and science curricula by using a thematic approach to learning. Our presence and support during classroom visits further affirmed their ideas, encouraging them to experiment more.

While visiting classrooms, we noticed that the discussions about multicultural stories became deeper as students compared and contrasted cultures. Students and teachers also began to seek additional information about various cultural groups through the use of classroom visitors, films, videos, or books. Perhaps our model of becoming a "learner among learners" at our in-service sessions cultivated their comfort with this role in their class.

Importantly, our support, guidance, and assistance seemed to empower teachers to take ownership of the program. This possibility is confirmed by principals and administrators who shared that teachers began to provide in-service sessions for teachers in their schools or to make presentations about the multicultural literacy program at local, state, and national conferences. Once teachers saw how the program affected their students, they became inspired to share their knowledge with others. It is possible that having opportunities to share with teachers at the in-service sessions increased teachers' confidence in their abilities to share the program with larger audiences.

Changes in Student Cultural Attitudes and Literacy Performance

The results suggested that the innovative program positively affected treatment students' cultural attitudes and reading performance. In each analysis, for both school districts, the treatment group consistently showed greater mean performance on the cultural attitude and literacy measures. Statistical analyses, however, showed significant effects in gain scores only for the treatment group on the vocabulary and total reading performance measures for students in school District A during year 2. The substantial amount of variability associated with the gain scores frequently overwhelmed the mean differences in gain scores between the treatment and comparison conditions. This variability, evidenced by the large standard deviations, existed for all measures, including the gain scores.

Changes in Student Cultural Attitudes. The interview results indicated favorable changes in treatment students' attitudes toward other cultures for the combined school districts, especially after the second year. Consistent with the findings of Au (1993, 1995), Norton (1991), and Bishop (1987, 1992), the use of multicultural literature seemed to promote appreciation and respect for the values and contributions of diverse cultures. The change in attitudes toward other cultures also might be attributed to the multicultural reading and writing curriculum, which included many opportunities to extend students' knowledge about other cultures. For example, the findings from informal observations showed that students participated in meaningful cultural experiences as they contrasted and compared cultural elements in multicultural stories or investigated the histories or traditions of cultural groups in depth after reading a multicultural story.

Similarly, the findings from student interviews showed students' motivation to read, write, and extend their cultural knowledge. As one student shared, "I love it because you can just imagine that you're visiting enchanted lands, and you can go to any country in the entire world just by reading." Another noted, "I like these books because they have more to do with culture and the way things are in different lands and in history." The students' responses to interview questions further illustrated that they were gaining cultural knowledge through these experiences. For example, one student commented, "You get to learn about people you have never heard of, and you get to learn about people you have heard of, like Harriet Tubman."

The changes in the students' cultural attitudes also might be attributed to the professional growth of their teachers. The teachers shifted from merely gaining an awareness of multicultural literature and its connection with culture to the effective use of multicultural teaching strategies in their classrooms. Following the suggestions of Hoffman (1996) and Banks (1994), we emphasized the need to avoid categorizing or trivializing the cultures of others during our in-service sessions. We tried to help teachers see that multiculturalism should be holistic and comparative, with opportunities to investigate intra- and cross-cultural variability. Similar to Banks (1994) and Hoffman (1996), we further modeled the fact that cultural knowledge is an ongoing process by providing multicultural learning experiences and strategies in progressive stages during our in-service sessions.

These findings underscore the need to heighten teachers' cultural knowledge and beliefs in staff development programs. Cultural knowledge has not been a part of their educational background. Historically, European American values and views have pervaded our educational system. Staff development programs need to be aware of the progressive stages of multicultural learning and address them over time through in-service instruction and classroom visitations.

Changes in Student Literacy Performance.   Despite marginal statistical effects, it seems plausible to attribute changes in students' reading performance to the multicultural literacy curriculum implemented in the classrooms of the treatment group. Consistent with Au (1993, 1995), Banks (1994), and Sleeter and Grant (1994), changing the content of the curriculum to include multicultural literature and cultural experiences might have facilitated the academic performance of the culturally and linguistically diverse students in school District A. The reading materials, the learning context, and the social interaction patterns reflected the linguistic and cultural backgrounds of these students (Au, 1998; Bishop, 1987; Moore & Diamond, 1990; Steffensen et al., 1979) and could have served to increase their reading performance.

Merely using multicultural literature, however, is not sufficient (Banks, 1994; Hoffman, 1996). Consistent with the research findings (Au, 1995; Banks, 1994; Bishop, 1987), multicultural literature merely provides the literacy learning foundation for culturally and linguistically diverse students. Meaningful, in-depth transactions with multicultural literature are needed if there are to be changes in students' reading performance. Similar to the students in other research studies (Au, 1993, 1995; Cummins, 1986), the students in our program had multiple opportunities to read and write authentic texts in varied grouping arrangements, and to collaborate, discuss, and interpret the multicultural books they were reading. Other researchers (Bishop, 1987, 1992; Hoffman, 1996) have reported that a culturally rich curriculum increases self-esteem, which, in turn, influences academic performance. Similarly, as the culturally and linguistically diverse students in our study began to feel that their cultural heritage or language was affirmed, perhaps their self-esteem increased, enabling them to improve their literacy performance.

Opportunities to collaborate, discuss, and interpret the stories also appeared to increase students' vocabulary development. Consistent with the findings of Blachowicz and Fisher (1996), teachers distinguished meanings of words as they read stories aloud to students, or they made meaning more explicit through discussions and collaborative reading activities in a variety of grouping arrangements. Other researchers have emphasized the importance of wide reading (Blachowicz & Fisher, 1996), wide writing (Diamond & Moore, 1995; Tompkins, 1994), and using new words in a variety of writing activities (Diamond & Moore, 1995; Stahl & Kapinus, 1991; Tompkins, 1994). While reading, students read some books independently, some in whole class settings, some in small groups, or some in pairs. They also participated in many writing strategies, using the new words they encountered in the stories in varied grouping arrangements. It appeared that the combined activities resulted in improved vocabulary development in school District A.

Although the pattern of findings on literacy performance was similar in school District B, the students in the treatment group did not demonstrate significantly higher reading performance or vocabulary development. One possible explanation for this finding might be that this school district was predominantly European American, with a limited number of culturally and linguistically diverse students. The literature that most of these students typically encountered included characters, settings, and themes that reflected them and their experiences. Only a small number of these students might have experienced cultural incompatibility with the curriculum. Although the culturally and linguistically diverse students might have benefited from the program, this would not be reflected in the gain scores because their numbers were so small.

Another explanation might be that most students in school District B were ranked as educationally and economically advantaged. The majority of these students came from homes that included many opportunities to read and write and multiple opportunities for enriched literacy experiences. It is possible that the higher level skills that these students were acquiring were not adequately captured by standardized achievement tests. Perhaps the impact of a multicultural literacy program on literacy performance will be greater in schools with a high concentration of culturally and linguistically diverse students or in schools with a high concentration of students living in poverty.

Another possible explanation for the marginal findings might be that the program was implemented only 2 days a week. Perhaps a stronger treatment, implemented 5 days a week, would result in greater gains on the cultural attitude and literacy measures in both school districts. These are questions for future studies to investigate in more depth.

Relation Between Changes in Teacher Behavior and Changes in Student Performance.   Although it may be early to draw definite conclusions, the pattern of findings in our study is promising. Specifically, changes in teacher behaviors and attitudes, which evolved through the teachers' own professional growth, over time were reflected in students' literacy performance and cultural attitudes. Consistent with the findings of other researchers (Hall, 1979; Hord et al., 1987; Newlove & Hall, 1976), changes in student performance appeared to occur when teachers were implementing the innovative program at least at a Routine Level of Use. Studies performed by Levin (1988) and Hall and Loucks (1977) have further shown that achievement gains are not usually observed during the first year of implementation. According to these researchers, achievement gains may require several years before they are documented. Similarly, our study showed that achievement gains in students' literacy performance occurred after 2 years of MLP implementation in school District A.

Documenting Changes in Student Performance.   In their extensive review of literature-based studies, Tunnell and Jacobs (1989) further cautioned that research does not consistently indicate differences in reading performance through the use of standardized measures. Similarly, the extremely large standard deviations associated with gain scores in the standardized measures of our study greatly reduced the power of the statistical tools used to test the treatment effect.

Although the achievement gains in our study suggest a pattern of findings, it also is important to acknowledge that it is difficult to know what factors accounted for the changes because the multicultural program included multicultural literature, cooperative learning, and whole language type instruction.

IMPLICATIONS

This study has concrete implications for both research and practice. First, it demonstrates that a multicultural literacy program can be implemented when ongoing evaluation procedures become tools for modifying and changing the program to meet the evolving needs and concerns of the school, the community, the classroom, the teacher, and the students. Second, it shows that a multicultural literacy program can improve the literacy performance of students, especially students from diverse cultures and lower poverty levels. Third, the findings demonstrate that a multicultural literacy program can increase students' appreciation and understanding of other cultures.

The Change Process and Program Implementations

Over the years, large amounts of time, money, and effort have been devoted to school reform movements that target students who are culturally and linguistically diverse and those who live in poverty. In his presidential address for the National Reading Conference, Duffy (1991) emphasized that "despite reform and isolated pockets of progress, classroom instruction is basically the same now as it was when I started in 1957" (p. 2). Too often, teachers return from in-service sessions feeling insecure in their abilities to use innovative strategies. Others may discover problems as they try the strategy. As a result, they frequently return to traditional practices, which they think will be easier to implement.

In contrast, evaluation of the multicultural literacy program implementation showed that classroom instruction was changing. These findings provide additional insight into the change process and ways to facilitate the change process. In the following discussion, we highlight some of these insights for others to explore and investigate in more depth.

Importantly, teachers are not always aware of how they can adjust and respond to differences in learners' cultural knowledge and language. While acquiring these new skills, they need a supportive context that identifies and meets their evolving needs and concerns. The spacing of classroom visits across time provides them guidance and support so that their classroom instruction can begin to change. The visits also increase opportunities for collaboration between teachers and researchers. Working together, coteaching lessons, and creating new lessons, they can discover ways to promote cultural knowledge of students and to integrate multicultural perspectives into the curriculum.

Once teachers are comfortable and familiar with new instructional techniques, they need to become involved with the staff development program for new teachers. In our study, teachers first shared their teaching practices with other teachers at the in-service sessions, then began to help conduct in-service sessions and classroom visits. These approaches might help teachers become reflective decision makers who modify and adapt instruction to meet their students' needs. Staff development programs can be enriched by involving teachers in the change process.

In addition, we learned that a multicultural staff development program needs to be an ongoing process for several years. Similar to Au (1995) and Purves (1994), we discovered a need to reflect and discuss the multicultural literature, to participate in extended discussions related to the social issues and the cultural contexts of the literature. Teachers need multiple opportunities to participate in deeper investigations of diverse cultures and ways to integrate this knowledge across the curriculum. For many teachers, this is a new way of thinking and acting. Their prior experiences with cultural knowledge are frequently limited.

Implementation of a multicultural program also requires that multicultural issues and perspectives be addressed according to the context of the community. For example, in their research Vogt, Jordan, and Tharp (1987) found that peer assistance, which reflected the Hawaiian children's home experiences with sibling caretaking and companion groups, increased the literacy learning of Native Hawaiian children. This same approach, however, did not work in classrooms of Navajo children who tend to work individually and do not socialize with children of the opposite gender. Similarly, how the implementation of a multicultural program is approached in homogeneous school districts may be different.

Equally, important, we found that the use of ongoing evaluation procedures provided tools for modifying and changing the program to meet the evolving needs and concerns of the community, classroom, and students (Diamond & Moore, 1995; Hall, 1979; Hord et al., 1987). The Stages of Concern Questionnaire and the Levels of Use Interview, for example, eliminated guesswork and intuition by helping us to identify resources and materials for our in-service sessions, accommodate the evolving needs of our teachers, and determine intervention strategies during classroom visitations. Having multiple sources of data further enabled us to see how the program was being implemented from multiple viewpoints, including those of teachers, students, principals, and administrators. The sources also helped us consider ways to adapt the program to accommodate the teachers, students, classrooms, and community.

IMPROVING LITERACY THROUGH TEACHING PRACTICES

Analyses and trends suggest that the use of a multicultural literacy program is one way to address the needs of the changing populations in our country. Aligning the curriculum with the cultural experiences of the learners (Au, 1993, 1995; Banks, 1994; Sleeter & Grant, 1994) heightens their academic performance. According to researchers (Au, 1995, 1998; Hoffman, 1996; Sleeter & Grant, 1994), there also is a need to identify culturally congruent teaching practices and culturally responsive teaching activities to form a foundation for working with students of culturally and linguistically diverse backgrounds. We found that certain teaching practices seemed to facilitate the literacy performance of students participating in our study. Examples of these teaching practices include the following:

1. Incorporating students' language and culture into the curriculum through multicultural literature to facilitate their reading and writing development.
2. Organizing learning to emerge from the cultural background of students and to remain compatible with the culture of students.
3. Creating opportunities for students to discuss and reflect on the multicultural literature and its cultural elements, offering them opportunities to extend their knowledge and understanding of cultural issues.
4. Integrating the curriculum to focus on themes, which often is consistent with the learning styles of students from diverse cultures, enabling students to develop basic skills, while acquiring new knowledge in challenging and meaningful ways.
5. Organizing instruction to foster heterogeneous, collaborative learning to promote higher order cognitive and linguistic discourse, sharpen understanding of information, and facilitate assistance from others in acquiring new skills or information as needed.
6. Creating opportunities for active rather than passive participation of all students to minimize disciplinary procedures and maximize literacy learning.

7. Organizing literacy learning to evolve from meaningful, purposeful contexts, including hands-on, interactive activities (i.e., choral readings, reader's theater, writing, dramatization, reflective discussion) to foster the acquisition of literacy development and its application across all content areas.

Although the findings from our study must be considered with caution, they provide a foundation for future studies. Discovering how students, especially students of diverse cultures, develop literacy will continue to challenge researchers. Achievement gaps continue to exist between Euro-American students and culturally and linguistically diverse students.

Future studies need to examine how gender, race, socioeconomic status, ethnicity, and ability are related to literacy performance. We need more empirical evidence to determine what teaching practices facilitate literacy learning of these students. There also is a need for qualitative research studies that investigate more closely the effects of various learning configurations, in particular cooperative learning groups, on literacy learning of culturally and linguistically diverse learners and students in poverty. Additional studies need to be designed to determine how to develop culturally responsive teaching activities and identify cultural source materials. Similarly, studies need to investigate ways to foster the professional development of teachers so they can critically analyze multicultural texts, curricula, activities, and teaching practices.

The findings from these future studies will enable us to create culturally responsive instruction so that all students can achieve. We cannot wait for social, economic, or political reforms (Au, 1995). We must develop multiple perspectives about literacy that conform to cultural contexts now.

REFERENCES

Alvermann, D., & Ridgeway, V. (1990). Implementing content area reading with limited finances. In G. Duffy (Ed.), *Reading in the elementary school* (pp. 200–208). Newark, DE: International Reading Association.

Au, K. (1993). *Literacy instruction in multicultural settings*. Fort Worth, TX: Jovanovich College Publishers.

Au, K. (1995). Multicultural perspectives on literacy research. *Journal of Reading Behavior: A Journal of Literacy, 27,* 83–100.

Au, K. (1998). Social constructivism and the school literacy learning of students of diverse backgrounds. *Journal of Literacy Research, 30,* 297–319.

Banks, J. (1994). *Multiethnic education: Theory and practice* (3rd ed.). Boston: Allyn & Bacon.

Beiger, E. (1995/1996). Promoting multicultural education through a literature-based approach. *The Reading Teacher, 49,* 308–311.

Bishop, R. (1987). Extending multicultural understanding through children's books. In B. Cullinan (Ed.), *Children's Literature in the reading program* (pp. 60–67). Newark DE: International Reading Association.

Bishop, R. (1992). Multicultural literature for children: Making informed choices. In V. Harris (Ed.), *Teaching multicultural literature in grades K–8* (pp. 37–53). Norwood, MA: Christopher-Gordon.

Blachowicz, C., & Fisher, P. (1996). *Teaching vocabulary in all classrooms.* Englewood Cliffs, NJ: Merrill.

Campos, J., & Keatinge, B. (1984). *The Carpinteria preschool program: Title VII second year evaluation report.* Washington DC: Department of Education.

Cohen, E. (1987). *Designing group work: Strategies for the heterogeneous classroom.* New York: Teachers College Press.

Cohen, A., & Swain, M. (1976). Bilingual education: The immersion model in the North American context. In J. F. Alatis & K. Twaddell (Eds.), *English as a second language in bilingual education.* Washington DC: Department of Education.

Conley, M., & Tripp-Opple, K. (1990). Improving staff development through cooperation. In G. Duffy (Ed.), *Reading in the elementary school* (pp. 209–221). Newark DE: International Reading Association

Cummins, J. (1986). Empowering minority students: A framework for intervention. *Harvard Educational Review, 56,* 18–36.

Delpit, L. (1995). *Other people's children: Cultural conflict in the classroom.* New York: The New Press.

Diamond, B., & Moore, M. (1995). *Multicultural literacy: Mirroring the reality of the classroom.* New York: Longman.

Duffy, G. (1991). What counts in teacher education? Dilemmas in education-empowered teachers. In J. Zutell & S. McCormick (Eds.), *Fortieth yearbook of the National Reading Conference* (pp. 1–18). Alexandria, VA: The National Reading Conference.

Florez, V., & Hadaway, N. (1986). *Bridging linguistic and cultural differences through reading: Multiethnic literature in the classroom.* (Report No. CS 008 692). Paper presented at the Annual meeting of the Southwest Regional Conference of the International Reading Association, San Antonio, TX (ERIC Document Reproduction Service No. ED 278959).

Hall, G. (1979, November). *Using the individual and the innovation as the frame of reference for research on change.* Paper presented at the Australia Association Research in Education, Melbourne, Australia.

Hall, G., & Hord, S. (1987). *Change in schools: Facilitating the process.* Albany: State University of New York Press.

Hall, G., & Loucks, S. (1977). A developmental model for determining whether the treatment is actually implemented. *American Educational Research Journal, 13,* 263–276.

Harris, V. (1991). *Teaching multicultural literature in grades K–8.* Norwood, MA: Christopher-Gordon.

Hoffman, D. (1996). Culture and self in multicultural education: Reflections on discourse, text, and practice. *American Educational Research Journal, 33,* 545–569.

Holmes Group. (1990). *Tomorrow's schools: Principles for the design of professional develop-ment schools.* East Lansing, MI: The Holmes Group.

Hord, S., Rutherford, W., Austin, L., & Hall, G. (1987). *Taking charge of change.* Alexan-dria, VA: Association for Supervision and Curriculum Development.

Ladson-Billings, G. (1994). *The dreamkeepers: Successful teachers of African American chil-dren.* San Francisco: Jossey Boss.

Levin, H. (1988). *Toward an evaluation model for accelerated schools.* Stanford, CA: Stanford University.

Lipson, M. Y. (1983). The influences of religious affiliation of children's memory for text in-formation. *Reading Research Quarterly, 18,* 448–457.

Loucks, S., Newlove, B., & Hall, G. (1975). *Measuring levels of use of the innovation: A man-ual for trainers, interviewers, and raters.* Austin: Research and Development Center for Teacher Education, University of Texas at Austin.

McDiarmid, G. (1993). What to do about differences? A study of multicultural education for teacher trainees in the Los Angeles Unified School District. *Journal of Teacher Edu-cation, 43,* 83–93.

Moore, M. A., & Diamond, B. J. (1991, April). *Promoting literacy and cultural awareness: A multicultural literature-based approach.* Paper presented at the annual American Educa-tional Research Association, Chicago, IL.

Newlove, B., & Hall, G. (1976). *A manual for assessing open-ended statements of concerns about an innovation.* Austin: Research and Development Center for Teacher Education, University of Texas at Austin.

Norton, D. (1991). *Through the eyes of a child: An introduction to children's literature.* Colum-bus OH: Charles Merrill.

Pisano, A., & Tallerico, M. (1990). Improving writing instruction through staff develop-ment. *Journal of Staff Development, 11,* 18–21.

Purves, A. (1994). The ideology of canons and cultural concerns in the literature curricu-lum. In S. M. Miller & B. McCaskill (Eds.), *Minority education: Anthropological perspec-tives* (pp. 83–111). Norwood, NJ: Ablex.

Routman, R. (1994). *Invitations: Changing as teachers and learners, K–12.* Portsmouth, NH. Heinemann.

Reyhner, J., & Garcia, R. (1989). Helping minorities read better: Problems and promises. *Reading Research and Instruction, 28,* 84–91.

Sleeter, C., & Grant, C. (1994). *Making choices for multicultural education: Five approaches to race, class, and gender* (2nd ed.). New York: Macmillan.

Sparks, G., & Simmons, J. (1989). Inquiry-oriented staff development: Using research as a source of tools, not rules. In S. Caldwell (Ed.), *Staff development: A handbook of effective practices.* National Staff Development Council, Oxford, Ohio.

Stahl, S., & Kapinus, B. (1991). Possible sentences. *The Reading Teacher, 45,* 36–43.

Steffensen, M. S., Joag-Dev, C., & Anderson, R. C. (1979). A cross-cultural perspective on reading comprehension. *Reading Research Quarterly, 15,* 10–29.

Stevens, R., Madden, M., Slavin, R., & Farnish, A. (1987). Cooperative integrated reading and composition: Two field experiments. *Reading Research Quarterly, 22,* 433–454.

Stevens, R., & Slavin, R. (1995). The cooperative elementary school: Effects on students' achievement, attitudes, and social relations. *American Educational Research Journal, 32,* 321–351.

Stevens, R., Slavin, R., & Farnish, A. (1991). The effects of cooperative learning and direct instruction in reading comprehension strategies on main idea identification. *Journal of Educational Psychology, 83,* 8–16.

Tompkins, G. (1994). *Teaching writing: Balancing process and product.* New York: Merrill.

Tunnell, M., & Jacobs, J. (1989). Using "real" books: Research findings on literature-based reading instruction. *The Reading Teacher, 42*, 470–478.

Vogt, L. A., Jordan, C., & Tharp, R. G. (1987). Explaining school failure, producing school success: Two cases. *Anthropology and Education Quarterly, 18*, 276–286.

APPENDIX A

Multicultural Books Included in Classroom Sets (Teachers selected 20 at a time)

Aardema, V. (1981). *Bringing the rain to Kapiti plain.* New York: Dial.

Adams, E. (Ed.). (1982). *Korean Cinderella.* Seoul, Korea: Seoul International Publishing House.

Adoff, A. (1982). *All the colors of the race.* New York: Lothrop, Lee, & Shepard.

Aliki. (1988). *Corn is maize.* New York: Harper & Row.

Aliki. (1988). *A weed is a flower.* New York: Simon & Schuster.

Babbitt, N. (1969). *Search for delicious.* Toronto: Farrar, Straus, & Giroux.

Bains, R. (1982). *Harriet Tubman: The road to freedom.* Mahwah, NJ: Troll.

Baylor, B. (1972). *When clay sings.* New York: Aladdin Books.

Baylor, B. (1986). *I'm in charge of celebrations.* New York: Macmillan.

Baylor, B. (1989). *Amigo.* New York: Macmillan.

Behrens, J. (1986). *Fiesta!* Chicago: Children's Press.

Belpre, P. (1978). *The rainbow-colored horse.* New York: Warne.

Boholm-Olsson, E. (1988). *Tuan.* New York: R & S Books.

Brown, T. (1986). *Hello, amigos.* New York: Henry Holt.

Brown, T. (1987). *Chinese New Year.* New York: Henry Holt.

Clark, M. G. (1980). *Freedom crossing.* New York: Scholastic.

Cleaver, E. (1985). *The enchanted caribou.* New York: Atheneum.

Coerr, E. (1977). *Sadako and the thousand paper cranes.* New York: Dell.

Crowder, J. (1986). *Tonibah and the rainbow.* Bernalillo, NM: Upper Strata.

Demi. (1980). *Liang and the magic paintbrush.* New York: Henry Holt.

Demi. (1987). *The hallowed horse.* New York: Dodd Mead.

dePaola, T. (1978). *The popcorn book.* New York: Holiday House.

dePaola, T. (1983). *The legend of the bluebonnet.* New York: G. P. Putnam's Sons.

Dorros, A. (1991). *Abuela.* New York: Dutton Children's Books.

Feelings, T. (1974). *Jambo means hello.* New York: Dial.

Feeney, S. (1985). *Hawaii is a rainbow.* Honolulu: University of Hawaii Press.

Flournoy, V. (1985). *The patchwork quilt.* New York: Dial.

Goble, P. (1978). *The girl who loved wild horses.* New York: Macmillan.

Goble, P. (1990). *Dream wolf.* New York: Bradbury Press.

Greenfield, E. (1988). *Nathaniel talking.* New York: Writers & Readers.

Grifalconi, A. (1986). *The village of round and square houses.* Boston: Little, Brown.

Haskins, J. (1990). *Count your way through the Arab world.* Minneapolis: Carolrhoda.

Heide, F. (1990). *The day of Ahmed's secret*. New York: Lothrop, Lee, & Shepard.

Knight, M. B. (1992). *Talking walls*. Gardiner, ME: Tilbury House.

Krumgold, J. (1953). *And now Miguel*. New York: Harper Trophy.

Lewin, T. (1993). *Amazon boy*. New York: Macmillan.

Longfellow, H. W. (1983). *Hiawatha*. New York: Dial.

Lord, B. (1984). *In the year of the boar and Jackie Robinson*. New York: Harper & Row.

Louie, A. (1982). *Yeh-shen: A Cinderella story from China*. New York: Philomel.

Macaulay, D. (1975). *Pyramid*. Boston: Houghton Mifflin.

Macaulay, D. (1977). *Castle*. Boston: Houghton Mifflin.

Margolies, B. (1990). *Rhema's journey: A visit to Tanzania*. New York: Scholastic.

Martin, B., Jr., & Archambault, J. (1987). *Knots on a counting rope*. New York: Henry Holt.

Martin, R. (1992). *The rough-face girl*. New York: G. P. Putnam's Sons.

McKissack, P. (1986). *Flossie and the fox*. New York: Dial.

McLean, V. (1987). *Chasing the moon to China*. New York: Redbird.

McLean, V., & Klyce, K. (1989). *Kenya! Jambo!* Memphis, TN: Redbird Press.

Miles, M. (1971). *Annie and the old one*. Boston: Little, Brown, & Co.

Mohr, N. (1978). *Felita*. New York: Bantam Skylark.

Mora, P. (1992). *A birthday basket for Tia*. New York: Macmillan.

Musgrove, M. (1976). *Ashanti to Zulu: African traditions*. New York: Dial.

Myers, W. D. (1988). *Scorpions*. New York: Harper Keypoint.

Myers, W. D. (1993). *Malcolm X: A biography*. New York: Scholastic.

Polacco, P. (1990). *Babushka's doll*. New York: Simon & Schuster.

Ringgold, F. (1992). *Aunt Harriet's underground railroad in the sky*. New York: Crown.

Sales, F. (1989). *Ibrahim*. New York: J. B. Lippincott.

San Souci, R. (1987). *The enchanted tapestry*. New York: Dial.

San Souci, R. (1987). *The talking eggs*. New York: Dial.

Say, A. (1990). *El chino*. Boston: Houghton Mifflin.

Say, A. (1991). *Tree of cranes*. Boston: Houghton Mifflin.

Seattle, Chief. (1991). *Brother eagle, sister sky*. New York: Dial.

Seeger, P. (1986). *Abiyoyo*. New York: Macmillan.

Sneve, V. D. (1989). *Dancing teepees*. New York: Holiday House.

Spier, P. (1990). *People*. New York: Doubleday.

Stanek, M. (1989). *I speak English for my mom*. Morton Grove, IL: Albert Whitman.

Stanley, F. (1991). *The last princess: The story of Princess Ka'iulani of Hawaii*. New York: Four Winds Press.

Stanley, D. (1988). *Shaka, king of the Zulus*. New York: Morrow Jr. Books.

Steptoe, J. (1988). *Mufaro's beautiful daughters*. New York: Lothrop, Lee, & Shepard.

Taylor, M. (1975). *Song of the trees*. New York: Dial.

Taylor, M. (1976). *Roll of thunder hear my cry*. New York: Bantam.

Taylor, M. (1987). *The friendship and the gold cadillac*. New York: Bantam Books.

Taylor, M. (1990). *Mississippi bridge*. New York: Dial.

Tsuchiya, Y. (1988). *Faithful elephants*. Boston: Houghton Mifflin.

Waters, S. (1990). *Lion dancer: Ernie Wan's Chinese New Year*. New York: Scholastic.

Wells, R. (1992). *A to zen: A picture book of Japanese culture*. Saxonville, MA: Picture Book Studio.

Williams, K. L. (1990). *Galimoto*. New York: Lothrop, Lee, & Shepard.

Winter, J. (1988). *Follow the drinking gourd*. New York: Alfred Knopf.

Xiong, B. (1989). *Nine-in-one grr! grr!* San Francisco: Children's Book Press.

Yarbrough, C. (1979). *Cornrows*. New York: Coward-McCann.
Yep, L. (1975). *Dragonwings*. New York: Harper Trophy.
Yep, L. (1989). *The rainbow people*. New York: HarperCollins.

APPENDIX B

Lesson Plan 1.1: Appreciating Cultural Differences and Similarities by Celebrating People

OBJECTIVES: The students will be able to

1. appreciate the similarities and differences of people from different cultures.
2. state four ways people are similar and four ways people are different.
3. write a biopoem about themselves or a family member.

PARTICIPANTS: All grade levels, whole class, small groups

MATERIALS: Book: *People*, by Peter Spier; paper, pencils, crayons, drawing paper

INSTRUCTIONS:

1. Students will list four ways people are similar and four ways they are different.
2. Students will share their lists in groups of three or four.
3. Each group will share its lists with the total group as teacher records information on large chart paper.
4. Teacher and students will read the book *People* interactively, with teacher asking questions as the book is read.
5. Students and teacher will discuss additional ways people are similar and different, adding new information to the large chart.
6. Each student will interview a classmate, following the biopoem format.

7. Students will share the biopoems orally. Differences and similarities among the students may be highlighted during this time. Once the biopoems are shared orally, they can be revised and edited for publication.

8. Biopoems may be illustrated and displayed on a bulletin board, framed by each student's thumbprints.

Lesson Plan 2.1: Cultural Feature Analysis

OBJECTIVES: The students will be able to
  1. read orally one of the selected books.
  2. identify elements of the story (e.g., culture represented, setting, main characters/traits, family relationships, message).
  3. compare and contrast the elements in the stories.
  4. discuss cultural features that become apparent as a result of comparison and contrast of the elements.

PARTICIPANTS: Fourth and fifth grades, earlier grades with some modification

MATERIALS: Books, *The Patchwork Quilt, Knots on a Counting Rope, Annie and the Old One*, and *Cornrows*

INSTRUCTIONS:

1. The teacher and students will interactively read a book of the teacher's choice, preferably one with a clearly defined plot. Teachers and students will discuss elements of the story.

2. Students will be divided into four cooperative learning groups. Each group will have an equal number of high, average, and low ability students.

3. Each group will read a selected book. It is suggested that one of the high ability students read the book, with the other students joining in.

4. Students in the group will identify the culture represented, setting, main characters/traits, family relationships, and message. Teacher will circulate among the groups to facilitate the process.

5. Students will record the information about the story elements on the feature analysis handout.

6. Each group will share its information with the whole group. The teacher will record on the feature analysis chart on the overhead.

7. The teacher will lead the students in comparing and contrasting elements of the stories, bringing out cultural features of the elements that can aid in understanding people of various cultures represented by the books.

CULTURAL FEATURE ANALYSIS

TITLE	CULTURE	SETTING	CHAR. & TRAITS	FAMILY REL.	MESSAGE

12

Pitfalls and Potential: Multicultural Literature and Teacher Study Groups

Frances A. Levin
New Jersey City University

Michael W. Smith
Dorothy S. Strickland
Rutgers University

As educators, we frequently make assumptions. We assume that by exposing teachers and students to multicultural literature, they will be more open to learning about other cultures. We assume that cultural self-respect and respect for differences are attainable goals. Moreover, we assume that if teachers and students read and discuss multicultural literature, they will develop an ethical respect for other cultures and a heightened cultural awareness. Do these assumptions represent truth? Or are they merely the imaginings of optimistic educators who recognize that something must be done, some curriculum undertaken, and some dialogue initiated to confront the cultural barriers that typify today's classrooms.

Despite efforts to diversify the teaching population, teachers in the United States remain largely Euro-American, female, monolingual, and from lower- and middle-income backgrounds (Cazden & Mehan, 1989). Conversely, many of their students originate from linguistic-minority backgrounds and lower-income families, resulting in a cultural chasm between teacher and student (Ladson-Billings, 1994). The need, therefore, for teachers to possess ethical respect and a heightened sense of cultural awareness is indisputable. Whether such ends can be achieved through the process of reading and discussing multicultural literature is a consideration of our research. Through our research of teachers reading, discussing, and writing about multicultural literature, we have found some avenues to the building of cross-cultural understanding, and as expected, we have uncovered many new questions.

THEORETICAL FRAMEWORK

In this chapter, we present two research studies that exemplify the major goals of our respective work. Through our work with preservice and in-service teachers, we have studied the use of multicultural literature to help teachers and students develop an ethical respect for others. We also have examined talk about text that is at odds with the patterns of discourse that typify school discussions, and we have sought models of staff development that provide teachers with the time for self-inquiry (Brown & Kysilka, 1994; Ladson-Billings, 1994; Reissman, 1994), reflective practice (Council for English Education [CEE], 1994), ownership (Sanacore, 1993), and the opportunity to grow personally and professionally.

Our discussion is based on an examination of ethical respect as related to the teachers studied, the use of multicultural literature as a means of moving toward ethical respect, the discourse of the teachers, and the study group format as a viable, professional development experience. The first study was conducted by Smith and Strickland in 1995. The second study, which built on their work was carried out by Levin in 1997. Although the studies were not identical, they shared similar research questions and design. Both studies involved teachers reading multicultural literature in a study group or book club format and an examination of group process dynamics.

Ethical Respect

Ethical respect, as termed in our studies, is the manner in which readers are engaged with the authors of and the characters in a text. By ethical respect, we mean more than identifying with the characters. Downie and Tefler (1970) helped to clarify our definition of respect:

> Let us try to tie together the various components in our attitude of respect. Insofar as persons are thought of as self-determining agents who pursue objects of interest to themselves, we respect them by showing active sympathy with them. In Kant's language, we make their ends our own. Insofar as persons are thought of as rule-following, we respect them by taking seriously the fact that the rules by which they guide their conduct constitute

reasons which may apply both to them and to ourselves. In the attitude of respect, we have then two necessary components: an attitude of active sympathy and a readiness at least to consider the applicability of [others'] rules both to them and to ourselves. (pp. 28–29)

Cultivation of ethical respect is contingent upon the reader's ability or willingness to hold certain assumptions. One of the most critical is the propensity to consider all characters of equal worth until the text proves otherwise. Kane (1994) explained that "treating others as innocent till proven guilty" (p. 25) constitutes respect. Taylor (1992), in his noteworthy essay on multiculturalism, The Politics of Recognition, explained that respect recognizes the equal dignity of all citizens with the presumption of "equal worth" (p. 72). Acceptance of this assumption means the reader is capable of leaving his or her biases behind. That is, the reader initially judges authors and characters on their own terms rather than in terms of the expectations and values he or she brings to the text.

Cornel West (1994), author of the national bestseller, Race Matters, recounted his story of hailing a taxi on the Upper East Side of Manhattan. After a considerable amount of waiting, West realized no taxi would stop for him because he was an African American male, and therefore resigned himself to taking the subway.

Ethical respect for West's plight would cause the reader to think not only about the difficulty of getting a taxi in New York, but more specifically, about the difficulty associated with a Black male securing a taxi in a predominately White area. The reader is able to recognize the indignity of the situation.

In addition, the reader also must accept the rules that governed West's life. West believed that because he was dressed in a particular way, as a successful man, perhaps his experience would be different and a taxi would stop for him. The rules that governed his behavior told him that if he had been dressed in casual clothing, such as a T-shirt and jeans, he would have known to take the subway in the first place.

The reader who has ethical respect for this character understands the reasons for West's choices and considers the level of thought that may go into seemingly mundane situations. Paying this character ethical respect means examining what these competing positions mean to the reader. It may mean that the reader reflects on the social inequity of society, its effect on certain groups, and how the reader concerns him- or herself with larger cultural issues, thereby broadening his or her cultural understanding and acceptance of the character's humanity.

Teachers reading West's story may identify with the experience first on a personal level, perhaps by recalling a time when they experienced a similar situation. Through our analysis of the study group discourse, we found this to be the case. Teachers, at least initially, almost instinctively related the texts to personal experiences in order to interpret the situation. We believe that to begin the process of formulating ethical respect, a closer look at the author and the characters is necessary. Using multicultural literature to further that goal offers readers a variety of perspectives.

Teaching Multicultural Literature

When we consider the practice of using multicultural literature to foster an ethical respect for others, we mean developing in readers the presumptions of equal worth and causing them to adopt the ends of others as their own. This way of thinking represents a slight departure from conventional goals pursued by many advocates of multicultural literature. Some researchers have suggested that exposure to and awareness of different cultures may have far-reaching implications in diverse classroom communities (Trueba, Jacobs, & Kirton, 1989). Sleeter and Grant (1987), in a study of multicultural workshops, found that awareness and sensitivity training were the focus of most multicultural workshops.

Although we recognize the importance of exposure and awareness, these are not the ultimate goals of multiculturalism. As Banks (1994) asserted in the transformations approach, teaching readers to analyze varied perspectives of the text helps them better understand the characters, their actions, and the rules governing their behavior. We also believe that considering a variety of perspectives can further the development of ethical respect.

Our perspective also counters the concept of universal experiences, what Taylor (1994) termed the difference-blind perspective, as the ultimate goal. This perspective recognizes that we all are the same under the skin regardless of our race, religion, or ethnicity, and that an understanding of certain universal themes we all share fosters a healthier attitude toward others. Although there is certainly truth in that statement, it often prevents readers from recognizing the unique culture and conventions of each group. Therefore, we are in favor of the reader assuming the character's role on the basis of the character's rules and position instead of the reader placing himself in the role of the character using his or her own life experiences.

Patterns of Discourse

One of the questions in our research focused on whether the typical patterns of discourse in a school situation would be evident in a study group. As Cazden (1988) explained, school discourse at all levels is dominated by the initiation–recitation–evaluation (IRE) model. This IRE pattern begins with the teacher asking a question, receiving a response from the student, and then evaluating that response. We wondered whether teachers involved with a study group would begin to use a new model, one that is more congruent with the goals of literature circles, such as shared responsibility and conversational dialogue. Eeds and Hudelson (1995) addressed this issue by emphasizing the value of teachers participating in literature discussion groups as a means of entering into the lives of others, making meaning of one's own life and providing a literary experience for teachers. From this literary experience, they contended that teachers are better able to provide this model for their students. We attempted to offer this model in the hope that teachers would participate in discussions differently, behaving as readers instead of teachers, and perhaps eventually incorporating that learning into their own classroom discussions.

Teacher Study Groups

Our research also considered whether teacher study groups have intrinsic professional development value. We wondered whether this format was an effective model for engaging teachers and for promoting their professional development. Providing teachers with appropriate staff development has been a continual challenge for teachers, administrators, and staff developers. Yet, study groups, in one format or another, have been used for many years (Sprague & Makibbin, 1994).

The concept of study groups is not a new one. The first recorded study group in America dates back to Benjamin Franklin, who organized meetings of businessmen to review moral and successful business practices (Sprague & Makibbin, 1994). Teachers, however, began "reading circles," study groups that provided continuing education, in the late 1800s (Powell, Berliner, & Casanova, 1992). The reading circles offered a forum for discussion of current educational issues. Groups of teachers studied various texts and responded to their readings through discussion and sharing.

We decided to use a study group format because it provided, in our estimation, a potential means of fostering ethical respect. Four recent studies by Flood et al. (1994), Florio-Ruane and deTar (1995), and Florio-

Ruane and Raphael (1997), and Athanases, Christiano, and Lay (1995), offered information that helped to situate our studies. Their work, like ours, focused on reading multicultural literature in a study group format.

Flood et al. (1994) studied several teacher and student teacher book clubs in which participants responded to a series of texts focused on multicultural literature. Both teacher and student teacher groups believed they grew in their sensitivity and awareness of various cultures. The teacher and student teacher groups also noted a development of collegiality and trust among participants as they shared their thoughts with the group.

In a later study, Florio-Ruane and deTar (1995) studied a group of future teachers who read, responded to, and discussed ethnic autobiographies in a teacher study group setting. They analyzed the group discourse and determined that conversation in their club offered a difficult, in terms of the personal nature of the discussions, yet "fertile ground" for both learning and research.

In a more recent study, Florio-Ruane and Raphael (1997) learned that the use of autobiographical text has great potential to put teachers in meaningful contact with alternative ways of being and becoming literate, and to sensitize them to the ways individuals from varying backgrounds experience literacy in and out of school.

In addition to long-term research studies (1 year or more), Athanases et al. (1995) studied a 3-day institute in which 19 educators read literature by ethnically diverse authors, discussed responses, and planned ways to use the works in class. Two themes emerged: (a) the value of empathy and (b) the need for reconciliation among groups divided by differences, biases, and histories of injustice. After the experience, the educators shared ways of addressing their classroom concerns. The group process was found to be successful in the effort to bring multiculturalism into the classroom.

As a result of these studies and our professional experiences, we reasoned that multicultural literature discussed in a study group format could have a potential impact on a group of teachers in their development of ethical respect for various cultures. We surmised that by reading and discussing all types of multicultural literature, teachers would gain a heightened awareness of cultures, and perhaps develop an ethical respect. It is from this premise that we approached our work. As it evolved, we recognized that although the teachers gained certain benefits from their involvement in the teacher study group, our research objectives were not fully realized.

DESCRIPTION OF RESEARCH

Participants in Study 1

The 11 teachers who participated in the Literacy and Diversity Study Group initiated by Smith and Strickland (1996) involved 4 African American women, 1 African American man, 3 European American women of various ethnicities, 3 European American men of various ethnicities, and 1 Latina woman. These teachers taught in an urban area designated by the state to receive special funding because a significant proportion of the students resided in high poverty areas with a history of low achievement.

Context. This study group had eight monthly meetings over the course of one academic year. Seven of the meetings centered on the discussion of picture books, young adult novels, or **adult short stories**, each with a multicultural focus. The final meeting was devoted to discussing the experience of being a part of the study group. The group met in the school library at one of the participating schools. Refreshments were supplied by one of the participants. The group was asked to write a brief journal entry for each of the sessions. Smith and Strickland (1996) suggested journal prompts for each entry, which are highlighted, along with the books and stories discussed, in Table 12.1.

Data Collection and Analysis. Each session was audiotaped and transcribed, although technical problems made one of the tapes inaudible. Thus, there were seven transcriptions: six discussions of literature and one final discussion on the experience of being in the group.

Each of the literature discussion transcriptions was divided into two units of analysis: content unit and turn. A content unit was defined as a segment of discourse designed to make a single point. Preliminary analysis of the data suggested that content units had one of six foci: personal, personal–textual, textual, global, teaching, or teaching–textual. Subsequent analysis confirmed that these six foci were descriptive of all but one of the content units. That content unit was eliminated from the data set.

Analysis of the relation among turns was based on the coding system used by Marshall, Smagorinsky, and Smith (1995) to analyze the nature of participants' responses in literature discussions.

Table 12.2 describes the coding categories and offers a definition of each. The length of each turn also was analyzed in terms of communica-

TABLE 12.1
Texts and Writing Prompts

Month	Text	Writing Prompt
October	"A Visit to Grandmother" by William Melvin Kelley (adult short story)	Free response
November	*The Whispering Cloth* by Pegi Deitz Shea (picture book) *Been to Yesterdays* by Lee Bennet Hopkins (poems for young people)	Select a poem or passage that you like. Write a response to that poem or passage.
January	*My Name is Maria Isabel* by Alma Ada Flors (children's novel) *Too Many Tamales* by Gary Soto (picture book)	Free response
February	"Everyday Use" by Alice Walker (adult short story)	Track your understanding of the main characters in a three-column response. Put the character's name in the first column, a passage that affected your understanding of the character in the second column, and how your understanding has developed or changed in the third column.
	Maniac Magee by Jerry Spinelli (adolescent novel)	Free response
March	"Two Kinds" by Amy Tan (adult short story)	Free response
April	*Number the Stars* by Lois Lowry (adolescent novel) *Amazing Grace* by Mary Hoffman (picture book)	Free response
May	no reading	What makes a good discussion?

tion units, which are units of discourse that have the force of a sentence, but may be as short as one word (yes or okay). The content units were analyzed for knowledge base and further analyzed with in comparison to information from interviews and observations.

Participants in Study 2

Eight teachers participated in Literacy and Diversity Study 2, all of whom were European American women. There was one media specialist and seven elementary school teachers, representing grades one through six. The participants taught in a school located in a predominantly White district. However, their school had a diverse population and the lowest socioeconomic level in the district. All of the teachers in the school were

TABLE 12.2
Description of Coding Categories: Study 1

Content Units

Personal: Content centers on speaker, speaker's family, speaker's cultural background, and the like, without reference to the text under discussion.

Personal–textual: Content centers on how speaker, speaker's family, speaker's cultural background, and so forth relate to the text under discussion.

Text: Content centers on characters, elements of text, and author's craft.

Teaching: Content centers on how speaker has taught or will teach without reference to the text.

Teaching–textual: Content centers on how speaker would teach the text under discussion or how the text has affected speaker's view of teaching.

Global: Content centers on generalizations about people, teaching, and texts beyond the text under discussion.

Nature of the Response

Elaborate: Turn that substantively changes the previous turn by building on previous content or by offering an interpretation of what the speaker is saying

Mention: Turn that refers to previous turn in order to gain floor and then departs from substance of previous turn

Question: Turn that asks previous speaker to clarify or develop the previous turn

Restate: Turn that makes effort to repeat or summarize previous turn

Agree: Turn that simply states agreement with previous turn

Disagree: Turn that simply states disagreement with previous turn

Evaluation: A positive or negative comment on previous turn

Orchestrate: Turn seeks to relate subsequent turn(s) to previous turn

No: Turn has no clear relation to previous turn

White. Although the principal had actively recruited minority teachers, he had been unable to attract any to this school. Therefore, the cultural backgrounds of the teachers were quite different from those of the school population.

Context. This Literacy and Diversity Study group met 10 times during the course of an academic year. Meetings were held every 3 weeks on Friday afternoons in the school library, barring school holidays or activities.

The participants read multicultural children's literature and stories from *Braided Lives* (1991), a multicultural anthology written by a group of teachers, as well as journal articles and book chapters relating to multicultural literature. A listing of the book titles can be found in Table 12.3.

The first meeting began with the writing of a cultural autobiography, using this prompt: "Write a brief autobiographical sketch providing information about your cultural background and how it impacts who you are today." At the end of each session, 10 minutes was devoted to writing a

TABLE 12.3
Study Group Meetings and Texts Read: Study 2

September 27, 1996	Cultural autobiographies
	Multiculturalism: article from *Reading Today*
	My Name Is Maria Isabel, Alma Ada Flors
October 18, 1996	*House on Mango Street*, Sandra Cisneros
November 1, 1996	*Baseball Saved Us*, Ken Mochizuki
November 15, 1996	*The Whites in My Head, to Be a Slave*, Freeman
December 13, 1996	*Number the Stars*, Lois Lowry
January 24, 1997	*Zlata's Diary*, Zlata Filopovic
	Roll of Thunder, Hear My Cry, Mildred Taylor
February 14, 1997	*The Watsons Go to Birmingham, 1963*, Christopher Curtis
March 7, 1997	*Children of the River*, Linda Crew
April 18, 1997	*Mrs. Katz and Tush*, Patricia Polacco
	The Always Prayer Shawl, Sheldon Oberman
	Plain and Fancy, Patricia Polacco
	Chicken Sunday, Patricia Polacco
	Amazing Grace, Mary Hoffman
	Honey I Love, Eloise Greenfield
	Smoky Night, Eve Bunting
May 2, 1997	*Been to Yesterdays*, Lee Bennet Hopkins

reflection on the day's discussion as a way of modeling the "debriefing process" (O'Flahaven, 1994) in literature circles. A historical record was written by Levin after each meeting in an effort to chronicle the session's events. The study group was structured to parallel a literature circle (Daniels, 1994; Eeds & Wells, 1989).

Participants responded to the readings in a response journal and discussed the text during meetings. The researcher was an active participant–observer during each meeting, providing materials as well as refreshments.

Data Collection and Analysis.   Each of the 10 sessions was audiotaped and transcribed. Each content unit was coded according to the following categories: personal, text, teaching, global, teaching–textual, collegiality and support, and barriers to change. This protocol was developed for the purpose of coding the discourse in terms of the broad conceptual framework of a study group and as a way of looking at how teachers make connections from personal interpretation to teaching. Seven discrete categories were established to sort and clarify the transcription data. Table 12.4 explains the protocol used.

The participants also were interviewed and observed in their classrooms both before and after the study to determine their professional and personal growth. The interviews were coded using analytic memos and constant evaluation of all available information.

TABLE 12.4

Coding System for Teacher Study Group Meeting Transcriptions

A. Personal–textual
1. Related text to themselves
2. Related text to family
3. Related text to cultural background
4. Related text to socioeconomic background
5. Other
B. Text
1. Analyzed character's motivation
2. Analyzed character's thinking
3. Analyzed character's actions
4. Analyzed character's personality
5. Analyzed author's craft
C. Teaching
1. Stated how they presently teach
2. Stated new idea or understanding
3. Stated a new strategy that they tried in their classroom
4. Discussed a classroom experience
5. Reflected on classroom practice or philosophy
D. Global
1. Made generalizations
2. Made cultural generalizations about their own culture
3. Made cultural generalizations about other cultures
4. Made universal generalizations
E. Teaching–textual
1. Stated how they use a particular text
2. Stated a new understanding relating to the use of a text
F. Collegiality and support
1. Offered recognition and encouragement
2. Provided validation to peers of current or new practices
3. Helped fellow teachers in terms of materials or advice
4. Sought validation from peers
G. Barriers to change
1. Verbalized curricular restraints
2. Expressed contentment with present practices
3. Displayed disillusionment toward new ideas
4. Voiced limitations of materials
5. Perceived administrative constraints
6. Articulated time concerns
7. Communicated general pessimism

RESULTS

Although the studies were similar in design and nature, it is important to note that the cultural composition of the groups differed. The Smith and Strickland (1996) study group comprised a very diverse population of teachers, including African American men and women, European American men and women, and a Latina woman. The Levin study, in contrast, consisted of all European American women. The schools in both studies contained a highly diverse student population. Originally, we were concerned that our results might vary because of the difference in group composition. However, this was not the case.

Although we believe our goal for developing ethical respect was not realized, we did experience benefits from our studies. We found that the teachers in both studies engaged in discussions different from those typically found in classroom discourse. We found that the teachers enjoyed their experience in the study groups and believed they profited from them. The participants believed they benefited both in terms of content and collegiality.

Changing Prevailing Patterns of Discourse

It was found that both studies successfully engaged teachers in discussions that challenged the typical patterns of discourse in school discussions. Table 12.5 shows that the two teaching categories represented only 25% of the total content units in study 1, and only 23% of the total content units in study 2, which suggests that in both studies the teachers were engaged in the discussions as readers rather than teachers.

Table 12.5 also shows that although the texts were the focus of the discussions, the participants explored connections between their lives and the texts, using the stories as a springboard for sharing their personal experiences and beliefs. These connections in the discussions resembled grand conversations rather than the gentle inquisitions (Eeds & Wells, 1989) that teachers in search of correct answers often maintain.

TABLE 12.5
Comparison of Percentages of Content Units by Category

Study 1					
Personal	Personal/ Textual	Textual	Teaching/ Textual	Teaching	Global
18	8	30	12	13	18

Study 2						
Personal/ Textual	Text	Teaching	Global	Teaching/ Textual	Collegiality & Support	Barriers to Change
27	22	15	15	8	6	7

TABLE 12.6
Percentage of Responses by Type

Elaborate	Question	Restate	Agree	Disagree	Eval	Orch	No
57	9	1	3	3	1	6	20

Table 12.6 shows the extent to which the discussions were different than the kinds of discussions that, according to Cazden (1988), occur in schools. According to the analysis of the responses, the discussions were precipitated by statements rather than questions, which comprised only 9% of the total turns. This suggests a pattern at odds with typical school discussions.

In fact, 57% of the turns were coded initially as elaborations. A subsequent analysis of the elaborations found that in two thirds of these turns, participants built on the previous turn, suggesting the kind of collaborative discourse that Flood et al. (1994) found in their study. In the other one third of the turns coded initially as elaborations, speakers mentioned the previous turn, yet used it as a springboard to introduce a point that did not depend on the previous turn. In addition, 20% of the turns were coded as having no relation to the previous turn.

Both analyses suggest the fluidity of the discussions. Participants were able to explore points of personal interest and to change the directions of the conversation, something ordinarily reserved for the leader of the discussion in school discussions of literature. Only 7% of the turns were coded as agree, disagree, or evaluation categories, another obvious departure from the IRE sequence. The number of elaborations suggests that the participants were able to develop their ideas and interpretations in the discussions. The group members' tendency to develop their own ideas is also suggested by the fact that the turns averaged 5.57 communication units.

We wondered whether the teachers' experiences in the study group would provide them with an imaginable alternative to the IRE sequence. In both studies, according to the participants' journal entries, our hopes were realized. Teachers unanimously noted that their participation in the group had affected the way they think about discussions. More specifically, two major themes emerged in their entries. One was the value of the personal nature of the discussions. This can be seen in the following excerpts from the interviews:

> I particularly enjoyed our round-table discussions about the many books and pieces of literature because they led to lively talks about our personal experiences.

It was so interesting to listen to everyone's opinions about the books and the teaching. I learned a lot, and some of it surprised me.

The teachers' comments indicated that they valued the opportunity to talk, listen, and learn from each other. The other emerging theme was that this format offered the time and possibility for camaraderie, as Flood and Lapp (1994) and their colleagues found. One participant articulated this benefit in an interview:

I have known most of these teachers for a long time, but now I realize how much more I know about them, not only as educators, but also as individuals. It's great!

Other benefits were visible in participants' comments regarding alternative conceptions of discussion gained through their involvement in the group. For example, teachers noted they learned that "everyone's thoughts and opinions are valuable," and that "it's good to hear other people's views on books and teaching—listening made me realize how easily I (or my students in class) could miss something in a book." The teacher's conception of discussion is what Cazden (1988) called "deliberate action" against the default option of IRE. This acknowledgment of the importance of discussion and listening to others may be a beginning step in actually changing the patterns of discourse in the participants' classrooms. Although the participants seemed to recognize that change does not come easily, their comments indicated a willingness to try. One teacher explained:

I still find it somewhat difficult. Short answers on the part of students paralyze the discussion. Nonetheless, I will continue making a great effort to bring "conversation" to my classroom.

For me, I enjoyed listening to the ideas of the other teachers. Even though I may not be able to do a literature circle or the exact type of activities that we did here in my class, this helped me get new ideas for my teaching.

Therefore, our analyses confirms that the study group format was effective in providing an imaginable alternative for discussions typically found in schools. It also was clear that the participants considered the value and qualities of discussions in a way different than they had before their involvement in the groups.

Other benefits also were realized by the group members. The participants found value in the study group format as a means of providing professional development.

The Teacher Study Group As Professional Development

The teachers considered the study group format to be an effective professional development tool for keeping abreast of new ideas or literature. Endorsed by teachers, the study group format, then, perhaps has the potential to become as popular and as significant as some other formats that monopolize professional development. As Little (1993) stated, "Professional development must be constructed in ways that deepen the discussion, open up the debates, and enrich the array of possibilities for action" (p. 130). Our experiences with study groups and the participants' interviews exhibited Little's (1993) criteria.

In terms of the group content, the teachers were consistent in their belief that they gained new perspectives on the literature. They credited other participants with helping them to look at issues differently. Hearing other viewpoints and discussing the literature helped to clarify the texts and to suggest avenues for their possible usage.

A teacher in the Levin study group summed up the general experience of group members:

> I learned much more about multicultural literature with this group than I ever would have in workshops or in-service meetings. Here I read the books, had time to think about them, and then expressed my opinions and listened to other people's opinions. You don't have that kind of time in a regular in-service. (exit interview)

Similarly, in Smith and Strickland's (1996) study, when the group discussed the components of a good discussion, many stated that being part of a group helped them get a better sense of what discussions should be like in their own classrooms.

Although participant satisfaction is important, there are other criteria, as outlined by the Council for English Education (CEE, 1994), that determine the success of a study group. The CEE maintains that the following 10 criteria are important in assessing the effectiveness of particular professional development approaches. The outlined criteria include reflective practice, ownership, theorized practice, collaboration, agency, time, administrative collaboration, school and community partnership, pluralism and democracy, and explicit and tangible support.

We found that the study group format has the potential to fulfill all the criteria outlined by the CEE. Furthermore, if a study group is perceived to be important by its participants, then indeed it should be a strong choice for a format of professional development. Because there traditionally has been such negativity on the part of teachers regarding the effectiveness of in-service programs, it would appear that participant satisfaction is one aspect of this process that should not go unnoticed (Garmston, 1991; Sparks & Loucks-Horsley, 1992).

The teachers' perceptions of the value of the study group were overwhelmingly positive. Through interviews and written debriefings, teachers repeatedly described study groups as effective means of professional development for many reasons, believing them to be more beneficial than more traditional staff development formats. The study group offered time to learn and the rare opportunity to interact with other teachers.

The teachers' comments indicated that the study group provided the opportunity to talk, listen, and learn from each other, and the time and possibility for camaraderie, a finding corroborated by Flood and Lapp (1994) and their colleagues. One participant in Levin's study articulated this benefit:

> I have known some of these teachers for years and yet, I now feel like I really know them—what they feel, how they teach, etc. I think when you develop a new kind of relationship, you feel more comfortable talking about problems and things. (exit interview)

Collegiality also was apparent in Smith and Strickland's (1996) study. In one instance, a participant in the group offered an analysis of the group's function, saying, "At first I felt like this was group therapy. But I realized that I've learned a lot about the people in the group and about myself."

Although our beliefs regarding the value of study groups were confirmed, this was not the case regarding our hope for the development of ethical respect. The participants in both studies did not exhibit ethical respect for the characters of the texts they read.

Fostering an Ethical Respect for Others

The premise of our inquiry maintained that multicultural literature will help readers develop an ethical respect for others when they provisionally adopt the perspective of the literary characters in the text as their own. When the personal experiences or biases of the readers are too ingrained to be open to new considerations, as we found, ethical respect seems unlikely. Additionally, when the reader feels that his or her experiences are privileged over the character's experiences, the reader is not likely to feel ethical respect.

Both studies exhibited similar patterns in that the teachers made very different personal connections with the texts, often depending on the cultural background portrayed in the books. The participants made more personal connections when their background of experience was similar to that expressed in the texts. For example, in Smith and Strickland's (1996) study group discussion of "Everyday Use," none of the White teachers participated. When asked why, they noted that although they felt enriched by the discussion, they did not feel that their personal experiences were relevant to the conversation. Similarly, in Levin's (1997) study, one of the participants, in a discussion about *My Name is Maria Isabel* by Flors (1994) was surprised that a teacher would be so insensitive to a child. She stated:

> I read that book as a teacher, and I never would call a student Mary if her name was Maria, just for convenience. I once had six Lisa's in my class and I dealt with it.

The text offered her the chance to use her experiences to frame her thinking and understanding of the characters in the book.

Although training in reader response theory has taught us to recognize the importance of the reader's experiences, we found that the reader's experiences actually may interfere with the development of ethical respect. We found three categories that hindered this development, which we term preempting, keeping distance, and interfering.

Preempting. The participants in both studies made connections with the texts when possible. When the information in the story was too difficult to conceptualize, the teachers preempted the characters' stories with one of their own. They shared a personal situation similar to that of the characters' or one to which they could relate in terms of their own experiences. Their responses fell short of ethical respect for the character.

For example, in Levin's (1997) study, during a discussion of *Zlata's Diary* (Filipovic, 1994), which chronicled the war in Bosnia, some members of the group had difficulty identifying with Zlata, a 12-year-old girl who had suffered the indignities of living with war. The teachers connected with this book by linking the concept of war and Zlata's feelings to something they understood. Consequently, 40% of the discussion was personal talk related to the Vietnam War, how it felt to have a family member involved or stationed in another country, and how this affected the participant.

Although the participants felt great empathy for Zlata, they agreed that it was too difficult even to conceive of the distress and hardships encountered by Zlata, which inhibited ethical respect for her character. We recognize that understanding characters on their own terms when the reader's life experiences may not give enough insight into what others have experienced is very difficult. It was clear this was the case in the discussion of *Zlata's Diary*.

Preempting also was apparent in Smith and Strickland's (1996) study in the discussion of "Two Kinds" by Amy Tan (1989). This story of a Chinese American mother and daughter at odds may have presented situations in which the participants were unable to relate. An immigrant mother who pushed her daughter in very negative ways may have been too foreign or difficult for the participants to consider because they barely discussed the characters or the actual story. "Two Kinds" was discussed during the same meeting as *Everyday Use* by Alice Walker (1994), and the participants chose to focus on *Everyday Use*. When the one of the researchers remarked about the relationship between the mother and daughter in "Two Kinds," one of the participants ignored the statement and referred back to earlier talk about *Everyday Use*.

Distancing. We found that study group participants sometimes distanced themselves from the characters and the authors of the texts. They seemed to make more personal connections when their background of experience was similar to what was expressed in the texts. For example, in Smith and Strickland's (1996) study group discussion of *Everyday Use* by Alice Walker (1994), the participants were asked to track their understandings of the three main characters: the mother and her two very different daughters. An excerpt from the discussion of *Everyday Use* shows how the speaker made the author, Alice Walker, a part of the discussion on the character of the daughter, Dee:

> She really did not have a strong appreciation of her culture, because, I guess to me, what Alice Walker always repeats in a lot of her work is that the first and foremost appreciation of your culture begins with your mother; I mean how can you appreciate or even act like you're going to appreciate your culture unless you have this respect for your mother? That doesn't make sense.

Another teacher continued:

> Well, I think that you have to first get to the point where you can find dignity in all kinds of work. And see, it's easy to say now, but when you have to, it takes a lot to appreciate your mother who's not doing what you think she should. Maybe not what someone else is doing. You really have to grow to be able to see past that. If you notice, the picture that was painted, everything on the outside was rough, but you had to go a little deeper in order to see other qualities of the mother.

In this discussion, both Dee and her mother were evaluated on their own terms, which we have argued, is at the core of treating someone with respect. Yet, within this same discussion, we were aware of certain participants distancing themselves from the text. As noted, not one of the White teachers in the group participated in this conversation.

Similarly, in Levin's (1996) study, there were instances in which members of the group distanced themselves from the text because they were uncomfortable or unfamiliar with the subject. In *Been to Yesterdays* by Hopkins (1995), the use of objectionable words in the text became the topic of discussion in the group. The participants spent a considerable amount of time talking about their feelings related to certain words instead of discussing the rich characters or the moving story. One of the participants stated:

> I think it's awful to use the n-word in a class that has African American children. How insulting it would be for them to hear us use that word. And what about the parents? They'd be screaming their heads off!

This type of discussion dominated the book talk and prevented the teachers from talking about the characters or the story.

Readings from professional journals also triggered distancing. A reading of the article entitled "The Whites in My Head" by Freeman (1996) produced confessions from the teachers that they were unable to relate to the experience because of their membership in the majority culture. "The Whites in My Head" (1996) is an article written by an African American woman who expressed anger that even as an adult, she visualizes characters in books as White because none of the books she read as a child had African American characters.

One of the participants was angered by the author's indignation about the lack of African American presence in literature. Another of the participants argued that specific cultures ought to help themselves, but then softened and said, "Maybe if we introduce young kids to multicultural literature, that'll help." Reading this article created unresolvable issues for the teachers, which gave them the impetus to distance themselves from the story being told. Their lack of acknowledgment of the author's feelings indicated a lack of ethical respect for the author.

Interference. At times, the readers' experiences interfered with their ability to develop ethical respect for the characters in the text, as was evidenced by a discussion of *Roll of Thunder, Hear My Cry* by Taylor (1976), and *The Watsons Go To Birmingham, 1963* by Curtis (1995). Many of the teachers in Levin's (1996) study had preconceived notions about African Americans that were very difficult to eradicate. The participants focused on what they believed to be a lack of interest in education for African Americans and used these opportunities to speak personally about different children in their school. Their talk revealed obvious cultural prejudices against some of their students. When the group began the discussion of *Roll of Thunder, Hear My Cry*, one participant talked about the boy in the book who was always in trouble. That incited several teachers to bemoan the problems of some of their students. One participant said:

> You know, it's the same with James (pseudonym). He comes to school dirty and tired. His grandmother takes care of him, his mother is on crack, his father is god knows where. What chance can he have?

Their talk about various students in the school dominated the discussion and left little time to delve into the lives of the characters in the book.

Prior experiences with the African American population in the community had given many of the teachers a markedly negative view of their family life and education. Many believed this was not a prejudice, but rather factual information. These feelings seemed to be deeply embedded, yet not verbally acknowledged. The participants in Levin's (1996) study were unable to experience ethical respect because of these strongly held beliefs.

In contrast, when the participants in Levin's (1996) study discussed *Children of the River* by Crew (1991), significant empathy was evident in the discourse. One teacher stated, "I really never thought too much about people coming to a new country and all that is involved." Another mentioned that her view of immigrants all living together in one house had changed, admitting, "I used to think, 'Oh those people, why don't they just live normally?' but now I feel pretty guilty about thinking that. I mean, what choices do they have?" The teachers did not seem to hold as deeply rooted prejudices for Cambodians or Jews as they did for African Americans, therefore, making ethical respect somewhat attainable for some cultures, but not for others.

The participants gained a heightened awareness of certain aspects of multiculturalism. The teachers spoke of how they began to look at the texts from a new vantage point and learned about new cultures. When asked in the exit interview whether they had taken anything from the study group back to their classrooms, several teachers said they understood the plight of new immigrants in a more complete way. One participant expressed, "When a child comes into my class and cannot speak English, I think I will have more patience and understanding toward them."

Empathy and sensitivity to new immigrants is an affective type of growth that was realized by the participants. Unfortunately, their sensitivity and awareness was restricted to cultures with which they had experienced limited, or at least not negative, exposure before this study. Participants failed at times to reconfigure preset beliefs. It must be stated that their unwillingness, conscious or unconscious, to allow new information to challenge preformulated views was never explicitly addressed in the group. One wonders if the researchers had intervened and discussed what seemed to be obvious bias whether the teachers might have realized that their biases most likely would affect their teaching and their students.

Therefore, although the study groups may have increased awareness of some cultures, they did not progress to the point at which preconceived notions were considered and questioned. It could be argued that with increased time or interventions, more progress could have been realized.

Although we would argue that ethical respect is an ultimate goal, we also see it as a process. The first step must include cultural awareness of the characters in the text to begin the process of understanding or adopting the experiences of the characters. The reader must have that awareness to understand the conventions and laws guiding the characters. This is a beginning. As the cultural differences between teachers and the populations they serve grows (Florio-Ruane & deTar, 1995), we recognize that a heightened cultural awareness must be a precursor to ethical respect (Jackson, 1994).

CONCLUSION

From our perspective, our studies were successful in several ways. First, we saw the value of teachers taking time to talk to each other in personal and professional ways. Second, we experienced the teachers' excitement in being part of their own professional development, engaged in meaningful discussions that were not characterized by the IRE pattern. Third, we recognized that the teachers became better acquainted with multicultural literature and previously unknown authors, and in some cases, experienced greater cultural awareness.

Our observations lead us to believe that the book group format of professional development can help teachers gain ownership of their own professional growth, a necessary component of meaningful staff development. The teachers pointed to the various benefits of scheduled time, reflective practice, and collaboration, which we hope will be continued by the teachers.

Although we were successful in challenging the patterns of discourse and in choosing of a professional development format, we were not as successful in our attempt to engender ethical respect through exposure to and discussion of multicultural literature selections. We found that the process of developing an ethical respect for others is a complicated one that cannot be completed by mere exposure to books, journals, group discussions, and stories about various cultures. We have seen that a heightened cultural awareness may be an important first step in the process of developing ethical respect, but it is not indicative of our ultimate goal.

We believe that the results of these two research studies challenge the commonly held view that multicultural literature in the classroom bridges the cultural barriers that exist between people. Although reading and discussing multicultural literature in a study group format can produce a heightened sense of cultural awareness, it fails, in our opinion, to establish ethical respect, an ingredient essential to the dismantling of cultural barriers.

We also recognize that there may be other ways of encouraging ethical respect in a study group. Perhaps if the participants' beliefs had been challenged by a facilitator or other group members, or if the discussion of prejudices had been made explicit, or if the prompts had demanded more specific attention to the characters and their cultures, then evidence of ethical respect might have been more visible. These interventions to the study group format certainly are worthy of continued research.

We have learned much from our studies and now are left with new questions to pursue and optimism for the development potential of teacher study groups. Our goal remains the development of ethical respect, with the hope of building cross-cultural understanding.

REFERENCES

Athanases, S. Z., Christiano, D., & Lay, E. (1995). Fostering empathy and finding common ground in multiethnic classes. *English Journal, 84,* 26–34.

Banks, J. (1994). Transforming the mainstream curriculum. *Educational Leadership, 51*, 4–8.

Brown, S., & Kysilka, M. (1994). In search of multicultural and global education in real classrooms. *Journal of Curriculum and Supervision, 9*, 313–316.

Cazden, C. (1988). *Classroom discourse: The language of teaching and learning.* Portsmouth, NH: Heinemann.

Cazden, C., & Mehan, M. (1989). Principles from sociology and anthropology: Context, code and classroom. In M. Reynolds (Ed.), *Knowledge base for the beginning teacher* (pp. 47–57). Oxford: Pergamon.

CEE Commission on Inservice Education. (1994). Inservice education: Ten principles. *English Education, 26*(2), 125–129.

Daniels, H. (1994). *Literature circles: Voice and choice in the student-centered classroom.* York, ME: Stenhouse Publishers.

Downie, R. S., & Tefler, E. (1970). *Respect for persons.* New York: Schocken.

Eeds, M., & Hudelson, S. (1995). Literature as foundation for personal and classroom life. *Primary Voices, 3*, 2–7.

Eeds, M., & Wells, D. (1989). Grand conversations: An exploration of meaning construction in literature study groups. *Research in the Teaching of English, 23*, 4–29.

Fishman, A. (1995). Finding ways in: Redefining multicultural literature. *English Journal, 84*(8), 73–79.

Flood, J., & Lapp, D. (1994). Teacher books clubs: Establishing literature discussion groups for teachers. *The Reading Teacher, 47*, 574–576.

Flood, J., & Lapp, D. (1995). What happens when teachers get together to talk about books? Gaining a multicultural perspective from literature. *The Reading Teacher, 48*(8), 720–723.

Flood, J., Lapp, D., Alvarex, D., Ranck-Buhr, W., Moore, J., Jones, M., Kabildis, C., & Lungren, L. (1994). *Teacher book clubs: A study of teachers' and student teachers' participation in contemporary multicultural fiction literature discussion groups.* Reading Research Report No. 22, National Reading Research Center, Universities of Georgia and Maryland.

Florio-Ruane, S. (1994). The future teachers autobiography club: Preparing educators to support literacy learning in culturally diverse classrooms. *English Education, 26*(1), 52–66.

Florio-Ruane, S., & deTar, J. (1995). Conflict and consensus in teacher candidates' discussion of ethnic autobiography. *English Education, 27*, 11–39.

Florio-Ruane, S., & Raphael, T. (1996, December). *Reading, writing, and talk about autobiography: The education of literacy teachers.* Paper presented at the annual meeting of the National Reading Conference, Charleston, SC.

Florio-Ruane, S., & Raphael, T. (1997, December 5). *Reading culture in autobiography: The education of literacy teachers.* Research report presented at the annual meeting of the National Reading Conference, Scottsdale, AZ.

Freeman, W. (1996). The whites in my head. *Voices from the Middle, 3*, 26–27.

Garmston, R. (1991). Staff developers as social architects. *Educational Leadership, 11*, 64–65.

Hargreaves, A. (1992). Cultures of teaching: A focus for change. In A. Hargreaves & M. G. Fullan (Eds.), *Understanding teacher development* (pp. 216–240). New York: Teachers College Press.

Harris, V. (1995, May 1). *Literacy and learning in a culturally diverse society literature recommendations.* Workshop presented at International Reading Association annual conference, Anaheim, CA.

Jackson, F. (1994). Seven strategies to support a culturally responsive pedagogy. *Journal of Reading, 37*(4), 298–303.

Kane, R. (1994). *Through the moral maze: Searching for absolute values in a pluralistic world.* New York: Paragon House.

Ladson-Billings, G. (1994). What we can learn from multicultural education research. *Educational Leadership, 5*, 22–26.

Levin, F. (1997). *Staff development: Promoting teachers as readers groups.* Unpublished doctoral dissertation, New Brunswick, NJ: Rutgers University.

Little, J. W. (1993). Teachers' professional development in a climate of educational reform. *Educational Evaluation and Policy Analysis, 15*(2), 129–151.

Maeroff, G. (1993). Building teams to rebuild schools. *Phi Delta Kappan, 74*, 512–519.

Marshall, J., Smagorinsky, P., & Smith, M. (1995). *The language of interpretation: Patterns of discourse in discussions of literature.* Urbana, IL: NCTE.

Minnesota Council of Teachers of English. (1991). *Braided lives: An anthology of multicultural American writing.* Minneapolis, MN: Minnesota Humanities Commission.

Murphy, C. (1991). Lessons from a journey into change. *Educational Leadership, 48*, 63–67.

O'Flahaven, J. (1994). Teacher role options in peer discussions about literature. *The Reading Teacher, 48*(4), 354–356.

Powell, J., Berliner, D., & Casanova, U. (1992). Empowerment through collegial study groups. *Contemporary Education, 63*(4), 281–284.

Rabinowitz, P., & Smith, M. W. (1998). *Authorizing readers: Resistance and respect in the reading of literature.* New York: Teachers College Press.

Raphael, T., & McMahon, S. (1994). Book Club: An alternative framework for reading instruction. *The Reading Teacher, 48*(2), 102–116.

Raphael, T. E., Goatley, V. J., McMahon, S. I., & Woodman, D. A. (1995). Promoting meaningful conversations in student book clubs. In N. Roser & M. Martinez (Eds.), *Book talk and beyond* (pp. 7–83). Newark, DE: International Reading Association.

Reissman, R. (1994). Leaving out to pull in: Using reader response to teach multicultural literature. *English Journal, 83*(2), 20–23.

Sanacore, J. (1993). Using study groups to create a professional community. *Journal of Reading, 37*, 62–66.

Sleeter, C., & Grant, C. (1987). An analysis of multicultural education in the United States. *Harvard Educational Review, 57*, 421–444.

Smith, M., & Strickland, D. S. (1996, November 17). *Complements or conflicts: Conceptions of discussions and multicultural literature in a literacy and diversity study group.* Paper presented at the annual convention of The National Council of Teachers of English, Chicago, IL.

Sparks, D., & Loucks-Horsley, S. (1992). Models of staff development. In W. Robert Houston (Ed.), *Handbook of Research on Teacher Education* (pp. 234–239). New York: Macmillan.

Sprague, M., & Makibbin, S. (1994). Study groups: A conduit for change in education. *Contemporary Education, 65*(2), 99–103.

Taylor, C. (1992). The politics of recognition. In A. Guttmann, C. Taylor, S. Wolf, S. Rockefeller, & M. Walzer (Eds.), *Multiculturalism and "The Politics of Recognition"* (pp. 147–152). Princeton, NJ: Princeton University Press.

Trueba, H., Jacobs, L., & Kirton, E. (1989). *Raising silent voices: Educating the linguistic minorities for the 21st century.* New York: Harper & Row.

Yokota, J. (1993). Issues in selecting multicultural literature. *Language Arts, 70*, 156–157.

Yokota, J. (1995, May 2). *Evaluating multicultural literature*. Workshop presented at the International Reading Association annual conference, Anaheim, CA.

BIBLIOGRAPHY

Crew, L. (1991). *Children of the river*. New York: Laurel Leaf Publishers.
Curtis, C. (1995). *The Watsons go to Birmingham, 1963*. Des Plaines, IL: Delacorte.
Filopovic, Z. (1994). *Zlata's diary*. New York: Penguin.
Flors, A. (1994). *My name is Maria Isabel*. New York: Simon & Schuster.
Hopkins, L. B. (1995). *Been to yesterdays*. New York: Boyds Mills Press.
Tan, A. (1989). *The Joy Luck Club*. New York: Putnam.
Taylor, M. (1976). *Roll of thunder, hear my cry*. Bergenfield, NJ: Dial Books for Young Readers.
Walker, A. (1994). *Everyday use*. New Brunswick, NJ: Rutgers University Press.
West, C. (1994). *Race matters*. New York: Random House.

Afterword

Arlette Ingram Willis
Violet J. Harris
University of Illinois at Urbana–Champaign

The panoramic multicultural and multiethnic landscape of the United States can be described as an environment full of splendor, a rich tapestry of color from dense hues to vibrant brilliance to subtle light tones. America has always been a nation of multiple cultures and languages, but until recently, notions of a "melting pot," or all cultures and languages assimilating into the dominant culture, overshadowed attempts to celebrate our diverse nation. It has been an exercise in futility, however, to conceive of our multicultural landscape as one unified nation composed of varied cultural–ethnic groups with an array of backgrounds, life experiences, values, beliefs, languages, traditions, and ways of knowing, all living in harmony without ever addressing our differences. A more unsentimental portrayal of U.S. cultural and linguistic landscapes evinces a nation fraught with a history of colonization, oppression, subordination, and alienation.

Over the past two decades there has been increased interest and research on issues of difference, often loosely labeled "multicultural," in literacy research and practice. This is an important shift in literacy research. Geneva Gay (1994) has observed that, "multicultural education for all students [is] an imperative, particularly if education is to fulfill its basic function of being personally meaningful, socially relevant, culturally accurate, and pedagogically sound" (no page no.). The attention drawn to broad and undefined notions of multiculturalism, however, has resulted in notions of race being unaddressed. Toni Morrison (1992) noted that, "race has become metaphorical—a way of referring to and disguising forces, events, classes, and expression of social decay and economic division far more threatening to the body politic than biological 'race' ever was" (p. 63). Thus, we have observed that many recent conference presentations and publications under the moniker of multiculturalism have neglected the history, research, and literature in the field.

A variety of ideological positions and methods that cover the expanse of education, including the intersection of multicultural issues in literacy research and practice, should include research and findings drawn from journals outside the literary field such as the *American Educational Research Journal, Harvard Educational Review, Journal of Negro Education, Teachers College Record, Theory Into Practice,* and *Journal of Child Development,* among others. Publications in these outlets often include alternative formats that offer an emic perspective and conceptions of the lived experiences, nuances, and assumptions of multiple cultures that are not always voiced, and that cannot always be accounted for by traditional forms of literacy inquiry. As a group, these alternative research formats challenge dominant ideologies and paradigms, as well as the assumptions of traditional academic research that attempt to marginalize their value and import. Much of the work published in nontraditional literacy outlets makes race and its impact on people of color living in the United States, including children and their education, central. For instance, the use of narrative formats helps to highlight the possible long-term cumulative affects of cultural insensitivity, which may be hard to measure using traditional methods.

Relying on a broader range of information may help to reduce ideological and conceptual shortsightedness in data analysis and interpretation. We believe that it is especially imperative for all researchers to acknowledge and draw from a broad range of information in their analysis and interpretation of cross-cultural settings. For example, solely referencing research conducted by European Americans to inform discussions of cross-cultural literacy events can lead to interpretative errors, misappropriation of emphasis, and stereotypical understandings. In addition, not referencing original conceptual and empirical work and relying too heavily on interpretations by others are problematic and endemic in our field with regard to multicultural issues in research and practice.

In our multiple roles as editors and reviewers, we often have received a set of reviews for an article only to learn that, unbeknownst to us, we have reviewed the same article as White colleagues at our institution or others. On more than one occasion, we have noticed that reviews often fall along racial lines. That is, often colleagues of color have similar responses to manuscripts, whereas our responses differ significantly from those held by our White colleagues. It is insightful, nonetheless, to note how our responses differ. We not only differ in what we believe is important in a manuscript, but also in what is missing. The experience has created opportunities for us to share our differing points of view in more detail, and to become more informed about the perspectives we use in our evaluations. Moreover, it can engender dialogues that continue, in part because we can trust one another to be honest and forthright, and in part because we see each other as equally qualified to make judgements about what should be published and why. These forms of relationship suggest the importance of dialogue and collaboration among colleagues of color and Whites whose research interests or opportunities have included research on multicultural issues.

TAKING THE FIRST STEPS

In general, research on multicultural issues in literacy research and practice falls into three broad categories: the insider–outsider point of view, the outsider pretending to be within, and the evolving personal narrative of the outsider. First, the insider–outsider refers to cultural and linguistic insiders who may conduct research among members of their cultural or linguistic group, but are outsiders within specific cultural, linguistic, geographical, gender, or class contexts. For example, Anya Dozier Enos (2001), a Pueblo scholar conducts research in Pueblo communities. She brings insider information about cultural, linguistic, and knowledge building that she has found to be helpful and insightful in her research. However, she also notes that each Pueblo community is distinctive. Enos has observed that for Pueblo people there is "the interplay between nature, art, and tradition in which each serves to strengthen the other, and all work to attach people to their Pueblo communities. The core, the center of this world, the center of *the* world is the Pueblo plaza" (p. 85, italics in the original).

Furthermore, Enos states that her research entrée into Pueblo communities included several preferred steps. First, she sought advice from the governor of her Pueblo. He wrote her a letter of support and introduction that she took with her as she sought permission from Pueblo elders in the communities wherein she wanted to conduct her research. She also understood the importance of honoring Pueblo life that dictates what information is not to be shared with outsiders:

I respect the orality and privacy of Pueblo tradition and believe that these customs are partially responsible for the strength and perpetuation of the Pueblo. Such information retains a certain vitality and appropriateness in the minds of our people because it is not recorded. Keeping information private eliminates the risk of misinterpretation by outside sources. It is only in the Pueblo context that such information has the meaning it is meant to have. Changing its form and or removing it from its context within the Pueblo would distort and corrupt its meaning and, therefore, its critical value for Pueblo culture. The loss of such information may result in incomplete research, but it is a necessary incompleteness. (pp. 88–89)

Second, many well-intentioned research projects on multicultural issues in literacy research and practice fall short of understanding the fundamental concerns mentioned by Enos. For example, there is a growing body of research that emits "subjective tolerance" that erases the richness and complexity of diverse cultures, multivocality, and experiences. This body of research advocates for addressing multicultural issues. However, there are several shortfalls: (a) Racial and cultural differences are presented as a binary to Whiteness; (b) discussions are framed to universalize themes without acknowledging and deconstructing the cultural and linguistic contexts; and (c) "authorized" references become the standard for discussion, with little regard for the integrity of the participants' lives, voices, experiences, and ways of knowing. Several of our White colleagues have confided that they much prefer to conduct their research among students of color because they find research among Whites "boring." They also have mentioned that there may be a greater likelihood of publication outlets for their research if it is focused on students of color as they attempt to offer a "new" perspective for understanding the literacy growth and development.

This does not seem to be a "new perspective" to us, but an old perspective in which researchers, often very well-intended researchers, presume that they can name and interpret the experiences of students of color, devoid of input by students of color. Unfortunately, too often in these studies, conceptual and theoretical frameworks have been used indiscriminately, thus serving to marginalize the literacy process further for populations under investigation. Audre Lorde (1998) has argued that "the master's tools will never dismantle the master's house" (p. 112). In addition, many studies demonstrate a weak grasp of race and gender issues within our racialized society as well as accompanying power/knowledge relations. We have been dismayed by researchers who fail to analyze and interpret data beyond their own frames of reference, which would not be so problematic if they simply offered a disclaimer or admitted that their viewpoint has been shaped and molded by their own experiences.

These shortcomings, in conducting cross-cultural research, are fueled in part by a normalizing and universalizing of the "American" literacy experience that presumes histories and levels of commonality among multiple groups in our society. Such narrow frames of reference for literacy, language, and ways of knowing among different schools, teachers, and students suggest that contextual factors are overlooked or misunderstood. Furthermore, the lack of contextualization creates images of participants of color, "without the responsibility of specificity, accuracy, or even narratively useful description" (Morrison, 1992, p. 67), that are static, one-dimensional, or flat, as opposed to active, three-dimensional, or rounded.

One of the more troubling concerns in multicultural literacy research and practice are studies that attempt to capture the manifold layers of linguistic variance in classrooms wherein multiracial students are enrolled. Discourse analysis requires considerable sophistication and experience with multiple interpersonal communication styles and languages. Cultural and linguistic outsiders can miss nonverbal and verbal nuances, intonation subtleties, and cultural and linguistic idioms that carry considerable meaning among culturally familiar speakers. Furthermore, oral language games in which speakers engage during conversations that require linguistic complexity and sophistication also can be misunderstood or interpreted as simplistic, rude, or inappropriate.

There are examples, however, of culturally and linguistically sensitive approaches to classroom discourse within culturally and linguistically diverse settings. Rick Ayers, a high school teacher at Berkeley High School in California, has taken a different stance by acknowledging and appreciating the variety and use of language spoken in his classrooms. In addition, he does not exclude nonstandard English, hip hop, slang, and other vernacular forms. For 6 years he has incorporated these forms into his courses by having students research, collect, and publish their language in a Berkeley High slang dictionary. Ayers also recognizes that his students are "brilliant and engaged in their home language, but when they are asked to write in 'school language' they are tongue-tied. I want them to recognize their strengths" (quoted in Ashfar, 2001). Ayers explains that, "language is dynamic, constantly changing. . . . There are people on the outer edge of language who are creating it, and there are the people who are just the guardians of the prescribed rule" (Ashfar, 2001). To strengthen their academic voices and to help his students learn to negoti-

ate various audiences, he asks students to write an essay in their vernacular as a starting point, then translate it into standard or academic English
as their audience shifts from self and peers to teacher.

Literacy research that addresses communities of color should include
rich descriptions and details of the research context. Demographic information about both the researchers and the participants should be part of
the contextal descriptions. Listing the race, class, gender, and linguistic
characteristics of the participants and the researchers only begins the
process of understanding the context. What is particularly troubling
about the use of racial and ethnic terms in many studies is the deficit
tone that unfairly positions students of color along with "at-risk" and
poverty labels. The careless use of labels to define students raises other
questions regarding the positionality of the researchers. It is important
and necessary for researchers to situate themselves within the context of
their studies. If race, class, and language are issues under investigation,
researchers must begin by deconstructing their positionality within the
research site. Much more information and insight are needed about
sociocultural and sociolinguistic frameworks as well as the interconnect-
edness of race, class, gender, language, and power and privilege in the
analysis and interpretation of cross-cultural literacy events.

Third, since Paley's (1979) *White Teacher*, there has been a plethora of
seemingly endless personal narratives that detail how unaware many
White researchers and educators are of the role they have played in the
miseducation of students from cultural and linguistic backgrounds that
differ from their own. The gist of these works too often is not the education or the future of the students, nor the unacknowledged biases of the
authors, but the illumination of a personal journey. Noteworthy as these
efforts are for the authors, and as informative as they may be for researchers, such works also should acknowledge the power/knowledge relations,
the discursive practices that maintain privilege positions, and the possible
role each author has as a change agent in the lives of children. We
strongly encourage researchers and authors to read similar works by researchers and educators of color for additional sources of insight, evolu-
tion, and possibility.

Personal narratives by literacy researchers can begin to have a more
profound effect on the field when all researchers move beyond shallow
demographic acknowledgments and begin to unpack the ways in which
their subjectivities affect participants and collaborators. In addition, there
should be a discussion of action—the obligations and responsibility they
have taken, or plan to take, as change agents. Continual growth and understanding in these areas are necessary as literacy researchers conduct

research among school populations composed of racially and linguistically diverse student populations. Furthermore, literacy researchers should not conceive of analysis and interpretations devoid of the opinions and insights of scholars and participants of color.

NEXT STEPS

Former U. S. Secretary of Education, Richard Riley, called a quality education the "new civil right" (Riley, 2000). Many politicians and leaders in education quickly embraced and extended this idea in their reference to literacy as a civil right for all U. S. school children. Interestingly, the idea of linking literacy to politics and to notions of the Civil Rights era recalls a history of struggle endured by countless Americans as they fought for and through the legal system for equal rights and opportunities for education and literacy. Yet, the intersection of politics and literacy has largely been ignored by literacy researchers who wish to believe that literacy research is not affected by politics, and that literacy itself is above the fray. By way of contrast, we envision literacy access and opportunity as a human right (Willis & Harris, 2000). We encourage all involved in the decision-making processes, from the federal government to classroom teachers, to assume their moral obligation and responsibility to ensure that all children have culturally appropriate and relevant access to and opportunity for literacy.

Finally, literacy research on multicultural issues must be informed by cultural and linguistic insiders. It also must be interpreted and validated within the group's ways of knowing. In the real world, this means developing collaborative and trusting relationships in which power and authority within the academy are shared.

REFERENCES

Ashfar, Y. (2001). *Berkeley high school slang dictionary provides "4-1-1" for confused ears* [Online]. Available: http://www.uwiretoday.com/offbeat. Accessed: June 7, 2001.

Enos, A. (2001). A landscape with multiple views: Research in Pueblo communities. In B. Merchant & A. I. Willis (Eds.), *Multiple and intersecting identities in qualitative research* (pp. 83–102). Mahwah, NJ: Lawrence Erlbaum Associates.

Gay, G. (1994). *A synthesis of scholarship in multicultural education* (Urban Monograph Series). Oak Brook, IL: North Central Regional Educational Laboratory [Online]. Available: http://www.ncrel.org/sdrs/areas/issues/educatrs/leadrshp/le0gay.htm. Accessed: November 3, 2000.

Lorde, A. (1998). Poetry is not a luxury. In P. Bell-Scott (Ed.), *Flat-footed truths: Telling Black women's lives* (pp. 147–151). New York: Holt.

Morrison, T. (1992). *Playing in the dark: Whiteness and the literary imagination.* Cambridge, MA: Harvard University Press.

Paley, V. G. (1979). *White teacher.* Cambridge, MA: Harvard University Press.

Riley, R. (2000). *Seventh Annual State of American Education Address, "Setting New Expectations," Southern High School, Durham, North Carolina* [Online]. Available: http://www.ed.gov/Speeches/02-2000/000222.html. Accessed: January 31, 2000.

Willis, A., & Harris, V. (2000). Political acts: Literacy learning and teaching. *Reading Research Quarterly, 35*(1), 72–89.

Author Index

Note: Page number followed by *n* indicates a footnote.

Subject Index

teacher education, and Sally Oran's students,
171

O

Oran, Sally
classroom, 167–168
prior knowledge of cultural contexts, 172
students
engagement, 178–179
learning about cultural context of schools,
180–181
modeling, 179–180
writing development, 176–177
Overtranslation, 162

P

Parents, perceptions of own role in literacy
learning, 132–134
Parents' Perception of Literary Learning Inter-
view Schedule (PPLLIS), 125,
127–132
Partner reading, 50
Pen pal exchange, see Letter exchanges
Picture books, see also Spanish in Latino pic-
ture storybooks
bilingual preschooler response to, 16–23
categories of, 146n
Picture-driven connections, 20–21
Polar Bear, Polar Bear, What Do You Hear?, 17,
18
Portfolio assessment plan, 109, 110
Predictable text, structurally, 17–18, 22
Preempting, 279–280
Preschool bilingual reader responses, 11, 13,
23–26
Pretending, 13
Primary Program Foundation Document, 124,
140
Prose format (meaningful prose), 18–19,
22–23

R

Reader response, 11–12
of preschoolers, 11–13
research on, 11
theoretical perspectives on, 11
Reader-shaped responses, 23–24
Reading, see also specific topics
distributed, 211

Reading circles, see Teacher study groups
Reading comprehension test scores, 242–245
Realistic fiction, 18–19, 23, 25
Recitation teaching, 203
Research, literacy
categories of multicultural issues in, 291
multicultural, 289–291
first steps in, 291–295
next steps, 295
Researchers, literacy
personal narratives by, 294
Respect, see also Ethical respect
defined, 264–265
Responsive teaching/responsivity, 203–205,
219–220, see also Monitoring interactive teaching
defined, 203
missed opportunities for, 214–215
Role sets, 50
Rough Rock, 102, see also Navajo community school

S

Scaffolding, use of, 190–193
Self-correction, 39
Semantic field, 155–156
Small group instruction, see Group literacy
instruction
Social justice, commitment to, 2–3, 103
Sociocultural factors, see also Home and
school
and literacy, 70–71
Sociocultural perspective, 2, 11
Sociocultural research perspective, 204–205
Spanish in Latino picture storybooks,
145–147, 163–164
characteristics of Spanish entries, 153
function, 159–161
grammatical aspects, 154–155
illustration, 161
length, 153–154
method, 157–158
placement, 158–159
semantic field, 155–156
type, 156
strategic effects, 163
theoretical framework, 147–148
author as cultural translator, 148–150
undesirable effects, 162–163
Storytelling, 84–86, 88–91
Structurally predictable text, 17–18, 22